HAIL, SIENA!
Siena Heights University
The First Hundred Years

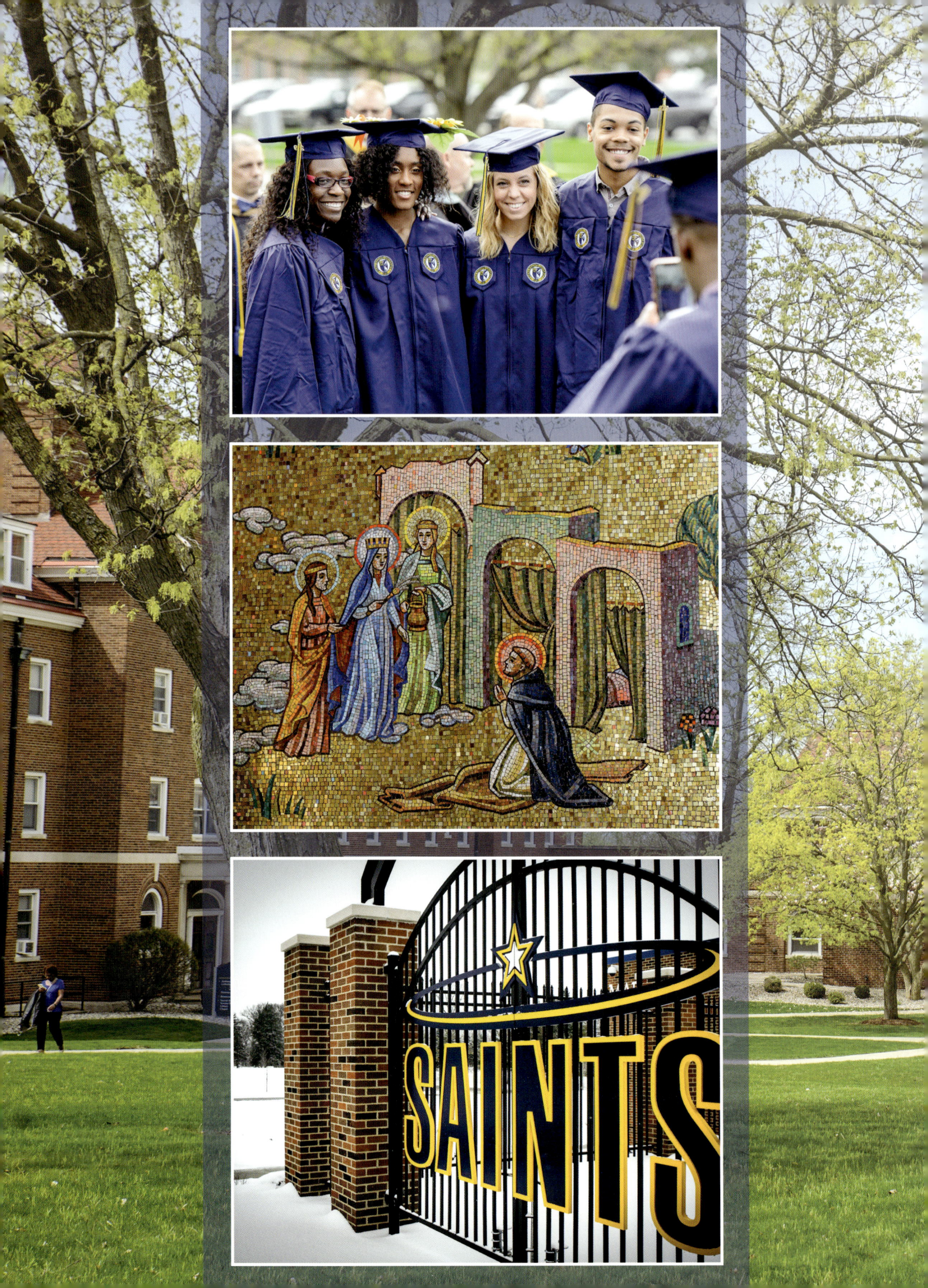

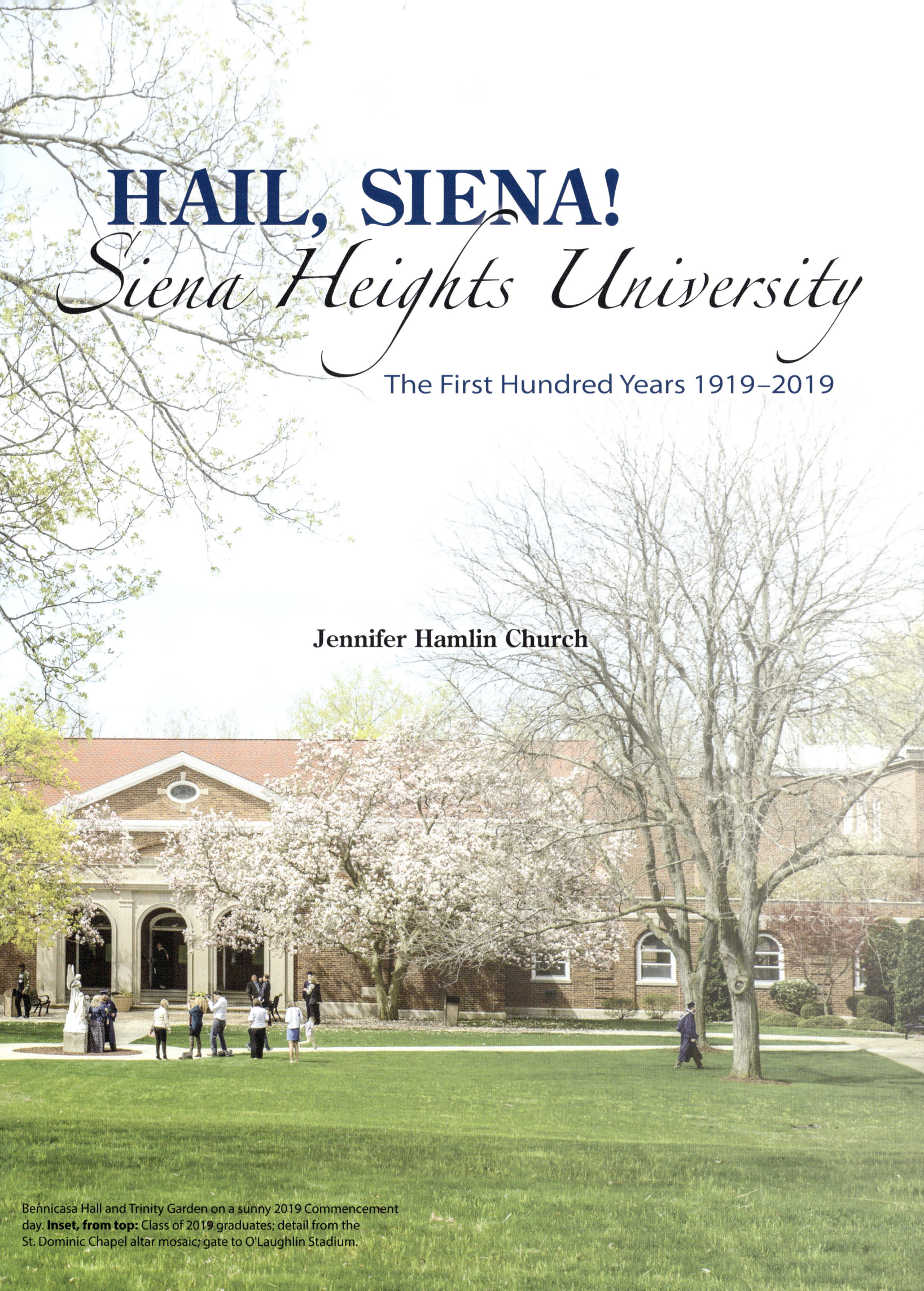

HAIL, SIENA!
Siena Heights University
The First Hundred Years 1919–2019

Jennifer Hamlin Church

Bennicasa Hall and Trinity Garden on a sunny 2019 Commencement day. **Inset, from top:** Class of 2019 graduates; detail from the St. Dominic Chapel altar mosaic; gate to O'Laughlin Stadium.

The mission of Siena Heights,
a Catholic university founded and sponsored by the Adrian Dominican Sisters,
is to assist people to become more competent, purposeful, and ethical
through a teaching and learning environment
which respects the dignity of all.

Siena Heights University
Adrian, Michigan 49221

With Degree Completion Centers across Michigan in
Southfield, Dearborn, Monroe, Jackson, Lansing, Battle Creek, Kalamazoo, and Benton Harbor;
Theological Studies in Partnership with the Diocese of Lansing;
And Online Degree Completion through the Office of Distance Learning.

Copyright © 2019 by Siena Heights University
1247 E. Siena Heights Drive
Adrian, MI 49221

All rights reserved, including the right to reproduce this work in any form whatsoever without permission in writing from the publisher, except for brief passages in connection with a review. For information, please contact Siena Heights University.

THE
DONNING COMPANY
PUBLISHERS

The Donning Company Publishers
731 S. Brunswick
Brookfield, MO 64628

Lex Cavanah, General Manager
Nathan Stufflebean, Donning Production Supervisor
Richard A. Horwege, Senior Editor
Terry Epps, Graphic Designer
Katie Gardner, Marketing and Production Coordinator

George Nikolovski, Project Director

ISBN 978-1-68184-235-6

Cataloging-in-Publication Data available from the Library of Congress

Printed in the United States of America at Walsworth

Dominican Hall and the McLaughlin
University Center by night.

CONTENTS

7   *Foreword*

9   *Acknowledgments*

        PART 1
10   *Digging for Roots*

             Presidential Profile: Mother Camilla Madden.

        PART 2
20   *The First Fifty Years: A College for Valiant Women*

             Presidential Profiles: Mother Augustine Walsh, Mother Mary Gerald Barry,
                Sister Benedicta Marie Ledwidge, Sister Petronilla Francoeur.
             Legends of the Faculty: Sister Ann Joachim, Sister Miriam Michael Stimson, Deans.
             Century of Study: Social Sciences, Math and Science, Graduate Education.

        PART 3
76   *Everything Changes! Transition and Tumult in the 1970s*

             Presidential Profiles: Hugh Thompson, Louis Vaccaro.
             Legends of the Faculty: Father David Van Horn, Sister Eileen Rice.
             Century of Study: Art, Teacher Education, the Bachelor of Applied Science.

        PART 4
114   *Engaging in a Widening World: The 1980s and 1990s*

             Presidential Profiles: Sister Cathleen Real, Richard Artman.
             Legends of the Faculty: Dedicated Adjuncts, William Blackerby.
             Century of Study: Humanities, Business, Performing Arts.

        PART 5
144   *Technology and the Common Touch: The 2000s and 2010s*

             Presidential Profile: Sister Peg Albert.
             Legends of the Faculty: Architects of Off-Campus Education.
             Century of Community Service.
             Athletics in the Modern Era.
             Legend of Athletics: Fred Smith.

        PART 6
184   *Hail Siena! Commencing into the Future*

190   *Sources*

192   *About the Author*

Foreword

How do you sum up 100 years of history in one book?

That was the question posed as Siena Heights University approached its 100-year anniversary. Ultimately, the answer was not how. It was who? You all know that during my tenure I have always emphasized the importance of people. All of us constitute who Siena has been, is, and will be in the future.

The choice was an easy one. Former alumni director Jennifer Hamlin Church spent two decades learning, sharing, telling—and making—history during her time at Siena Heights. A gifted storyteller, we tasked Jennifer with telling our story, from its earliest beginnings to the present day. As you will see in the following pages, she did a spectacular job.

As an Adrian Dominican Sister, I am keenly aware of the legacy that our founders left for us. From Mother Camilla Madden—the institution's first president—to all who followed, Siena Heights is what it is today thanks to the efforts, struggles—and prayers—of those who came before us. It is vital to document that history and heritage, and this book is a must-read for anyone who wants to understand the past, present, and future of Siena Heights.

During my time as President, I have made it a priority for the Siena community to learn the Dominican tradition as well as fully embrace the Siena Heights mission of being more competent, purposeful, and ethical while respecting the dignity of all. This book documents those common threads that have been woven into the fabric that is the legacy of Siena Heights.

As we prepare to celebrate the university's centennial, I am truly humbled to stand on the shoulders of the giants who are contained within these pages. I hope you enjoy, appreciate, and contemplate the contents of these pages as much as I did.

Thank you to Jennifer for telling the "Siena Heights Story," as well as the Centennial Committee for their efforts in making the 100th anniversary celebration truly one for the ages.

May the God of us all continue to bless Siena Heights University over the next 100 years and beyond!

Peace,

Sister Peg Albert, OP, PhD
President
Siena Heights University

Opposite: The statue of St. Augustine which has stood for decades in Trinity Garden was erected in honor of Mother Augustine Walsh, OP, second president of Siena Heights.

Grateful Thanks

This book would not have been possible without the work of the Adrian Dominican Sisters who established and maintained the Siena Heights archives: Sisters Helen Duggan, Marie Irene Miller, Jeanne Lefebvre, and Mary Beaubien, and all those who assisted them.

I am especially grateful to Helen Duggan, remembered by many as Sister Ann Charles, for the 150 oral interviews she conducted and transcribed a quarter century ago. Without the voices, memories, and experiences captured in those long-ago conversations, this book would be far less interesting.

Many thanks are due to the dedicated team of readers who offered feedback, insights, and encouragement throughout the writing process: Sister Peg Albert, OP, Arlene Bachanov, Norm Bukwaz, Julieanna Frost, Doug Goodnough, Bob Gordon, Kate Hamilton, Mary Small Poore, Mark Schersten, and Sister Sharon Weber, OP. Your help has been invaluable. Thanks, also, to the dozens of others who provided help with smaller portions of the text.

The Siena Heights University marketing office and the Archives of the Adrian Dominican Sisters willingly shared their rich photography resources. Bob Gordon, Amy Garno Anderson, Ken Thompson, and Deb Carter contributed images, as well. Thanks to all for your help in producing a visual treasure.

I am grateful to President Peg Albert, OP and the Executive Committee of the Administration, and to the Siena Heights 100th Anniversary Steering Committee and its History Sub-Committee, for endorsing this project; to the Adrian Dominican Ministry Trust for supporting the early stages of research; and to all the donors whose gifts through the years made this landmark anniversary possible.

Finally, I am forever in debt to the hundreds of Siena Heights graduates who shared their stories with me during my years in the alumni office, sparking my interest in the history of this special place; and to the Congregation of Adrian Dominican Sisters who have shown me that the search for truth never ends.

My goal was to provide a comprehensive and engaging overview of the first hundred years of Siena Heights. It was not possible, of course, to include every significant event, inspiring individual, or fabulous story; but I hope I have provided readers an appreciation of the fascinating history of this remarkable university. And I encourage *you* to share *your* story, enriching our collective understanding that much more.

J. H. C.

Opposite: Fresh snow and an ice storm transform the main campus on a glitering winter morning.

PART 1
Digging for Roots

To understand the Siena Heights story—to grasp the heart and soul of the university, and the values that have shaped it for a century—we must begin with Dominic and Catherine, and the Order of Preachers.

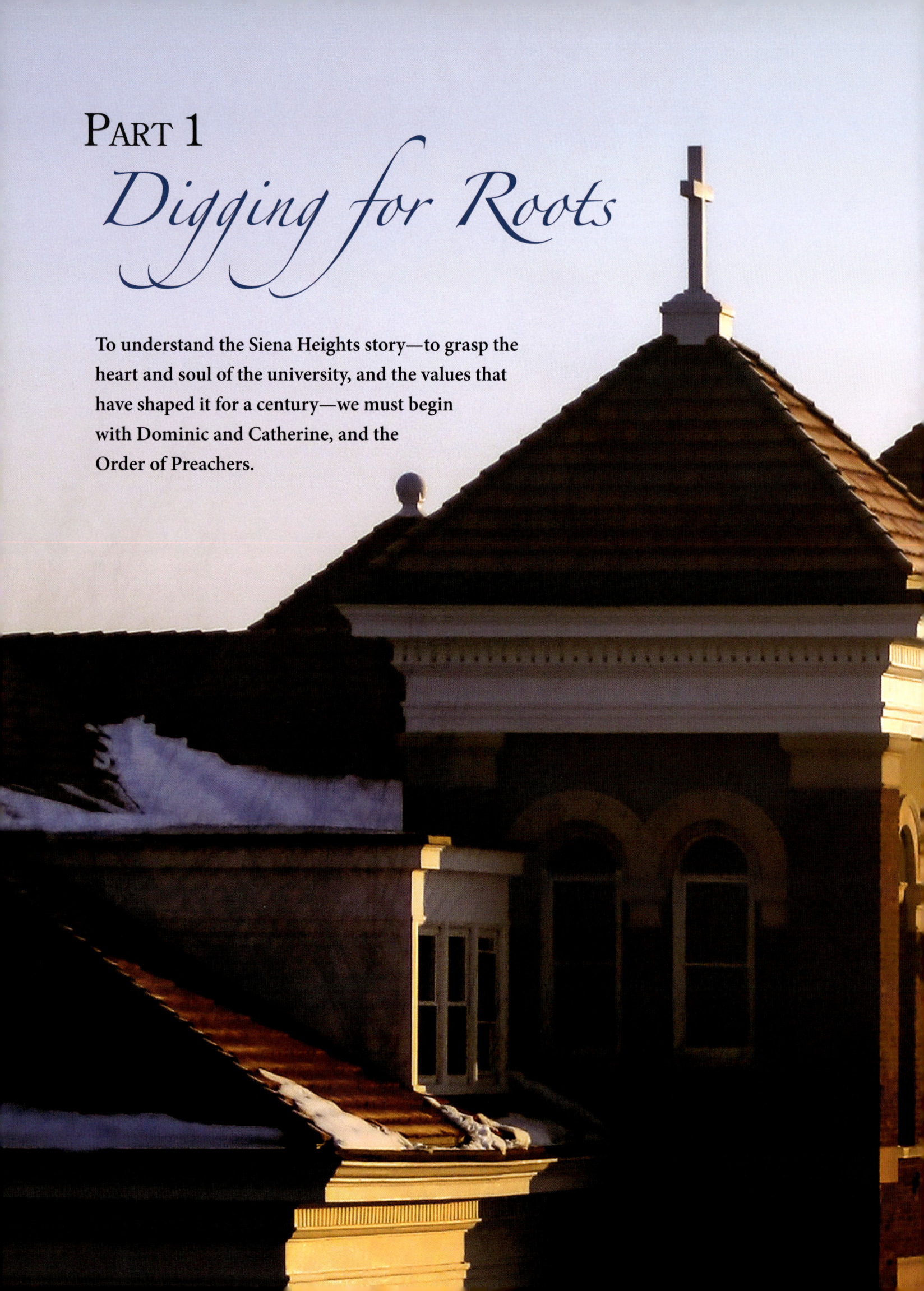

Sunrise over the rooftops of Sacred Heart Hall and its neighbor, the Dominican motherhouse Madden Hall, is a reminder of the life-giving bond between Siena Heights University and the Congregation of Adrian Dominican Sisters.

OLDER THAN ONE HUNDRED . . .

Siena Heights University celebrates its 100th anniversary in the academic year 2019–20, but our history goes back far more than a century. It has roots in the history of the Adrian Dominican Sisters and, before that, the history of Dominicans generally. The story begins with two people, now beloved as saints.

Dominic Guzman was born in the early 1170s in Caleruega, in Castile in Spain, and eventually became a priest. He was traveling in France in the early 1200s when he felt called to reach out to those in need. It was time, he said, to share the liberating truth of the gospel beyond the soaring walls of Gothic cathedrals. Instead of waiting for pilgrims to make the arduous journey to the doors of a distant church, he began to take the church to the people, wherever they were. He would preach God's Word in impoverished hamlets and hidden villages, on back roads and byways, anywhere he found people to listen. He would help them, serve them, teach them. In his lifetime he traveled and preached in Italy, Spain, and Southern France.

Dominic's idea—taking the church to the people—was a radical step, but it caught on. Others joined him. Soon they were called Dominicans. Eventually, they became the Order of Preachers. Today, all Dominicans, priests and sisters, attach to their name the initials OP, because they are still the Order of Preachers.

The earliest Dominicans embraced a two-pronged goal: to contemplate, and to give to others the fruits of that contemplation. This dual mission is still the core of Dominican life. Dominicans pray and study; that is the contemplation. But prayer and study are not enough; the second part of the work is as important as the first. They must share the fruits of contemplation. First, pray and study; then share what you have learned with others.

Dominic was canonized in 1234, becoming Saint Dominic just thirteen years after his death.

A century later, Catherine

From the beginning of his ministry, Dominic emphasized the importance of education and study. The Dominican Renaissance artist Fra Angelico painted this fresco of Dominic on the walls of the monastery of San Marco in Florence, Italy.

12 HAIL, SIENA! Siena Heights University

Benincasa was born March 25, 1347, the youngest of twenty-five children of Giacomo Benincasa and his wife, Lapa, in the hill town of Siena in Tuscany, Italy. Growing up, Catherine became an ardent follower of the ways of Saint Dominic. It is said that by the age of six, she was deeply committed to prayer; as she grew, she also became passionately responsive to the needs of her times. In her brief life, she worked for peace in many venues: within her family, in the plague-ridden hospitals of her community, in the corrupt politics of Siena, and even at the highest levels of the church, appealing humbly to the Pope to return to Rome and heal the schism dividing Christendom. She died in Rome on April 29, 1380, at the age of thirty-three. Canonized in 1461 by Pope Pius II, made a doctor of the church by Pope Paul VI in 1970, Saint Catherine—an uneducated girl from a humble family—became one of the most famous Dominicans of all time. She is the patron saint of firefighters, nurses, and the sick, and is beloved by the Dominican family.

St. Catherine of Siena

A mystic who had visions even as a child, Catherine Benincasa became known for her gift of contemplation, her devotion to the poor, and her involvement in the public issues of the fourteenth century.

Nearly five centuries after Catherine's death, the Convent of Holy Cross in Ratisbon, Germany, responded to a call for help from America by sending four Dominican sisters to New York City in 1853. These four immigrant women set down the roots of what would become eleven congregations of Dominican sisters across the United States.

A few sisters were sent from New York to Michigan in the early 1870s to teach in rural parish schools in the "thumb" area and in Traverse City. In 1879, the first four Dominicans came to Adrian, from the New York convent, to teach at the Catholic school at St. Mary's Church; four more sisters arrived the next year to teach at the St. Joseph's school. Then, in 1884, another six women arrived, charged with starting a hospital to respond to the injuries likely to occur in a railroad hub like Adrian. Now there were fourteen Dominican sisters in Adrian, many of them immigrants, some speaking no English. One woman was put in charge: Sister Camilla Madden.

Building and maintaining railroads could be dangerous. The Sisters of St. Dominic who arrived in 1884 to start a hospital anticipated many injuries in a railroad hub like Adrian.

Digging for Roots   13

A SCHOOL WOMAN

Camilla Madden was a committed educator. She had taught her younger siblings at home in Ireland, and taught in Ohio and Michigan schools before coming to Adrian. Although sent to establish a hospital, she "was really a school woman" at heart, said Sister Mary Philip Ryan, OP. Perhaps she had a plan from the beginning, because the local newspaper, *The Adrian Times and Expositor*, announced on March 21, 1884, that the Dominican sisters would open a hospital "and a college at the northern limits of the city."

But the college would not materialize for more than three decades.

Starting in a little farmhouse they called the Elm House, the sisters took in homeless residents as well as hospital patients. Anticipating more growth, Sister Camilla oversaw construction of a large brick building (the center portion of what is now Madden Hall). Prospects for the hospital were less promising than imagined, however, and the new building became primarily a home for the indigent aged. Camilla knew such an enterprise could not sustain itself financially. At the same time, she saw a greater need for education, especially for girls, than they had realized.

...continued on page 17

"Flexibility, adjustment, and risk, long recognized as distinctive marks of Dominican life, came naturally to Mother Camilla." *Nadine Foley, OP '45*

PRESIDENTIAL PROFILE NO. 1

Mother Camilla Madden, OP

President of St. Joseph's College: 1919–1924

Dominican Pioneer and Visionary.
Founder of the College.

Born in 1854 in Kings County, Ireland, Mary Madden was the eldest of nine children. She attended the local Irish schools before immigrating to America at age eighteen. In New York City, living with relatives who arrived earlier, she worked to send money home to her family. After hearing a Dominican father preach about vocations, Mary determined to become a Dominican sister. The priest directed her to Holy Rosary Convent on Second Street, but cautioned that she might need to learn German: the Holy Rosary sisters were an extension of a convent in Germany. Mary took her final vows in 1877 as Sister Mary Camilla. Eventually, three of her sisters in Ireland followed her to America and into Dominican life.

After four teaching missions elsewhere, Sister Camilla was sent to Adrian in 1884, charged with managing a hospital, establishing a permanent Dominican presence, and leading the new St. Joseph Province. Camilla—now Mother Camilla—struggled with the fact that she would not be teaching. She dearly missed the classroom, especially when she found herself planted in obscurity, among endless cornfields. When she determined there was no viable way to maintain the hospital, Camilla's love for education took root in the rural landscape.

She opened St. Joseph's Academy, a boarding school for girls, in 1896. She kept fees low to accommodate poor farm families, and the school grew rapidly. So did the community of sisters, with new postulants arriving each year. The reputation of the Adrian sisters as excellent teachers spread, too, and soon Mother Camilla was sending novices to teach in Catholic schools in other states.

In 1919, when Mother Camilla formally established St. Joseph's College, she already had two building projects in mind. Construction of the first, a magnificent classroom building, began immediately. When Sacred Heart Hall opened its doors in fall 1922, eight young lay women joined twenty-one Dominican novices for classes at the new college. Another four hundred younger girls were enrolled at the academy. The next year, work began on the second building, which would house an auditorium and gymnasium and be called Walsh Hall (later Sage Union).

Halfway through 1923, the Adrian Dominican Sisters became an independent congregation, separate from the New York convent. Perhaps Mother Camilla knew her work was done. Six months later, on January 8, 1924, she was dead. To honor the legacy of this remarkable immigrant, educator, and pioneer—founder of an academy, a college, and a congregation—the Adrian Dominicans renamed their motherhouse Madden Hall.

Mother Camilla founded a congregation, an academy, and a college.

> "The Reverend Mother Camilla was placed in charge and the influence of her holy zeal, her undaunted courage and energy were pronounced from the beginning."
>
> St. Joseph's College and Academy Catalogue, 1923–24

Mother Camilla and Sister Augustine Walsh turn the first spadeful of dirt at the 1921 groundbreaking for Sacred Heart Hall.

Adrian Dominican Sisters
Established 1884

The Elm House, where the Dominicans began their hospital in 1884, was "a bleak spot, set off by itself in the fields," according to Sister Mary Philip Ryan, OP. In 1886, the sisters moved the hospital into a brand-new brick building; ten years later, the hospital became St. Joseph's Academy. By 1902, with additions on both ends, the brick building began to resemble today's Madden Hall; the west wing (nearest in the photo) included an auditorium with a "marvelous stage" that was "the wonder of this part of the country," Sister Raymonda Culhane, OP recalled. After serving as a nursing home, and an infirmary for the college and academy, the Elm House was demolished in 1926.

Continued from page 14...

Sister Camilla wandered the nearby fields reflecting on her assignment and praying for guidance. She was expected to establish a permanent outpost for the sisters here. How would they support themselves? How should she proceed? Often her musings were interrupted by the whistles of locomotives. She would stop and listen to the trains rumbling in and out of Adrian, coming and going in all directions. How, she wondered, could she share the fruits of her contemplations?

Then it came to her. *Those trains should be bringing girls here,* she thought. *And we should be educating them.* The idea would not go away.

SCHEMING FOR AN ACADEMY

Times were hard for the pioneer Dominicans. Like the Biblical Ruth, they had been transplanted into the wilderness "amid the alien corn." They worked all day, not only teaching at the parish schools and caring for their residents, but tilling the fields where they planted fruit and vegetables, caring for the cows and chickens that provided milk, eggs, and meat. When that was not enough to feed them, they hitched the convent horse, Dolly, to a wagon and went on begging trips into the countryside. Sometimes they encountered prejudice against Catholics; but sympathetic farm families sent them home with produce or grain. It was enough to keep them going.

Despite the sisters' meager means, Camilla continued to dream about starting a school. Area priests encouraged her, but Bishop John Samuel Foley in Detroit opposed the idea, and without the Bishop's permission, she could not proceed. Eventually, working in partnership (some would say, in cahoots) with the supportive priests, she was able to secure Bishop Foley's reluctant approval. Unbeknownst to the Bishop, Camilla already had ordered—and received—desks and chairs for the new school. She was *that* certain God wanted her to do this work. With the Bishop's go-ahead in hand, she relocated the indigent residents of the hospital back into the Elm House, where they were lovingly cared for until their natural deaths. Then she outfitted the brick building with the new desks and chairs, and with beds; this would be a boarding school. And it would be called St. Joseph's Academy.

In 1896, the academy opened its doors. Six girls showed up. It was disappointing. But within a few weeks, the number rose to fifteen. And each fall confirmed that Mother Camilla's instincts were right. Enrollment grew dramatically. By 1903, after just seven years, St. Joseph's Academy was educating two hundred girls, from kindergarten through high school. Students came from farm communities in Michigan and Ohio but also from the east, west, and south, as far away as Georgia. The Dominican community was thriving, too; and each year, several academy girls were among the postulants choosing to enter the convent.

The sisters' horse, Dolly, provided transportation for business trips into the city of Adrian, as well as "begging trips" into the countryside.

Digging for Roots 17

A HIGHER DEGREE OF EDUCATION

As the academy and its reputation grew, the local community became less suspicious of the sisters. Distrust of Catholics diminished and St. Joseph's Academy was recognized as an excellent school for girls, not just a training ground for nuns. Mother Camilla gained a reputation as a fine educator, a gracious woman, and a person with good business sense. But she was not yet finished. Her dream in the cornfield had not ended with girls graduating from high school; they should be able to go further. Girls should go to college.

The success of the academy provided a foundation, and after two decades, Mother Camilla was ready to build on that foundation. But once again, there was an obstacle to overcome. This time, it was a matter of land. A college would require buildings, but where? The property east of the academy was too close to the railroad tracks. To the west, the farmland owned by Hannah and Edward Smith would be perfect, Mother Camilla thought, but there was a problem. The Smiths would not sell to the sisters. It was a matter of principle, the farmer said. And thievery, too.

For years, academy girls had raided the Smith orchard. The apples and pears were too tempting and too easy to pick for girls whose stomachs were always growling. Farmer Smith had no sympathy for hungry girls. They were stealing, he said; they had been stealing for years and the sisters were to blame. They could not buy his land.

Not to be deterred, Mother Camilla sought the help of friends, the Hays brothers, who were attorneys in Adrian. They found another buyer, someone with no interest in the land but willing and able to buy it . . . *and sell it back to the sisters!* Mother Camilla would have her college.

A COLLEGE FOR THE EDUCATION OF YOUNG LADIES

On February 25, 1919, Mother Camilla called a special meeting of her small governing group. There were five sisters around the table. The purpose of the meeting was to officially expand the sisters' existing education program from "St Joseph's Academy" to "St. Joseph's College and Academy." The college was an obvious outgrowth of the academy and would be a natural extension of it, providing opportunities for academy graduates as well as girls from other schools and postulants joining the Dominicans. The two schools—college and academy—would be part of a single organization. It seemed to make sense for both to carry the St. Joseph name.

The five sisters who signed the founding document became the college's first Board of Trustees. For legal reasons, they signed with the names they had received at birth. Mary Madden (Mother Camilla) would be president. Other trustees would be Mary Culhane, Mary Klein, Margaret McCauley, and Ellen Walsh—known to each other as Sisters Raymonda, Clementine, Agatha, and Augustine. Sister Augustine Walsh would become the college's second president and the congregation's second Mother General.

Articles of Incorporation for "St. Joseph's College and Academy" were filed in Lenawee County on March 20, 1919, and in Lansing a few days later. The purpose of the newly incorporated institution was specific: "the moral, literary, and scientific education of young ladies."

Above and right: The academy girls, from the youngest in the dining room to the first graduates in 1899, inspired Mother Camilla to dream of a college: "She had something in her, some vision, that women had to be educated to have their place in the world." *Mary Philip Ryan, OP*

Below: Located on a dirt road outside of town, surrounded by farm fields, the academy grounds were, nonetheless, enclosed by a protective fence.

Part 2
The First Fifty Years
A College for Valiant Women

"The symbolism of two new college buildings for a population of twenty-nine students in 1922 continues to speak to us today about faith in the future, and courage to responsibly act to co-create it."

—*Jeanne Lefebvre, OP '66*

When it opened in 1922, Sacred Heart Hall housed all college classrooms, and soon also housed the college dining room and a small store. Inset: Walsh Hall, opened in 1925, was sometimes called the music conservatory; it also housed a gymnasium. By the 1940s, college girls, gathered here on the fence overlooking Trinity Garden, lived in Archangelus Hall, seen in the background.

THE BEGINNING: 1919–1939
From Academy to . . . *College and Academy.*

For a few years after the 1919 chartering of St. Joseph's College, not much changed. The original brick hospital building, by now expanded with additions at both ends, still stood surrounded by farmland, serving as home, school, and offices for St. Joseph's Academy and for the sisters. Inside, a few sisters quietly began college classes, but from the outside, it was hard to see any difference at all . . . until construction began on one new building. And then another.

When Sacred Heart Hall opened in the fall of 1922, the Adrian newspaper hailed the four-story classroom building as "the pride of Adrian." Walsh Hall (later named Sage Union) opened three years later, providing an impressive concert hall, music practice rooms, and a gymnasium. Together, the two facilities created a new campus, proof that St. Joseph's College was open for business. In fact, though, the new buildings would be used by both the college and the academy; and all students of both schools still lived in Madden Hall. For years to come, popular perception around Adrian blended the two schools into one entity: "the Academy."

In the fall of 1922, the first group of eight lay college students walked through the doors of Sacred Heart Hall. Joining them were twenty-one young sisters, some of whom had begun their college studies already. Waiting for these twenty-nine students were the first three members of the full-time college faculty—all sisters, of course:

- Regina Marie Lalonde, OP, teaching English, French and Latin in Room 202
- Francis Joseph Wright, OP, teaching religion and philosophy in Room 206
- Bertha Homminga, OP, teaching science and home economics in Room 201

A PERFECT LOCATION

The 1923–24 St. Joseph's College and Academy catalogue served as the college's first marketing publication, assuring prospective students and their parents that "this institution is delightfully situated on one of the most favored sites in the vicinity of Adrian. The grounds, embracing sixty acres, afford ample opportunity for all kinds of athletic games, while the healthful location . . . with its well tilled farms, teeming orchards, and beautiful gardens, makes it an ideal spot for school girls."

Early catalogues boasted that the classrooms in Sacred Heart Hall provided "sufficient light and air that pupils can pursue their studies with no detriment to health." For many years, every classroom also had a crucifix on the wall. **Inset:** Sister Regina Marie Lalonde, OP.

Sister Regina Marie was only a novice herself, still wearing the white veil (worn by Dominican sisters before taking their first vows), when she met those first students. There were only a few chairs in Room 202 that day, nothing more; but several large desks arrived soon after. More furnishings and fittings came each week. A year later, the college could report in its catalog for 1923–24 that classrooms had not only "sufficient light and air that pupils can pursue their studies with no detriment to health," but also "every modern equipment . . . so that instruction in all the different branches can be supplemented by the most practical educational devices. The chemical and physical laboratories are well equipped."

The college girls were not immediately appreciated by the academy girls, who outnumbered them by several hundred. The high school seniors grumbled about losing their best privileges to a handful of newcomers. Now it was college girls living in the most preferred dorm on the top floor of Madden Hall and eating at the prime table in the dining room. And now, each morning after marching around "the Old Aud" (the Adrian Room in Madden Hall) for required exercise, the academy students had to wait while the college girls walked across to Sacred Heart Hall and began their classes: "Then *we* went over," Sister Catherine Philip Faeth, OP, remembered years later; the academy teacher "directed our passage and warned us by putting a finger to her lips that we should be quiet and not trouble the others."

Soon, though, annoyance turned to admiration, and the high school students embraced the college girls as adored role models. Sister Jean Cecile Hunt, OP, an academy freshman in 1926, recalled the presence of the college girls as "a great advantage because listening to them kind of said to us that our studies in high school meant something, they were leading someplace." All in all, she said, "We thought the college people were the best people that ever lived."

...continued on page 24

The First Fifty Years: A College for Valiant Women

By 1924, college girls, wearing the white caps and gowns they received as freshmen, rode in the St. Joseph's College float for the Parade of Progress.

Continued from page 23...

By 1923, when Marie Kruse stepped off the train from St. Louis, Missouri, to enroll as a freshman at the college, she found half a dozen second-year lay students and about ten other first-years like herself. After her parents had agreed she could attend a Catholic college, Marie had seen an ad for St. Joseph's in the *Sacred Heart Messenger* and was attracted by the Dominicans' white habits. Marie was only the first of many young women to be drawn to the college by the sisters' bright, white garb.

Marie and her fellow students lived a highly regulated college life, rising at 5:30 to the sound of the Madden Hall bell, retiring at 8:30 for nightly prayers. But like college students in all eras, they found ways to play as well as study, and like generations of students to follow, they tried to fool the nuns by pretending to be asleep at nightly bed check.

St. Joseph's College awarded its first degrees in 1924, to a few sisters who had begun their studies before the opening of Sacred Heart Hall. The first lay alumnae graduated a few years later. The Class of 1927 included Catherine Clark of Toledo, who came to college straight from the academy, and Helen Wolansky (later Urban), who traveled from New Jersey to enroll at St. Joseph's College. Helen's own daughter, Helena Urban (later Nosal), would be the first legacy alumna of the college, graduating twenty-five years later with the Siena Heights Class of 1952.

Change at the Top.

The 1923-24 college-and-academy catalogue described Mother Camilla Madden as a woman of "holy zeal" and "undaunted courage and energy," the "foundress" and "guiding spirit in all that pertains to the institution." She also was Mother General of the Adrian Dominican Sisters, who had only recently become an independent congregation, separate from their roots in New York.

Sister Joseph Therese (Marie) Kruse.

"A day or two before I went home for Christmas in 1923, I saw Mother Camilla coming out of the chapel with her black shawl wrapped around her. Smiling, she stopped me and asked, 'Where are you from, dear? What class are you in?'" Marie Kruse, just finishing her first semester, told Camilla she was from a small town outside St. Louis and looked forward to seeing her family over the holiday. "Then Mother Camilla invited me into her office and gave me a set of book marks, faith, hope, and charity. She made me very happy."

A few weeks later, on January 8, 1924, Marie returned to find Madden Hall's front doors draped in black. Mother Camilla had died earlier that day. "It was decided that the eight girls who were first to return would be her pallbearers. I had the great privilege

24 HAIL, SIENA! Siena Heights University

Academy and college graduates sat for a joint photo in the spring of 1929, in front of the "Grotto" that once stood on the college/academy grounds. Dark ribbon ties identify the St. Joseph College graduates.

of being one of them." A month later, Marie entered the Adrian Dominican Congregation, where, as Sister Joseph Therese Kruse, OP, she would wear the white habit that had drawn her to the college.

Sister Augustine Walsh, one of the five sisters who signed the original charter establishing the college, was elected Mother General in the spring of 1924. She now would be responsible for the congregation, the college, and the academy; she had big shoes to fill. Less outgoing than her predecessor and hampered by the periodic ill-health of asthma, Augustine was unlike Camilla in most ways except in her devotion to God and her Dominican commitment to education.

"Mother Augustine was very bright," Sister Mary Philip Ryan reflected later. "She had a great sense of education, and was herself a brain, but she was not . . . one who could go right up to the front very easily." So Augustine delegated management of the college to a trio of women who *could* comfortably step up. Mother Augustine would be president of St. Joseph's College, but Sisters Gerald Barry, Benedicta Marie Ledwidge, and Bertha Homminga would run it—and "those were the three women who got the college into the mainstream, both for certification and the granting of bachelor degrees," Sister Mary Philip said.

Even having delegated the administration to others, however, Mother Augustine would have a significant impact on the future of the college.

The First Fifty Years: A College for Valiant Women

Investing in Faculty Excellence.

Within a few years of Mother Camilla's death, the Adrian Dominicans were not only teaching girls at the academy and at the college, and children at the two Catholic elementary schools in Adrian, they also were providing sister-teachers for parish schools around the Midwest. The Adrian Dominicans in their white habits had become well-known for their intellect, their classroom skills, and the joy they brought to teaching. The number of parochial schools in America increased rapidly in the 1920s, as waves of Catholic immigrants arrived in the United States. More and more priests contacted Mother Augustine seeking teachers.

Facing this growing need for parochial school teachers—and anticipating the need for college faculty educated to the highest level—Mother Augustine made a decision late in her presidency that would influence the college and its academic reputation for years to come.

Instead of sending all novices (and even some postulants) out to teach before finishing their degrees, as had become the tradition, she selected the most promising novices each year to be "kept in for study." Instead of earning a bachelor's degree after many years of summer school, while teaching young children all through the school year, the sisters who were "kept in" would progress toward their degrees with the lay students, graduating as quickly as possible, fully prepared for teaching—or graduate school. Mother Augustine envisioned sending many sisters for doctoral studies. Since many American universities did not yet welcome women, or religious sisters, into their graduate programs, she would send them to universities overseas if needed.

...continued on page 28

Trinity Garden, dedicated in 1931, was designed as a "sunken garden" below Walsh Hall. The center statue originally was a fountain; water flowed from shell to shell into a reflecting pond—where, in winter, some college girls would try ice skating for the first time. The garden looked this way until work began on Benincasa and Archangelus Halls in 1937.

PRESIDENTIAL PROFILE NO. 2

Mother Augustine Walsh, OP

President of St. Joseph's College: 1924–1933

Gained Accreditation for the College.
Established Plan for Advanced Education of Faculty.

Born in February 1874, Ellen Walsh was the second of nine children in an immigrant Irish Catholic family in Tyre, in Michigan's "thumb" area. Farm life was challenging but Ellen's childhood was happy; the girls picked berries, the boys hunted and fished. Despite strong family ties, Ellen left home at age eighteen, feeling called to religious life. She arrived in Adrian soon after Mother Camilla's arrival, and was the community's first postulant, given the religious name Augustine. Augustine's brother Maurice became a priest, then Monsignor, and was a strong supporter of the Adrian Dominicans. Another brother, Peter, worked for the congregation for many years as overseer of buildings and gardens.

A prayerful and compassionate woman with a strong sense of justice, Augustine was one of the original faculty at St. Joseph Academy and served as secretary and assistant to Mother Camilla. Quiet, less outgoing than Camilla, and plagued by periodic asthma, Augustine was not everyone's choice when it was time to elect a new Mother General; but doubts about her leadership potential disappeared after she stepped into the position.

Mother Augustine initiated the practice of sending sisters for advanced education.

The job of Mother General of the congregation, which included serving as president of both the college and the academy, was by now very demanding. Thus, Augustine appointed three sisters to manage the college: M. Gerald Barry (correspondence and business), Benedicta Marie Ledwidge (academics), and Bertha Homminga (registration and records).

While overseeing and encouraging the three sisters in their successful efforts to achieve accreditation for the college, Augustine herself managed the congregation's widespread involvement in a fast-growing parochial school system. During her years as Mother General, the congregation opened nineteen new schools; the 1931–32 Catalog for St. Joseph's College and Academy lists *70 other schools* also "conducted by the Sisters of St. Dominic" at that time!

One of Augustine's greatest long-term contributions was her decision, shortly before death, to invest in doctoral education for promising sisters to prepare them for college teaching. Another was her commitment to shrewd money management. When she died in 1933, nine years to the day after Camilla's passing, the country was deep in economic depression but Mother Augustine left the college, academy, and congregation solvent—and with a fund to help the poor.

The college's second building, Walsh Hall (later Sage Union), which opened early in her presidency, was named in Mother Augustine's honor. The statue of St. Augustine in Trinity Garden is also a recognition of the college's second president.

> "Mother Augustine's success as a leader is shown by the fact that the community doubled its membership during her career as a mother general. The intellectual standard of the community is unsurpassed by any in the United States."
>
> *Adrian Daily Telegram, January 11, 1933*

Continued from page 26...

Although Mother Augustine did not live to see its results, her plan flowered under her successor's direction. In the college's first two decades, Sisters Regina Marie LaLonde and Ann Joachim studied languages and history respectively in Switzerland. Sister Miriam Michael Stimson studied research chemistry at Institutum Divi Thomae in Cincinnati. Sisters Philomena Murray (music), Marie McGowan (history), and Noreen McKeough (English) studied in Dublin, Ireland. Helene O'Connor (art) studied in Rome before founding Studio Angelico. They, and other Adrian Dominicans for decades to come, returned to Adrian to share the fruits of their graduate study—their contemplation—as members of the college faculty. Together, these highly educated women elevated the reputation of St. Joseph's College, later Siena Heights College, and inspired generations of students to strive for further academic achievement.

The full-time faculty grew quickly from the original three; by 1932–33, thirteen sisters were teaching and the curriculum had expanded to include music, drama, and other subjects originally dismissed as "ornaments" by Mother Camilla.

Mother Augustine was ahead of her time in her commitment to advanced education for women, but she was continuing the work begun by Mother Camilla. And when Augustine died, nine years to the day after Camilla's passing, she, too, was succeeded by a woman who would be a giant in her dedication to academic excellence. Sister Mary Gerald Barry, the first graduate of the college in 1924 and one of the three sisters to whom Augustine had entrusted its administration, became the third president in 1933. She would guide the college for more than two decades.

New Name. New Home. New Everything!

For several years in the late 1930s, college girls and their teachers watched as workmen dug the ground, laid the bricks, and transformed the area on the far sides of Trinity Garden. Previously edged by only Sacred Heart Hall and Walsh Hall, the garden was soon to be bordered by two more structures, a dormitory building and a dining hall. The deadline was tight. Many people were skeptical that the buildings would be ready for the 1938–39 academic year. But Mother Gerald prevailed. When students returned in the fall of 1938, Archangelus Hall and Benincasa Dining Hall opened their doors—and college life changed dramatically.

Left: Snow was still on the ground in early 1937 when Mother Gerald Barry and Sister Benedicta Marie Ledwidge broke ground for a new dining and dormitory complex. The project would provide living space for the college girls and separate dining areas for all, from college students to first-graders at the academy.

Right: In October 1938, students (in the caps and gowns they wore for formal occasions) and sisters gathered in Trinity Garden to dedicate Benincasa and Archangelus Halls.

From 1938 on, Archangelus lounge with its polished parquet floor was the site of many special occasions including this candlelit choral performance. In 1939, at an all-college assembly, Mother Gerald announced the college's new name from the raised landing. Through the 1940s and 1950s, the college maintained a small chapel for daily Mass at the opposite end of the lounge. (In 2019, the lounge has a new life as headquarters of the cheer and dance program.)

For girls used to living eight to a room—plus a nun—in Madden Hall, Archangelus was palatial—just two girls to a room, and a sister down the hall. Benincasa was another palace, spacious and beautifully outfitted, with moveable walls that defined separate eating areas for college girls, academy high schoolers, and the academy's youngest students.

In spring 1939, college girls and faculty gathered for a major announcement. "I can still see Mother Gerald standing at the railing at the top of the steps in Archangelus Lounge, announcing to the student body that the name of the college was being changed—not because we loved St. Joseph any less than Catherine of Siena, but because the academy was named St. Joseph, and sometimes there was confusion with the college having the same name," Sister Mary Arnold Benedetto, OP, remembered. "I wondered, though, where Mother Gerald got the 'Heights' from. I was used to lots of hills in Macon, Georgia, and I thought Adrian was quite flat."

On May 30, 1939, students, dressed in the academic robes they wore for all important occasions, raised the Siena Heights College flag for the first time.

The First Fifty Years: A College for Valiant Women

Legends of the Faculty

Sister Ann Joachim, OP '31

Sister Ann Joachim was a towering presence at Siena Heights for fifty years. A professor of history, economics, and political science from 1931 to 1971, and a prominent community leader until her death in 1981, she is one of the most colorful and best remembered teachers from Siena's first half-century. Tall and imposing with perfect posture throughout her life, "AJ" was an educator and attorney, legal counsel for the college for three decades, a multitalented athlete and coach, and a citizen activist committed to justice. She inspired hundreds of Siena Heights graduates during her lifetime; her memory continues to energize university students and alumni.

Born Petronilla Joachim in Cologne, Germany, Nellie (as she was called) came to Detroit with her family at the age of three. She began school a year later, because her older sister's first-grade teacher wearied of sending the tag-a-long Nellie home each morning. She began working part-time while still in grade school, when her father was ill and unable to work. She took a full-time job at fourteen, after her father's death, and attended business school at night. By fifteen, she was a legal secretary in a law firm. She quickly determined to study law herself, but for that, she would need a high school diploma. To speed up the process, she attended night classes simultaneously at two different high schools; by the time anyone questioned this approach, she already had passed the entrance exam and been accepted into the Detroit College of Law.

Graduating from law school at twenty-one, Nellie was the only woman present the day she sat for—and passed—the bar exam. She stayed with the same law office, earned an advanced degree, and eventually became a partner in the firm where she had started as a stenographer. Throughout those years of night school and daytime work, she always made time for her other interest: sports. She was a dedicated all-around athlete, becoming a tennis champion, a licensed pilot, a capable basketball player, and a sure shot with a gun.

Sister Ann Joachim brought many public figures to campus to engage students in public affairs of the day. When Michigan's G. Mennen "Soapy" Williams visited, she donned a bow tie in support of the bow-tied governor's liberal policies.

> "She was an incredible teacher. . . . She had an amazing appetite for life and for trying to better the community. Her personal actions, as well as her teachings, have stood out to me. It is what I have used most."
> *Carl Morton '71*

To the amazement of friends and family, Nellie decided at age twenty-seven to enter religious life. She had a dear friend who had joined the Adrian Dominicans; and she wrote later of feeling so drawn to serve God that she could not justify life outside the congregation. She entered the novitiate in January 1928; and took her first vows—and received her new name, Sister Ann Joachim (for Jesus' grandfather) Joachim (her legal last name)—in August 1930. A year later, this attorney with a law degree received her bachelor's degree from St. Joseph's College. She went on to earn a master's in history and political science from Loyola in Chicago, and a doctorate in history from the International Catholic University in Switzerland. Returning to America from Europe, she became the first woman religious admitted to practice law before the U.S. Supreme Court.

In addition to teaching history and social science, AJ was legal counsel for the college from 1939 to 1971. A practicing attorney, she also served as vice mayor of Adrian.

At Siena Heights, Sister Ann Joachim was known for many things. For years, all sophomores took her class in parliamentary procedure. Generations of students remember the chart on her classroom wall detailing the steps involved in passing a bill through Congress, "something that everyone had to know—or else!" Nadine Foley, OP '45, remembered. Many a student quaked in anticipation of her lengthy true-or-false exams, given orally with no repeats. That was her rule: "If you don't hear it the first time, there's no second chance!" She counseled seniors on finding work after graduation; Rita Geiger Schwing '52 was one of many alumnae AJ guided toward jobs in Washington, D.C. She also advised foreign students from up to nineteen different countries.

HAIL, SIENA! Siena Heights University

> "I was a lonely freshman when this tall Dominican nun came striding into Benincasa Hall cradling a shotgun! 'I'm going to get that crow yet!' she announced. Later, of course, I got to know her as an inspired teacher."
>
> *Marianne Egan McKeague '54*

She brought political speakers to campus, organized air raid drills, coordinated voter-registration efforts, and modeled for students the responsibilities of citizenship. She lobbied successfully to change the name of the road past the college to Siena Heights Drive. She spoke out against discrimination and stood up for the rights of immigrants and minorities. She worked tirelessly to keep the Norfolk and Western Railroad's Wabash Cannonball rolling through Adrian, where sisters and students regularly boarded or stepped off the train. She ran successfully for a seat on the Adrian City Commission because she wanted to make life better for the city's poor—and because she believed women should have a voice in government.

As did all teaching sisters in her era, Ann Joachim also patrolled the residence halls, enforcing rules and solving unexpected problems. Several alumnae remember her coming to the rescue when an unauthorized pizza delivery vehicle was stuck on the snowy driveway outside Archangelus Hall; Sister Ann pushed up her sleeves, pushed on the bumper, and helped the unfortunate driver get a start back up the hill!

Along with all that, Ann Joachim maintained her passion for athletics. She was the force behind sports in the college's earliest years and coached most of the teams that played basketball in the Walsh Hall gymnasium, where she was known to have a mean hook shot even in full habit.

> "Ann Joachim was the citizen-plus of the U.S."
>
> *Nadine Foley, OP '45*

During Alumni Weekend 1975, AJ was honored with this certificate from the National Register of Prominent Americans and International Notables. Her many achievements included becoming the first nun ever to be admitted to practice law before the U.S. Supreme Court, and publishing numerous judicial, sociological, and historical writings. Famous locally for her efforts to keep the "Wabash Cannonball" train in service, she was also an international figure, voted one of two thousand Women of Achievement in the world by the London Biographers.

Ann Joachim's remarkable legacy lives on in the Alumni Association's Sister Ann Joachim Award, given to graduates who take on society's difficult challenges, overcoming obstacles to achieve a better world while maintaining Dominican values. In 2014, AJ was inducted posthumously into the Athletic Hall of Fame, in recognition of her role as the founder of organized athletics—back when Siena Heights was still St. Joseph's College! In 2015, students on Siena's main campus honored Ann Joachim's memory during Homecoming with t-shirts depicting her campaign to save the Wabash Cannonball.

Even in full habit, Sister Joachim remained enthusiastic and involved in many sports!

> "The sisters hired me to do lawn care one summer. They fed me, too, and kind of took me under their wing. One day Sister Ann Joachim asked me if I had a shotgun, because they had too many pigeons. I said yes, and brought it the next day. I thought she wanted me to handle the problem. But no, she borrowed the gun. And she did fine. The next day, the sisters had squab for dinner."
>
> *Glenn Milner, Lenawee County Resident*

The First Fifty Years: A College for Valiant Women

Art students in 1939 assisted Belgian artist Ade Bethune in painting the frescoes outside Benincasa Hall that depict scenes from the life of St. Catherine Benincasa of Siena. Here, Catherine feeds the poor.

The Benincasa Frescoes and Studio Angelico.

In 1939, Siena Heights welcomed Belgian baroness Adelaide ("Ade") Bethune, an acclaimed artist and illustrator for the *Catholic Worker* newspaper in New York, to Siena Heights to design an original artwork for the walls outside the main entrance to Benincasa Hall.

As Sister Dorothy Ferguson, OP '42, recalled, "Mother Gerald had asked Sister Helene to provide some sort of appropriate decoration on the walls; they were pure white and something really was needed there." Sister Helene O'Connor, OP '34, was familiar with Ade Bethune's work, and knew it would be appropriate. "Helene wanted frescoes, rather than paintings, because paint very often tends to change color or to fade," Sister Dorothy continued. "You might have seen frescoes in Florence, Italy, that are a few hundred years old and still fresh."

Dorothy and several other art students worked as assistants with Baroness Bethune, taking down old (only one-year old!) plaster, preparing new plaster, and grinding pigment into a fine paste of paint. "Frescoes must be done on wet plaster," Dorothy explained, "so the fresh plaster could only be put on as much of the wall as could be completed in one day." Ade Bethune drew the "cartoon" in advance, then her student assistants traced the figures onto the wet plaster and carefully painted according to her color coding. "All of it really was done by Ade, because she had determined the colors that would go, and the coding. What we did was fill in the color. Then she did the final details. She drew in the features and also did the calligraphy with texts from the Dialogue of Saint Catherine."

At about the same time that Benincasa received its frescoes, Sister Helene moved the Art Department—which she named Studio Angelico after the Dominican priest and fresco artist Fra Angelico—from the basement of Sacred Heart Hall into the remodeled fifth floor attic of the building. Art would thrive on the fifth floor for three decades.

CAMPUS LIFE: THE NOT-TOO-ROARING '20s AND '30s
In Loco Parentis. **Extreme Version.**

When mothers and fathers sent their daughters to St. Joseph's College, they (and the girls) understood that the sisters were empowered to act as parents. As a result, campus life for those earliest alumnae was a far cry from what any student today would expect. Or accept!

Prior to 1938, all students lived in Madden Hall, in "dorms" that were large rooms with many beds, each with sheet-like curtains that were tied back during the day and let down at night for privacy. College girls lived together, separate from the academy girls, but every room included a Dominican sister (forerunners of the "wing nuns" who monitored Archangelus Hall). As academic dean, Sister Francis Joseph Wright also lived in a room with the college girls, checking bedtimes and bed-making along with academic achievements and failures!

The daily schedule was strict and demanding. Bells woke the students at 5:30 each day for morning prayer, followed by an hour of study before breakfast at 7:00 and Mass at 7:30. Attendance at Mass was not mandatory, especially for non-Catholics, of which there were always a few; but Catholic girls knew that any absence from Mass would be noted and investigated. Designated time slots for classes, study, meals, and three "recreation" periods filled the time before nightly prayer at 8:00 p.m. Bedtime was early, lights had to be out, and beds were checked to be sure each girl was where she should be.

When Sacred Heart Hall opened in 1922, everyone—college students, academy girls, and sisters—still ate in the basement of Madden Hall; the lay college students sat at tables in Refectory No. 3 next to Sister Annunciata's kitchen. Midway through the next year, however, college girls began having their meals in Sacred Heart Hall, Room 101 on the lower level. If you walked outside from Madden to Sacred Heart, the dining room was on the right at the foot of the stairs; if you came underground, it was the first room on the right as you emerged from the tunnel. Adrian Dominican novices brought the food through the tunnel from "Nuncie's" kitchen, then tried to keep it hot in Room 102 until serving time. Whether the college girls thought this was a step up or not is unknown!

...continued on page 34

For more than four decades, a protective iron fence surrounded the college, academy, and motherhouse grounds. Students needed permission, and sometimes an escort, to leave the grounds.

Until 1938, college students (like the academy girls) lived in Madden Hall, in dormitories like this one: large rooms resembling barracks, with curtains providing privacy for each of the many beds—in one of which slept the sister in charge.

Continued from page 33...

Like the academy girls, college students wore uniforms: a navy blue serge dress with a sailor-style collar Monday through Saturday, and a black dress of the same design with gold collar trim for Sundays. The St. Joseph's catalogue detailed strict instructions about what else to bring (or not) and even what to bring it in. Each girl's "one trunk and one traveling suitcase" was to include four pairs of sateen bloomers, among other things. Silk underwear was specifically banned "as we discourage all things that go for expense and not for training of character." In case anyone misunderstood, "the school reserves the right to return unsuitable articles."

Mail, too, was strictly monitored. Students were required to write home once a week, and outgoing mail was placed unsealed in a designated basket. Incoming mail was opened before it was given to the student; any money enclosed was removed and credited to the student's account, where it would stay until requested for a trip downtown or a weekend at a friend's home. Upon returning from the city—that is, Adrian—girls had to present their purchases for approval.

A wrought-iron fence surrounded the grounds in those years, and girls needed approval for any trip beyond it. Even a century ago, teenagers chafed against such restrictions. Catherine Clark '27 of Toledo, who comfortably traveled alone by interurban railroad any time she went home, recalled decades later: "We didn't have many privileges. We went to school on Saturday and had Thursday as a free day when we were permitted to go into town, usually accompanied by a sister. I always hated to ask permission. Sister Mary Pius was in charge one day when I said, 'Sister, I came to tell you I'm about to go downtown.' She said, 'Most people come and *ask* to go, but not Cath Clark!'"

Phyllis Muzillo Robison '36 (left) and Clorinda Bonfiglio Sullivan '36 celebrated their fiftieth reunion in 1986. **Above:** Classmate Marian Stimson, shown in her student days, enrolled with them in 1932—but graduated four years later as Sister Miriam Michael Stimson.

HAIL, SIENA! Siena Heights University

Not Much Social Life. Plenty of Pranks.

College girls in those early decades knew they were there to study, and they were grateful for the opportunity. The costs—$100 for one semester's tuition, room, and board in 1923–24, plus fees of $1 for the library and $5 for the gymnasium—sound laughably affordable today, but at the time, they were significant. Not many families could, or would, send their daughters to college.

When Sister Jean Marie Sheridan, OP, looked back at her life as a lay freshman in 1923, she noted that the life of the college girls was not much different from that of the postulants and novices. "Even our Saturdays were programmed," she said, "and social life was of our own making." Sister Helen Rita McCartney, OP, agreed, remembering her two years as a lay student: "We were there to study . . . but we did have very good times among ourselves, mostly laughing about nothing."

"We made our own fun and had lots of it," said Beatrice Cunningham Meyer '32, who was a freshman in 1926. "We used to sneak food from the dining room so we could have parties at night, maybe as late as 8:30!" She and her twin sister shared a first-floor room in Madden Hall with one four-poster bed; "because we were sisters, we were allowed to occupy the same bed." Sometimes they sneaked across the hall to the sisters' community room, bravely stretching a hand or foot over the threshold, just because it was forbidden. "We would have been expelled if we were caught!"

MAKING MISCHIEF IN MADDEN HALL

"A wicked thing we did was to sneak out into the hall and up the marble stairs. At the top of the stairs there was a pair of deer, mounted deer that Mother Augustine's brother had captured in his hunting days and had donated and put up there. We used to sneak up and turn their tails at a rakish angle. Of course, that was strictly forbidden and severely punished if ever one got caught."
Beatrice Cunningham Meyer '32 (1992 St. Dominic Award winner)

"We had two groups: the 'pray' girls and the 'play' girls. I had my roots in both. For the 'play' girls, fun was raiding the pantry and sliding down the marble stairs on pillows and roller-skating to town. That hill seemed a lot steeper back then. We'd skate into town, leave our skates at the post office, and then we'd do whatever we wanted to do."
Anna Bakeman Tompert '38 (1996 Outstanding Alumni Award winner)

"St. Joseph's College in 1938 was sort of like having your mother still with you. We had to get permission for everything we did. We didn't even have the privilege of someone not doubting us, because they didn't know us. It was a wonderful time!"
Sister Betty Dolan, OP '46 (freshman in 1938)

Above: Anna Bakeman, who came to college at age sixteen, admitted to having been both a "play girl" and a "pray girl." Still mischievous decades later, Ann Bakeman Tompert '38, veteran school teacher and author of many children's books, received the 1996–97 Outstanding Alumni Award.

Right: For several decades, a standard and mildly racy prank was posing with this sign, as if to encourage "parking."

The First Fifty Years: A College for Valiant Women

PRESIDENTIAL PROFILE NO. 3

Mother Mary Gerald Barry, OP

President of St. Joseph's/Siena Heights College: 1933–1957

Longest Serving President.
Architect of the Core Campus.
Creator of "Siena Heights" Name.

Michael and Catherine Barry of County Clare, Ireland, welcomed eighteen babies. Of the thirteen who lived past infancy, eleven would leave Ireland for the United States; and four—three sons and a daughter—would enter religious life. Bridget Catherine, born March 11, 1881, and known by her second name, left for America at age fifteen, joining several siblings already settled in Chicago; but she never lost her love of home. She visited Ireland as often as possible.

The Barry siblings found success in America. Two brothers settled in Florida, becoming highly respected as Bishop of St. Augustine and Monsignor in Miami Beach. Other brothers became attorneys, engineers, and businessmen. The sisters raised industrious families. In Chicago, the teenaged Catherine lived with and assisted the families of her brother Gerald and sister Susan, while simultaneously studying business and Gaelic. In her spare time, she studied with her brothers, Frank and James, who were in law school. Eventually, Catherine followed Frank to Nogales, Arizona, to work as an aide in his law practice and a companion to his wife. Those experiences in business and law would prove invaluable in her future.

Catherine Barry began to feel a call to religious life in her twenties, and after visiting her brother in Florida, expected to join the Sisters of St. Joseph in St. Augustine. But back in Nogales, she met several

Catherine Barry joined the Adrian Dominicans two years after this 1910 photo was taken.

Sister Mary Gerald and her twelve brothers and sisters: "Catherine and [ten of] her siblings were but a few of the many thousands of Irish emigres to the New World during the nineteenth century. Some were fleeing the Great Famine of the 1840s, while others left for political reasons, or because there were so few ways of making a living in Ireland, or simply because they were seeking a new adventure." Sister Nadine Foley, OP '45

Sister Mary Gerald (right) became a valued assistant to Mother Camilla.

Dominican teachers—and when she left Arizona in 1912, it was for Chicago and then on to Adrian, where she would be given her brother Gerald's name as her own: Sister Mary Gerald Barry. In 1924, she received the first degree ever awarded by the young St. Joseph's College; shortly thereafter, she was one of three sisters tapped by Mother Augustine to manage the college. In 1933, she was elected to succeed Augustine as the congregation's third Mother General, automatically becoming third president of the college.

Mother Gerald's contributions over a twenty-four-year presidency were remarkable: She built a PhD-educated faculty, by implementing Augustine's commitment to graduate education for the sisters. Through shrewd money management, she kept the college afloat through the Depression and World War II. She built an identity for the college, by providing dedicated dining and living space for college students in Benincasa and Archangelus Halls; and by renaming the college to distinguish it from the academy. She went on to build the core campus, adding the science and library facilities (together originally called Angelicus Hall) and Lumen Ecclesiae Chapel, named for St. Dominic, "the light of the church" (and renamed St. Dominic Chapel in the twenty-first century).

> *"Mother Gerald was a most remarkable woman. She was rough sometimes and said what she thought, but no one ever accused her of being unjust."*
> Sister Joseph Therese Kruse, OP

In these same years, Mother Gerald built and managed Catholic elementary and high schools across the country; started Barry College in Florida; began plans for St. Dominic College in Illinois; sent sisters to build schools and teach in the Dominican Republic, Puerto Rico, Peru, and the Bahamas; took over management of two hospitals (in Nevada and California); and initiated many of the congregation's social work and justice ministries.

In 1957, an exhausted Mother Gerald separated the presidency of Siena Heights from the job of Adrian Dominican Prioress. Continuing as head of the congregation, she appointed Sister Benedicta Marie Ledwidge, longtime academic dean, as fourth president of the college.

At her death in 1961, Mother Gerald was an internationally known church leader. Among those attending her funeral in Adrian were five archbishops, seven bishops, sixty monsignori, and two hundred priests. Her brother, Monsignor William Barry of Miami, presided.

> *"I was thirteen years old, riding my bicycle down Howell Road. I had to stop and watch. There were more nuns and priests than I had ever seen, hundreds of them, all in black, walking slowly to the cemetery. I was in awe. I thought the pope must have died."*
> Tracy R. Church '93, recalling Mother Gerald's funeral procession in 1961.

"With singular vision and with prudent wisdom and with missionary zeal, she has established new foundations and immeasurably improved the old." Honorary Doctorate citation from Loyola University

Basketball in the Walsh Hall gym (right) and (above) passion plays in Walsh Hall auditorium were highlights of student life in the early decades.

Arts and Early Athletics.

The earliest college students remembered plays and recitals in Madden Hall's "Old Aud," a combination auditorium, recreation room, and gathering place where girls received their mail in the evening. But the opening of Walsh Hall provided a spectacular new space specifically designed for music, drama, and athletics. Henceforth, the annual passion plays, orchestra concerts, lectures, and Friday night movies (on reel-to-reel projectors) took place in the sparkling new performance level. The basement became the site of loudly cheered basketball contests.

The lower level gymnasium, complete with windowed viewing areas at each end of the court, made possible an expanded physical education program and a lively new basketball tradition. The college and academy girls often played each other, with "the college nuns rooting for us and the academy nuns cheering for their girls. Lots of nuns used to turn out for our games," recalled Sister Mary Arnold Benedetto, OP '42. Sister Ann Joachim supervised the basketball program, and had "instructed us about reporting to the referee when you were sent in to replace another player. Dolores Gass dutifully reported, 'Gass for Benedetto,' and the referee jumped and said, 'What's the matter? Is she sick?'"

The Cunningham twins, Lillian and Beatrice, jumped at the chance to play basketball when they arrived in 1926—and distinguished themselves enough that both were invited to coordinate "physical training" at the college for two years in exchange for tuition. The twins' parents were only able to support them for the two years needed to earn a teaching certificate; but as the college's first "graduate assistants," both Lillian '30 and Beatrice '32 were able to complete bachelor's degrees. (Beatrice taught school for two years before returning to take over her sister's job). In the 1940s, Lois Hueneman Chazaud '49 would have a similar opportunity, earning part of her tuition by leading exercise classes for the postulants and working as a scheduling assistant for basketball coach Ann Joachim.

HAIL, SIENA! Siena Heights University

When Anna Bakeman Tompert '38 came to college at the age of sixteen in 1934, she found an active cultural life. "Sister Leonilla, bless her heart, was the drama teacher and she did some wonderful work. I remember doing an operetta, *Hansel and Gretel*, and I was one of the witches—you know, 'Nibble, nibble, mousie, who's nibbling at my housie?' That was a terrific show. The passion plays were wonderful, too."

The student body was small, so everyone got involved, Anna remembered: "Sister Thomasine was in desperate need of a violinist for her orchestra; and guess what, I rented the violin and learned to play. That's the truth." But when the musical piece called for a chorus, "after doing my bit in the orchestra, I was running out and getting on the stage for the chorus. I shall never forget that. I didn't have any time to get into trouble."

A Growing Campus and Well Regulated Home.

By 1938, Archangelus and Benincasa Halls had expanded the campus. College and high school students might pass each other outside the dining hall, but college life was definitely separate from the academy now. College girls were still closely monitored, though, and expected to maintain the high standards of "a well-regulated home where high principles prevail." Those standards included cleanliness and neatness in their rooms.

The hall nuns made daily inspections to ensure the girls kept Archangelus pristine. "I guess today's students are not expected to wash their windows, but we certainly did ours," Sister Mary Arnold Benedetto said of her student years. On her corridor, Sister Helene O'Connor checked the rooms daily. "We never won any prizes for neatness. In fact, Sister Helene used to leave little notes: 'Benedetto's ghetto,' 'Slum Clearance Project,' and so on. Or, 'Kindly remove the groceries from the front window.'"

"The magnolia trees on either side of Benincasa Hall were planted by Sister Mary George Nolan circa 1941. A delegation of sisters was present and all laughed heartily when she declared that the two twelve-inch trees would blossom to huge sentinels someday. Sister was right. Have a look!"
Sister Philomena Murray, OP, music faculty 1939–51

CHALLENGES AND ACHIEVEMENTS: THE 1940s AND '50s
The War Years.

As the 1940s began, the Adrian Dominican Sisters, with Mother Gerald at the helm, were exceedingly busy. Sisters were teaching in Catholic schools across the country. During one month in 1940, the congregation opened Dominican High School in Detroit and Barry College in Miami, Florida. A few months later, the Adrian Dominicans took over operation of a hospital in Santa Cruz, California (today's Dominican Hospital). And in Adrian, Siena Heights College and St. Joseph's Academy were thriving, both well known for academic excellence.

As a sign of confidence in the future, Sister Mary George Nolan, OP, business manager, planted magnolia trees on either side of the entrance to Benincasa Hall in the spring of 1941. "A delegation of sisters was present and all laughed heartily when she declared that the two twelve-inch trees would blossom to huge sentinels someday," recalled Sister Philomena Murray, who taught music from 1939 to 1951. "Sister was right, of course!"

World War II brought serious concerns to campus; but members of the Class of 1944 could not help but giggle after modeling the gas masks that prepared them for an attack.

The freshman class that enrolled at Siena Heights in the fall of 1941 would be unique in the college's history. Their first semester included America's entry into World War II following the bombing of Pearl Harbor on December 7, 1941. Their final semester included the celebration of V-E Day (Victory in Europe), on May 8, 1945. Between those historic bookends, the class of 1945 started a Student Council, wrote a constitution, volunteered with migrant workers and families, prepared for air raids, attended daily Mass, played basketball and bridge, walked to town, and studied a lot.

"There were not many proper parties," remembered Connie Berube Binsfeld '45, who came to Siena Heights from rural northern Michigan, "because it was very difficult to find boys." And there were worries, she added. "We had a lot of concerns about our families, our boyfriends, and former classmates, because that was the age group that was so very involved in the war. I think that did a lot to solidify an unusual closeness between the classes in those four years."

Sister Ann Joachim coached students as civil air wardens; this trio appeared to enjoy modeling their uniforms.

Growth in the 1950s.

At Siena, and across America, the decade following the war was a period of stability and growth. Enrollment at Siena Heights increased. The congregation attracted large numbers of young women interested in religious life. "There were large numbers of postulants, but the number of lay students also increased," said Sister Anne Marie Brown, OP '40, who served as director of admissions. "The students were high caliber and the faculty was totally involved."

In the fall of 1955, the freshman class was so large that a room in the basement of Walsh Hall behind the gym, was outfitted as a dorm. Eight freshman women, including Maurine Barzantni, OP '59, lived in a refitted locker room, which they called "St. Cecilia's," for the fall semester. "Basketball practice drowned out all concentration," Maurine remembered. "People coming to games, or to concerts upstairs, sometimes wandered in, too. Sister Ann Joachim gave us a very serious talk about allowing men in our dorm and damaging our reputation, which she hinted was already a little questionable." St. Cecilia's was a temporary solution, but Maurine and her friends left it with some sadness when space opened up in Archangelus for second semester.

Students in the 1950s remember studying biology with Sister Edwina Clare Crook; music with Sisters Denise Mainville and Marie Madonna; and Greek with Sister Ellen Vincent McClain. Theater students adored Sister Leonilla Barlage. Spanish students worked with migrant families alongside Sister Laurine Neville. English literature students studied with Sister Robert Louise; if they were lucky, they might be invited to join her Thomas More Book Club.

Founding faculty member Sister Bertha Homminga by now was renowned as the registrar who knew you by transcript as well as by name, and who could (and did) stop you in the hall to remind you of a graduation requirement yet to be met. Sister Regina Marie Lalonde, also one of the founding faculty, was still energetically teaching English and other languages; late in the decade, she installed a cutting-edge "language lab" on the third floor of Sacred Heart Hall.

The First Fifty Years: A College for Valiant Women   41

Legends of the Faculty

1919–2019 | 100 | SIENA HEIGHTS UNIVERSITY

Sister Miriam Michael (M²) Stimson, OP '36

Sister Miriam Michael Stimson—acclaimed chemist, scholar, teacher, and lifelong learner—was part of Siena Heights for seventy years. After attending the academy, where she grieved the death of her younger sister, also an academy student, she came to St. Joseph's College as a freshman in 1932. She graduated as a Dominican sister and a promising scientist. Mother Gerald sent her immediately to Institutum Divi Thomae in Cincinnati, where she was warmly received and earned her master's and doctoral degrees in chemistry in three years. She returned to Adrian in 1939 and began three decades as a celebrated professor of chemistry, teaching the valiant women of Siena Heights who nicknamed her M². She also established a research branch of the Institutum Divi Thomae at Siena Heights, operating out of a small laboratory in the basement of Sacred Heart Hall (now the alumni office).

Miriam brought many innovations to the teaching of chemistry, introducing micro methods and undergraduate research to the curriculum, and conducting her own research, including funded cancer research. In her early years as a chemist, she pioneered a technique for analyzing solids by means of infrared absorption, a development that proved critical to the discovery of the structure of DNA.

In 1953, she lectured at the International Colloquium in Spectroscopy held at the Sorbonne in Paris; Miriam was only the second woman invited to lecture at the Sorbonne, the first having been Madame Marie Curie. Later, she was invited to Rome for an audience with the Pope. She was also the first woman invited to lecture at the University of Notre Dame.

Miriam attended St. Joseph Academy for the last two years of high school; her younger sister, Alice Ruth, came, too. As she had throughout their childhood, Miriam would be watching out for her sister. But early in their second year, Alice Ruth died of heart failure, a grief that would stay with Miriam through her life.

> "She was very concerned about those of us teaching high school science. If you taught in a small high school, you taught all the science courses, and perhaps advanced math. That took a broad education. So she made provisions for us to learn literally everything. . . . She made sure that we understood the evolutionary process."
>
> *Sister Virginia O'Reilly, OP '73/MA*

Reflecting on changes in education and research, Miriam once noted, "I was taught simply to play around, and see what comes out. . . . 'This looks a little abnormal'. . . we had to ultimately put the results of experiments into the explicit format."

Alumnae from the 1940s and 1950s remember Miriam in the chemistry lab in full habit, an imposing, demanding, and deeply caring mentor. They also remember her patrolling the residence hall; she was unbending if she caught a young woman smoking! After Vatican II, alumni returning to campus met a new M²—"Just call me Miriam"—dressed in slacks, hair flying, welcoming former students to her home for snacks and conversation.

In the late 1960s, Sister Miriam accepted a research and teaching post at Keuka College in upstate New York. She returned to Siena Heights in 1978, serving as director of graduate programs until 1991 and developing a graduate program in addiction counseling. Her research took her to Leningrad, Azerbaijan, Armenia, and Moscow; and in 1989, she was invited to lecture at Jilin University, Manchuria, in the People's Republic of China.

> "While preparing materials for *The Soul of DNA*, I discovered that each person who knew Miriam had a slightly different interpretation of her, depending upon when they knew her and in what capacity. As for myself, I will always remember Miriam as a woman who transformed her tears into knowledge."
>
> *Jun Tsuji, Biology Faculty and Miriam's Biographer*

HAIL, SIENA! Siena Heights University

Miriam involved students, including Patricia Levinski Sommerfeldt '54, in her research, starting in her original lab in Sacred Heart Hall 103 (in 2019, the alumni office). In the late 1950s, she moved her spectrophotometer research into a new lab in the science-library addition.

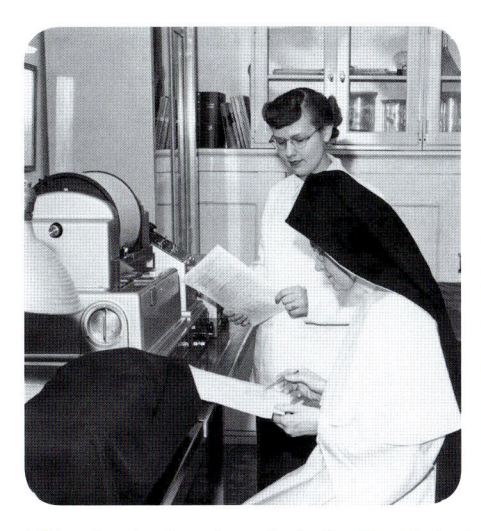

> "Miriam wasn't your stereotypical nun. Her veil gave way to signature hats. She wore overalls to work the earth in her beloved garden. She was a very colorful person, who was ahead of her time in many ways."
> *Sister Joan Sustersic, OP '66*

Sister Miriam's research attracted attention from many circles, including these professors and PhDs from the University of Michigan, Institutum Divi Thomae, Chrysler, and Parke Davis, who gathered in Miriam's first research lab to learn more about her work.

Upon retiring in 1991, Miriam was named professor emerita. For the next decade she kept an office in Sacred Heart Hall which she visited daily, reading scientific journals, following national and international news, corresponding with former students, conversing with faculty, and keeping administrators on their toes with her proofreading and policy ideas. When the college changed its name in 1998, it was Miriam—whom President Rick Artman introduced as "an institution herself"—who unveiled the new sign for Siena Heights University.

Chemistry professor and academic vice president Sharon Weber, OP '69, one of Miriam's former students, remembers her as a remarkable teacher. "I used to tell my own chemistry students that even the chairs in the science hall could explain chemistry if they would just listen. . . . Miriam was *that* good."

Known for her love of big hats and fresh vegetables, and for an undiminished joy in living, Miriam maintained a lively intellectual life throughout her eighty-nine years. She received the university's highest honor, the Siena Medal, six weeks before her death in 2002. In 2004, biology professor Jun Tsuji published Miriam's biography, which he had been working on for several years, titled *The Soul of DNA: The True Story of a Catholic Sister and Her Role in the Greatest Scientific Discovery of the Twentieth Century*. The book was nominated for the Margaret Rossiter History of Women in Science Prize.

The First Fifty Years: A College for Valiant Women   43

New Labs, a Library, and Lumen Ecclesiae.

The 1950s saw a spurt of building at Siena Heights.

The science laboratories and the library—which, along with every other educational facility, had been housed in Sacred Heart Hall since 1922—were in serious need of upgrading. The third floor library extended out into the hallway—and college girls often studied in the evenings with bats flying above them! Science classes met on the fourth floor, while research took place in Sister Miriam's ground floor research lab; supplies were stored in the basement stairwell.

In spite of these inconveniences, Siena Heights was earning national recognition for scholarship and science. But physical improvements were overdue.

A major addition, built onto the north wall of Sacred Heart Hall in 1955, provided space on its bottom two floors for mathematics and the sciences; the top level became a spacious library. The addition was intended to be named Angelicus Hall, but for some reason, the name never stuck; more than fifty years later, the facilities, expanded by another addition in 1981, are still called the Library and the Science Wing.

Almost immediately, construction began on another project: a stand-alone chapel, to be located between Sacred Heart and Madden halls. Up to this time, the college had used the sisters' Holy Rosary Chapel for significant occasions, and maintained a small chapel for daily use at the far end of Archangelus Lounge, which could be sectioned off with a folding wall. The simultaneous growth of both the college and the congregation prompted the decision to build a dedicated chapel for Siena Heights and the academy.

Early chemistry students studied on the fourth floor of Sacred Heart Hall. In the 1950s, students and postulants helped move the Science Department out of Sacred Heart and into the new addition, where they and their teachers enjoyed new lab facilities.

Alumnae of the 1950s remember these building projects well, because the students were part of the labor force! Once the Sacred Heart addition was completed, the college girls—postulants and lay students—were pressed into service to move the contents of the library and the labs into their new homes. When the chapel was complete, the student movers went into action again, transporting materials from Archangelus into Lumen Ecclesiae Chapel, named in honor of St. Dominic, "the light of the Church."

The new construction put the talents of another visiting artist to work, as Benincasa had done earlier. The artist this time was Melville Steinfels. For the science wing, Steinfels designed and painted the fresco of Dominican Albert the Great, patron saint of scientists, that appears on the south wall of the upper floor; once again, art students watched as he painted on wet plaster and explained the ancient technique. In the chapel, Steinfels designed and executed the three gold mosaics behind the chapel altar, as well as the Stations of the Cross on the aisle walls.

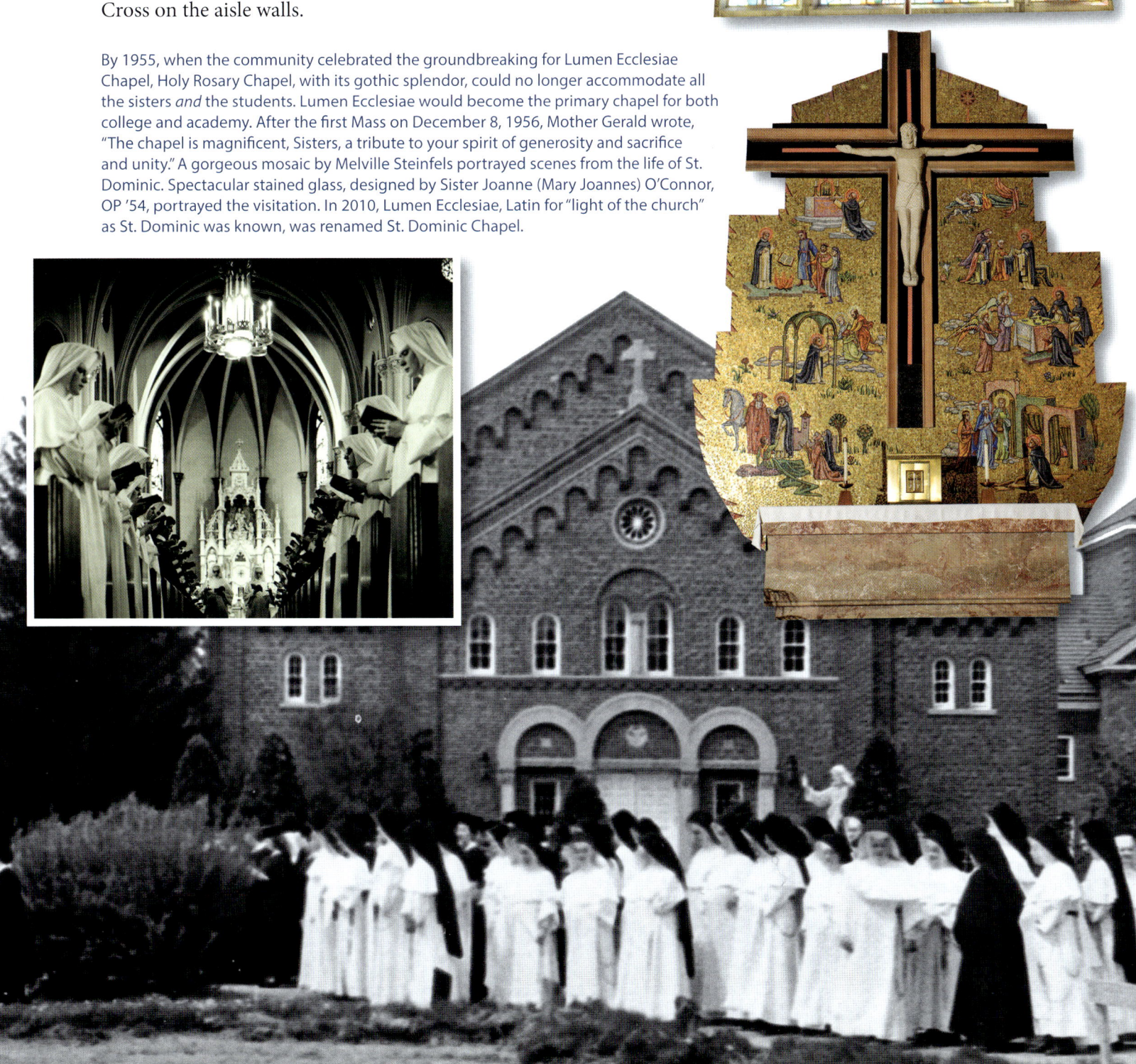

By 1955, when the community celebrated the groundbreaking for Lumen Ecclesiae Chapel, Holy Rosary Chapel, with its gothic splendor, could no longer accommodate all the sisters *and* the students. Lumen Ecclesiae would become the primary chapel for both college and academy. After the first Mass on December 8, 1956, Mother Gerald wrote, "The chapel is magnificent, Sisters, a tribute to your spirit of generosity and sacrifice and unity." A gorgeous mosaic by Melville Steinfels portrayed scenes from the life of St. Dominic. Spectacular stained glass, designed by Sister Joanne (Mary Joannes) O'Connor, OP '54, portrayed the visitation. In 2010, Lumen Ecclesiae, Latin for "light of the church" as St. Dominic was known, was renamed St. Dominic Chapel.

Skirting the issue: When not in uniforms, college girls still wore skirts—whether returning from student teaching in the 1960s or leaving campus for the weekend in the 1940s and 50s. (All students left for alumni weekend each fall, so returning alumni could stay in their carefully cleaned rooms.)

SIENA GIRLS, VALIANT WOMEN: STUDENT LIFE, 1940s TO 1960s
Valiant Woman. Cultured Woman.

From the beginning, the "valiant woman" in Proverbs 31 had been held up to college students as Biblical proof that women had intellects and identities of their own—and that the development of those gifts was both a form of Christian service and a responsibility to society.

In 1940, the *Catalogue* stated: "The Siena Heights graduate is expected to be 'a valiant woman' and 'to put out her hand to strong things.' Hence, there is little room at the college for the frivolous-minded. Earnestness of purpose and consistency in effort are expected." The statement appeared in catalogs well into the 1960s—along with the assurance that this did not make Siena Heights a gloomy place: "on the contrary, the dominant note on the campus is a spirit of joy."

Part of becoming a valiant woman, however, was learning proper manners and etiquette. Alumnae from these decades remember this required weekly class: "The Cultured Woman." "We called it Cultured Vulture," Henriette Nagle '59 remembered. Despite finding it all quite hilarious at the time, Henriette, who went on to chair the Fine Arts Department at a large New York high school, was grateful years later: "Because of those skills learned, I have spoken to six hundred parents at a time with calm and, I hope, intelligence."

Decades later, in the twenty-first century, Siena Heights University still tries to assist students with the manners and behaviors expected in professional settings. "Dress for Success" and the annual "Etiquette Dinner" are among the popular practical workshops offered on the main campus for students, male and female, anticipating job interviews and business lunches.

HAIL, SIENA! Siena Heights University

Life with Sister!

If Archangelus was the college girls' home away from home, the sisters were their surrogate mothers, aunts, and grandmothers, living on the same corridor, making sure no one stayed up too late, or slept too long, or failed to clean her room. In the dining hall, sisters monitored their table manners. In class, they were their teachers and mentors. Watching the girls compete in basketball, the sisters were their biggest fans. In a life together "24/7," as we might say today, the sisters also became their friends.

Everyone shared the same laundry room in the basement of Archangelus, where students and sisters often ironed together. The Dominicans would iron their habits and veils; the girls pressed their uniforms. "We wore long-sleeved blouses in the winter, and you couldn't get away with just ironing the cuffs and the collar," Joan Robie '55 remembered. "You never knew if a nun was going to ask you, 'Let's see the rest of your blouse.'" The girls learned not to take shortcuts!

But living side by side with the Adrian Dominicans was a highlight of college, as Diana Albera Luciani '58 remembered. "I had been around nuns all my life, but never in such close quarters." At Siena, she discovered that "they were human beings just like us. They got headaches and cramps, they liked to visit and share goodies, and they were good listeners if you had problems. They got mad at each other, and lost their cool occasionally with the students. But these women were not afraid to be themselves and I respected them all the more for it."

...continued on page 48

AJ (Sister Ann Joachim) enjoys the outdoors (inside the fence) with students in the 1940s.

RULES AND REGULATIONS

1920s—St. Joseph's College and Academy Catalogue, 1927–28

- "Students who are rude in their habits or conversation, or who disregard rules, will be expelled from the institution.... Politeness, obedience, mutual respect, and kindness are obligatory on all."
- "No student is allowed to borrow or lend money, clothing, jewelry, music, books, etc."
- "All letters or packages sent or received by the students are subject to inspection, thus preventing objectionable correspondence."

1940s—Siena Heights College Handbook of Student Regulations, 1944

- "A student's room reflects her character; it should be immaculate at all times."
- "Fountain pens may not be carried about inverted or without the caps. Care should be taken not to shake the fountain pen so that the ink splatters on classroom or corridor floors."
- "Shades should be drawn carefully whenever students are studying in negligee."

1960s—Siena Heights College Student Guide, 1960

- "Students are reminded to be courteous, unselfish, and cheerful at meals. Consideration for others demands that the conversation at table be pleasant and quiet."
- "Formal study is held from 7:30 p.m. to 10:00 p.m. on Monday, Tuesday, Wednesday and Thursday evenings, and from 8:00 p.m. to 10:00 p.m. on Sunday."
- "There is no formal study period on Friday or Saturday evenings. On these nights, the lights may be left on until 11:00 p.m. But students must be in their own rooms and quiet must be observed after 10:00 p.m."

The First Fifty Years: A College for Valiant Women

Continued from page 47...

Appreciation went in both directions. Sister Alice Joseph Moore, who taught education in the 1950s and 1960s, enjoyed the closeness that came from living with the students. "One Friday night, a student came to my room at 11:00 p.m. to ask if she could trust me with a story. I said, 'I hope so.' Off she went while I was concerned about what the story would be. She returned with a large bath towel. She turned back a fold and there was the tiny head of a beautiful animal. It was a six-month old fox. Her dad worked in Battle Creek for a cereal company; they test the nutrition of the cereal by the shine of the coat of the young foxes. She had kept the fox in her room all week to show her friends. It wouldn't be any fun at all if some sister didn't see it! Those were great years!"

Diana Albera Luciani '58 expressed the views of many students of the time: "I came away with tremendous respect for the strong-willed, intelligent, self-confident, independent nuns who had dedicated their lives to the education of young women. I would call them feminists in the most noble sense of the word."

Fabulous Fathers.

In its first fifty years, the college welcomed many priests as chaplains and professors. Alumnae remember a variety of brilliant, quirky, inspirational, and fun-loving "Fathers."

The Irish-born Father Anthony Philbin became chaplain to the sisters in 1919, just as the college was founded, and served for fourteen years. Sister Jean Marie Sheridan, OP, a college freshman in 1923–24, remembered him teaching the earliest religion classes and presiding at daily Mass in Holy Rosary Chapel.

Monsignor James Cahalan succeeded Father Philbin in 1933 and remained as chaplain until his death in 1952. He served "the sisters, the students at both the college and the academy, and the postulants and novices, as confessor, teacher, and counselor," Nadine Foley, OP '45, recorded. Both Father Philbin and Monsignor Cahalan are buried in the Adrian Dominican cemetery.

Father Clarence Dorsey joined the team of priests on campus in 1939 and served for almost a decade, "beloved by students and sisters alike," Sister Nadine said.

Father Edward C. LaMore, OP, joined the faculty in 1940, becoming a great mentor to Siena students. Sister Nadine recalled him saying, again and again, "Don't let anyone tell you that you can't learn something because you are a woman." The priest "had a tremendous impact on us," Nadine said, always reminding the students that "as a woman, you were not diminished."

Anastasia Evelyn Capoun '48 (left) and Bette Jaminet Rowe '48 are honored on this occasion by Father E. C. LaMore, a much loved priest and professor who inspired many Siena Heights women to pursue high achievement. After graduation, Evelyn rose to become director of social services at St. Vincent Hospital in Toledo, and a member of the Siena Heights College Board of Trustees.

"We all loved Father LaMore," Jacqueline Egan '47 agreed. "He was such a gentleman, so gracious, and such a wonderful teacher. I remember taking other courses in philosophy that I probably wouldn't have done if it hadn't been for him."

In the 1950s, Fathers Colum Burke, OP, and James Quinn, OP, joined Sisters Benedicta Marie, Mary Kevin, Patrick Jerome, and Cyril Edwin on the Theology and Philosophy faculty. Father Quinn, an Irishman, had a great sense of humor, Joan Robie '55 recalled. He "would lecture either standing on top of a table, or sitting on the table in tailor fashion." But, she added, his teaching was not casual: "He was very demanding, and just brilliant."

When Sister Helen (Ann Charles) Duggan, OP '41, joined the faculty in 1956, one of her extra duties was managing the chapel in Archangelus Lounge. "One of the two Dominican priests at the time, Father Conlon, used to literally run into the chapel when he came for Mass in the morning," she said. The lounge's parquet floor was badly warped badly by then, "and we used to worry he was going to plough over. I don't think he ever fell; it must have been a miracle."

What to Wear? What to Wear?

By the 1940s, the sailor-style dresses worn by the first college students had been replaced by a navy blue serge suit, which lasted—despite changing fashions—through the 1950s. "None of us had more than one uniform, so you can imagine what the skirts looked like, sitting in those blue serge suits day after day. We found out that if you used vinegar, you could take the shine off," Joan Robie '55 said, recalling an ironing trick that kept the uniforms presentable.

...continued on page 50

Uniform appearance: Members of the Class of 1952 relax between classes on the steps of Archangelus Hall, wearing the famous blue serge suit. Members of the Class of 1964 wear the stylish charcoal gray suit, even to watch Mary Jo Embach Mapes '64 put her horse through its tricks in front of Sacred Heart Hall (she boarded the horse at the fairgrounds). Uniforms "made life so much easier," Anna Marie Moriarty '67 reflected decades later. "Rich or poor, we all looked the same!"

Uniforms were not required for tennis—but slacks and shorts were forbidden. The girls played in skirts.

The First Fifty Years: A College for Valiant Women

Continued from page 49...

By the early 1960s, the uniform was updated, replaced by a charcoal gray suit. Sister Dorothy Brown, OP '32, was dean when the students "mobbed me one day and said, 'Couldn't we have a new uniform?'" The updated uniform "did change their image quite a bit," the dean admitted. "The neat-fitting jacket and straight-line suit were much more to their dignity."

The other "uniform" students wore through most of the first five decades was the academic cap and gown. Students received their caps and gowns as freshmen, in a formal ceremony in Walsh Hall called "investiture," which signaled the official beginning of their academic journey. Thereafter, they wore academic robes regularly, for Mass on the first Sunday of every month, as well as on special feast days and for particularly serious lectures or events. Shirley "Tootie" Horn '68 remembers most of the student body once traveling to the funeral of a classmate, all wearing their robes out of respect. "The family was very moved," she said.

Even the charcoal gray suit disappeared, however, when uniforms were abandoned completely in the late 1960s as the college prepared to welcome a coeducational student body. The tradition of wearing caps and gowns for serious events also went by the wayside. Henceforth, students would don academic robes only for graduation.

College girls also brought gowns to campus for dances, appearances on the Walsh Hall stage, and special ceremonies in Trinity Garden—or the photo opps beforehand!

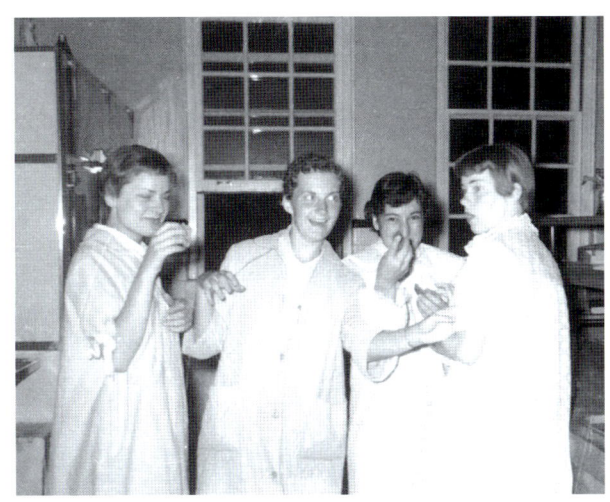

Bathrobes were required when leaving one's dorm room at night—especially to raid the kitchen for a late night treat, as this guilty group (including future Ohio Supreme Court Justice Alice Robie Resnick '61, left) did at 1:00 a.m.

Students received their caps and gowns at Freshman Investiture in Walsh Hall, then wore them for four years at special Masses and serious academic events.

Dances, Snowballs, and Innisfail.

Dances were something special at Siena. Boyfriends, brothers, and boys from nearby or not-too-far-away colleges attended the dances, sometimes arriving by bus. In the earliest years, Sister Ann Joachim would attempt to match girls and boys, primarily by height; but after ending up several times with one very tall girl and one very short boy, she abandoned that practice. Most dances were held in Archangelus Lounge, which eventually became known as Archangelus Ballroom, and were remembered as highlights of the year. Formal events, like crowning the Valentine queen, also took place in Archangelus.

Outdoor fun in the winter included ice skating in an area near Walsh Hall that was flooded and frozen each year. (At least one alumna also recalled learning to skate on the frozen pool that surrounded the angel sculpture in Trinity Garden in its earliest years.) The first snowstorm of the year generally prompted a lively snowball fight, especially with new students from Puerto Rico and the Dominican Republic.

Dolores Viola Sandri '56 and her date enjoy a Parisian evening.

The First Fifty Years: A College for Valiant Women

The first snow—and snowballs—were especially memorable for students from Latin America. Northerners, like the 1949 students shown at left, brought ice skates for the "rink" frozen near Walsh Hall.

In warmer seasons, students enjoyed tennis on the old courts that stood not far from Archangelus Hall, and picnics in Island Park. Another highlight, through the 1940s and 1950s, was the occasional trip to Innisfail, a camp owned by the Adrian Dominicans where whole classes shared rustic life with their sister chaperones. Catalogues of the era describe Innisfail as "a valuable extension" of the college:

Innisfail: This delightful woodland retreat is situated on two of the loveliest lakes in the famous "Irish Hills" a few miles from Adrian. . . . It affords opportunity for bathing, boating, and fishing for the students who spend an occasional week-end there. On the crest of a wooded hill between the two lakes, a spacious villa, equipped with electric lights and running water, containing private rooms, dining hall, and chapel, offers the delights of life in the open with the conveniences of the city.

As shown by these 1950s students, Innisfail offered opportunities for rowing, fishing, and relaxing outdoors in slacks!

52 HAIL, SIENA! Siena Heights University

Going to Town!

Walking into Adrian—"the city"—was another big part of life, and as the decades passed, the rules governing trips downtown relaxed slightly. By 1960, students could attend movies—as long as they were "rated 'A' by the Legion of Decency," according to the 1960 Student Guide. Consuming intoxicating liquors, except in the presence of parents, was subject to severe penalty, and the Guide "urgently recommended" that students avoid any restaurant that served beer or liquor. Beyond those restrictions (and the reminder that slacks and shorts "may never be worn without a skirt or coat" on the street), the code of off-campus conduct had been simplified to this caution:

By the 1960s, students like Carol Wrobel Krawczak '61 and Dorothy Youngblood Newlon '61 might have gone into town to buy the latest craze—a hula hoop!

> *The Administration reserves the right to restrict the off-campus privileges of students who spend an excessive amount of time in town, or who conduct themselves without restraint and dignity while riding in taxis, walking to the city, or in the city itself.*

And there was this P.S.: *Students may not visit in parked cars.*

WINDS OF CHANGE IN THE 1960S
Politics and Protest.

Across the country, the 1960s were years of tumultuous change. The decade began with John F. Kennedy moving into the White House, the first Catholic and youngest man to be elected president of the United States. When he challenged Americans to "ask what you can do for your country," Kennedy ushered in a spirit of hope, service, and social action. But the 1960s were marked, as well, by assassinations, civil rights unrest, political protest, and the Vietnam War.

...continued on page 54

Sister Bertha Homminga (seated at desk), one of the three founding faculty in 1922 and registrar for forty-seven years, was honored by Siena Heights with an honorary doctorate in 1969. Known for her incisive mind and prodigious memory, Sister Bertha "had a reputation for being able to look at you and tell you what your major was and what kind of grades you were receiving," according to Sister Marie Wiedner, OP '55.

The First Fifty Years: A College for Valiant Women

Continued from page 53...

"I remember being in the cafeteria the night the Cuban missile crisis flashed before the public," recalled history professor Sister Teddy McKennan, OP. "In those days, it was radio, and President John Kennedy gave a very serious address which was broadcast to us over the loudspeaker at our mealtime, telling us that the government had discovered that there were Soviet missiles in Cuba and that he had declared an embargo around the island and we were waiting for Khrushchev's response, which seemed likely to be a nuclear response. I remember that the students from the Dominican Republic were in tears and perhaps there were some girls from Puerto Rico then, too. It was a very tense moment."

Students and faculty alike would remember another day, too, in November of 1963. "I was lying on my bed upstairs on the second floor," Patricia Molly Pacquette '64 said. "My roommate came in and said, 'Kennedy's been shot.' I said, 'You are kidding.' She said, 'I am not.' People always know exactly where they were when they heard the news."

In the early 1960s, though, Siena Heights was still a quiet campus. College girls were more often called women, and lights could stay on until 10 p.m., but sisters still checked the rooms at night.

Above: Sister Benedicta Marie Ledwidge helped guide Siena Heights from the 1920s into the 1960s. **Below:** Sister Petronilla Francoeur, OP embraced the new decade, its changes and promise, but left the presidency in 1969 after an automobile accident.

New President, New Attitude.

Sister Benedicta Marie Ledwidge, longtime dean of the college, had been appointed president of Siena Heights in 1957; but by the early 1960s, she was experiencing serious health problems. In 1965, Benedicta Marie stepped down, and Sister Petronilla Francoeur, OP became the college's fifth president, infusing the office with enthusiasm and energy.

Petronilla became president just as Pope John XXIII concluded the Second Vatican Council. Vatican II, as it was commonly called, brought revolutionary change to the church. Priests set Latin aside, turned to face the congregation, and began saying Mass in English—or Spanish or Polish, whatever the local language. Laypeople stepped into parish leadership roles. Nuns and priests looked outward, going into the community and serving where people were in need. The Adrian Dominican Sisters were eager to embrace the changes. They began wearing shorter habits, then exchanging habits for ordinary street clothes. They tackled issues of social justice and quickly became more active and visible in the community.

Buoyed by the spirit of openness and change, Sister Petronilla began updating the college. Born and raised in Adrian, she knew Lenawee County well and quickly encouraged interaction between "town and gown," and collaboration with Adrian College. She removed the wrought-iron fence that had always separated the campus from its surroundings, and welcomed area teachers to evening classes in a growing graduate education program.

As a sign of the new times, Sister Petronilla adopted a logo for college communications. The traditional escutcheon associated with Siena Heights as a Dominican institution was still used on academic documents, but the "maple leaf image" appeared on letterhead, bulletins, and forms. The maple leaf, which identified the college with Adrian (the Maple City), rested on a triangular foundation signifying the educational, social, and spiritual dimensions of the college. The date 1919 noted our founding.

A new student residence—Ledwidge Hall, honoring Benedicta Marie—was opened with much fanfare; rooms were tastefully furnished with matching curtains and bedspreads that students were strongly urged to handle with care. The Art Department moved out of the fifth floor of Sacred Heart Hall, transferring its name to a brand-new building: Studio Angelico. Work began on a new theater. Envisioning a transition to a lay Board of Trustees, Sister Petronilla gathered a small group of business leaders to serve as a lay Advisory Council and assist with the change. Things were happening.

HAIL, SIENA! Siena Heights University

PRESIDENTIAL PROFILE NO. 4

Sister Benedicta Marie Ledwidge, OP

President of Siena Heights College: 1957–1965

Only President to Have Served as Academic Dean. Scholar and Friend of Students.

Sister Benedicta Marie Ledwidge's impact on Siena Heights is far greater than the eight years of her presidency might imply. Beginning in the 1920s, when Mother Augustine appointed her one of three sisters who would manage the young college, Benedicta Marie was an administrative leader of St. Joseph/Siena Heights for four decades. She served as dean for seventeen years, and executive vice president for another six years, before becoming president. Throughout those years, she was close to the students, and loved and respected by them.

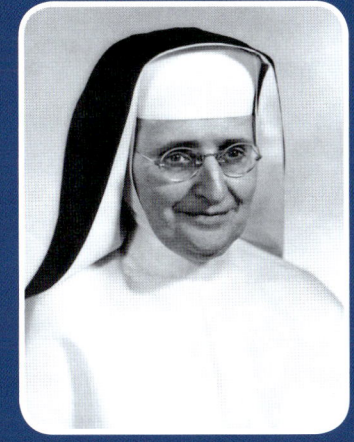

Born in 1888 near Pinckney, Michigan, Clare Ledwidge began life as a twin, but her sister died in infancy. She expressed interest early in a religious vocation. After teaching for several years, she entered the Sisters of St. Joseph in Kalamazoo, but her tenure was brief; she withdrew because of ill health. Several years later, recovered and now thirty-two, she joined the Adrian Dominicans and was dispatched to teach at schools in Chicago, Dearborn, and at St. Joseph's Academy in Adrian. "I have such an incorrigible love of teaching," she once said, that even after a holiday, she had no regrets returning to the classroom.

> "Who of us is not truly grateful for having shared a part of life with her?"
>
> *Sienae (Siena Heights Alumni Association Newsletter), May 21, 1968*

As dean of the college from 1934 to 1951, she was "the moving spirit of Siena Heights," said faculty member Sister Mary (Patrick Jerome) Mullins, OP '33, who called Benedicta Marie "a woman of deep wisdom and quiet leadership who urged all of us to make the college a home for love and a school for excellence." She "was very gentle with the students, and very protective of them," Sister Mary Philip Ryan, OP, agreed, adding, "She had an unusual wit, a classic wit. She spoke very well. And she was a very fine writer."

Although she was the first president of the college not to serve simultaneously as Mother General of the congregation, Benedicta Marie carried significant responsibilities as Vicaress General (assistant to Mother Gerald) and maintained dual offices in Sacred Heart Hall and the Motherhouse. Born in the nineteenth century, Benedicta Marie's vision was firmly focused on the future. Asked about weaknesses in American education in the 1960s, she noted that too few educators recognized "that we live in a transition between a jet age and a space age."

When failing health led to Sister Benedicta Marie's resignation in 1965, the college trustees voted to name the new residence hall in her honor. She died April 1, 1968, shortly before Siena dedicated Ledwidge Hall.

> "She came from a family of teachers, and she held teaching as one of the noblest professions. The student was her primary consideration."
>
> *Sister Corinne O'Connor*
> *(quoted in Nadine Foley's* To Fields Near and Far*)*

Difficult Questions.

As the 1960s wound toward the 1970s, Siena Heights, like many small colleges, found itself facing new financial challenges. And like other women's colleges, Siena Heights began to consider whether admitting male students might help solve these new problems.

Ruth LaFontaine '72 arrived on campus as a freshman in 1968. Coming from a small town, anxious to focus on her studies and her future, Ruth thought an all-girls college would provide the best chance for her to excel. Suddenly, the leaders of the college began encouraging conversation about coeducation—what it might be like, what the students thought. "I chose Siena Heights partly because it was all women," Ruth admitted. "There was a lot of discussion, and many of the girls felt men should not be allowed."

In the end, it came down to finances. "I had to say, 'Let men come in if we are losing money. We do not want the school to close,'" Ruth said, but "you knew the whole focus would change."

The decision to admit men as full participants in undergraduate education was the most significant change in the college's first half-century. No longer would this be a "college for young ladies." It would take a few years before the change was really noticeable, but henceforth, Siena Heights would be a coeducational institution. The era of the "Valiant Woman" was ending.

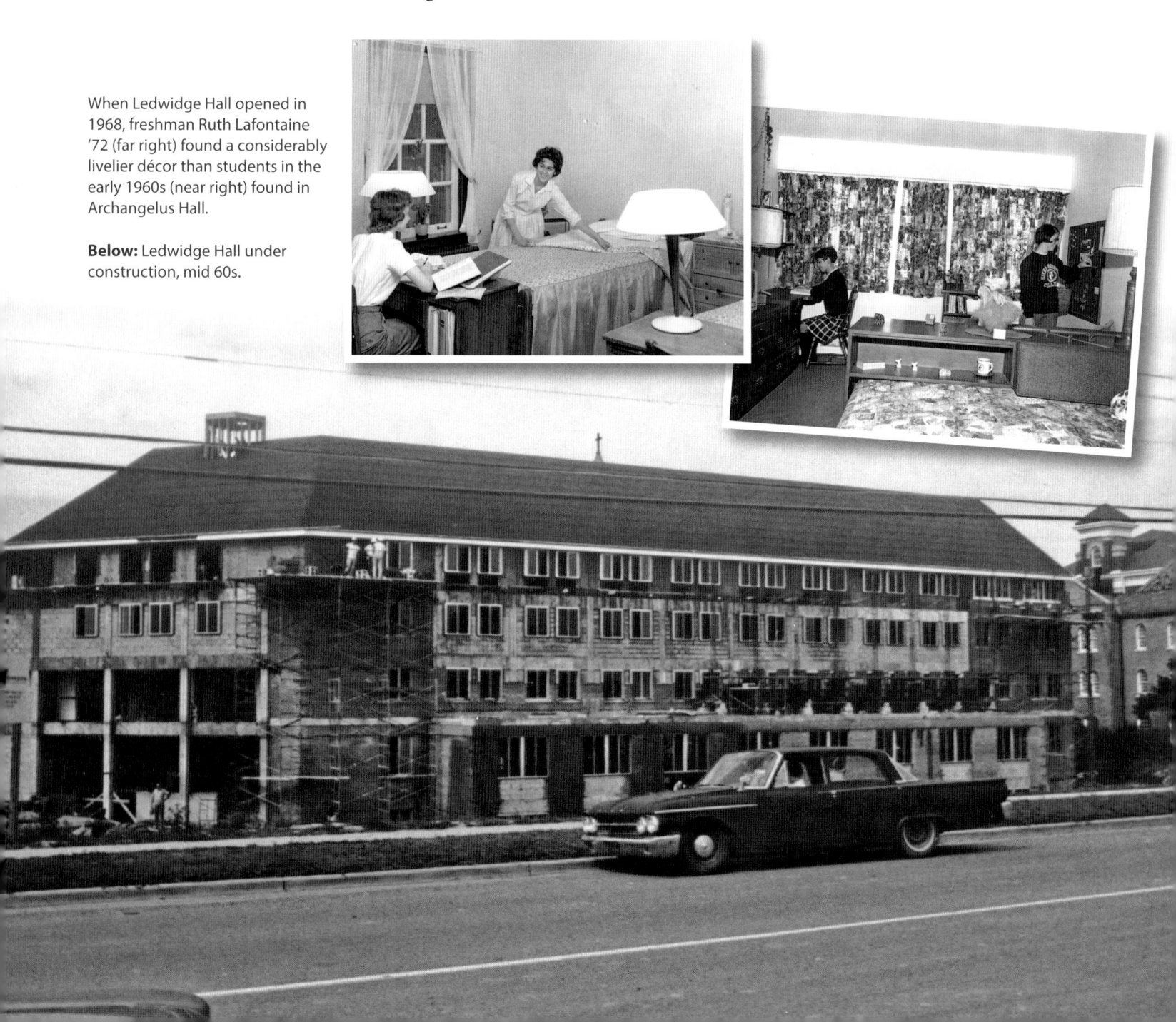

When Ledwidge Hall opened in 1968, freshman Ruth Lafontaine '72 (far right) found a considerably livelier décor than students in the early 1960s (near right) found in Archangelus Hall.

Below: Ledwidge Hall under construction, mid 60s.

Unexpected Developments.

In 1969, two unforeseen events jolted the Siena Heights community:

- First, pristine new Ledwidge Hall suffered a major fire, destroying the top floor and causing extensive smoke damage throughout the building. Residents were temporarily relocated to Regina Hall on the sisters' campus.
- Second and more important, in November of that year, lingering injuries from an automobile accident ended Sister Petronilla's presidency.

On December 3, 1969, Rosemary Ferguson, OP, prioress of the congregation, addressed the administration, students, and faculty of the college. Human life is characterized by "the counterpoint of constancy and change," she said. "A change has come into the lives of all at Siena Heights College, in the unexpected resignation of Sister Petronilla Francoeur for reasons of serious ill health," she continued. "There are many things for which we could justly commend and thank Sister Petronilla, but I have singled out this one aspect of her service for mention here: her effective efforts toward involving the college in today's world, and the world in a college for today."

Sister Rosemary went on to make two significant announcements:

- As of January 1, 1970, Richard Reaume, a respected member of the faculty, would serve as acting president of the college.
- Sister Petronilla's plan to reconstitute the Board of Trustees would proceed during the spring, and "it will be the first and main responsibility of the future Board of Trustees to search out a permanent president."

The search could take two years, she said. In fact, the next president arrived in August 1971.

When art teacher Father David Van Horn arrived on campus in the fall of 1970, he found what still appeared to be "essentially an all-women's school." He caught only occasional glimpses of the handful of male students, and observed that, except for himself and painting teacher Tom Burke, the college seemed to have an all-sister faculty.

No one really knew it, Father Van Horn said years later, but change was on its way:

"Siena Heights wasn't going to be this sleepy peaceful place very long."

The early 1960s logo (above) expanded "Veritas" (truth) into the Latin version of "the truth will set you free." The maple leaf logo (below), used from 1965 to 1974, emphasized community, the tree of life, and the college's location in the maple city.

The First Fifty Years: A College for Valiant Women

PRESIDENTIAL PROFILE NO. 5

Sister Petronilla Francoeur, OP

President of Siena Heights College: 1965–1969

Change Agent for the Sixties.
Embraced Coeducation and Welcomed the Community.

Sister Petronilla Francoeur was the last president to be appointed solely by the leadership of the congregation of Adrian Dominican Sisters. In just five years, she would lay the foundation for the college's future by embracing coeducation, nurturing improved community relations, and envisioning an independent Board of Trustees. Her tenure was brief, but she served as a vital link between Siena's first fifty years and its next half-century.

A member of the Francoeur family of Adrian, Sister Petronilla was a popular professor of French, Spanish, and English at Siena Heights during the late 1940s and early 1950s. After twelve years teaching languages and chairing the graduate program at Barry College in Miami, Florida, she was appointed president of Siena Heights on January 30, 1965.

In her first year at Siena Heights, she welcomed a record class of 250 freshmen, including students from Central America, Honduras, Iran, Santo Domingo, and Thailand, as well as Puerto Rico and fourteen of the states. That same fall, the college welcomed fifteen new instructors to the faculty, the largest increase to date. She also hired Siena's first full-time public relations director and awarded its first honorary doctoral degree, to Mother Genevieve Weber, OP.

"Petronilla was an educator with vision, a good listener, and open to considering the ideas and suggestions of the various segments of the college community."
Sister Noreen (Mary Paul) McKeough, OP '36

During her five years, Sister Petronilla ended the requirement for students to wear uniforms, introduced coeducation to the undergraduate program, revised the academic calendar, oversaw construction of Ledwidge Hall and Studio Angelico, established the first faculty senate, enhanced "town-gown" relationships, and recruited a lay Board of Advisors, the first step toward an independent Board of Trustees. In October of 1968, Petronilla was seriously injured in an automobile accident; a year later, she resigned as president, when it was clear she would be unable to resume active involvement in the office.

In December 1969, Sister Rosemary Ferguson, OP, prioress of the congregation, announced to students and faculty that Professor Richard Reaume had been named acting president of Siena Heights. She also announced the imminent formation of the Board of Trustees Petronilla had envisioned, whose "first and main responsibility" would be to search for her permanent successor. A few years later, Francoeur Theater was named in honor of this groundbreaking fifth president.

"Sister Petronilla brought a breath of fresh air. Times were changing, and she was an agent advancing those changes."
Sister Anne Marie Brown, OP '40, administrator/faculty

Petronilla brought energy and fresh ideas to the presidency during her brief tenure. "She was active, aggressive, and full of enthusiasm." *Sister Claudia Hinds, OP, graduate faculty 1963–74*

AN EVOLVING CURRICULUM
Veritas Enfolds You.

For decades, though not quite a century, the flagpole in front of Sacred Heart Hall has stood on a base engraved with the Dominican shield and, in large block letters, the Dominican motto, *VERITAS*, Latin for truth. The Siena Heights Alma Mater, written in the 1940s and still sung today, sounds an echo: "We bear . . . the torch and the shield of truth . . .*Veritas* enfolds you."

Inspired by Dominican intellectual Saint Thomas Aquinas, Adrian Dominicans have always understood that the search for truth goes beyond "my truth" to "your truth," other truths, and to God who is truth, all of which bears on our collective truth. The never-ending search for truth may lead over time to insights that alter our understanding and sometimes our views.

The notion of *disputatio*—the lively discussion of differing views that promotes mutual understanding if not complete agreement—is at the heart of the "teaching and learning environment" mentioned in the Siena Heights mission statement. In such a setting, everyone learns, whether professor or student, and everyone contributes to the teaching.

New eras have produced new ideas about what students should know to graduate into the lifelong search for truth. But *veritas* and *disputatio* have provided the foundation for academics at Siena Heights since its founding.

The VERITAS flag pole base—a gift of the Detroit Alumnae Chapter in 1932, renovated with support from the Class of 2009—also includes, in Latin, the words: To praise. To bless. To preach.

The First Fifty Years: A College for Valiant Women

Even in the 1920s and 1930s, College *and* Career.

From the start, the college offered two courses of study, one leading to a bachelor's degree after four years, the other leading after two years to a secretarial certificate or a teaching certificate (teaching did not then require a degree). A four-year degree in secretarial studies was another option. All of these were respected educational paths.

The Dominicans knew what careers were, and were not, available to women in the 1920s and 1930s. Unmarried lay women could teach or work in some clerical positions. Married women had almost no place in the work force, but they had other responsibilities: building families, educating children, contributing to church and community. Sisters in the Order of Preachers, of course, would work—*preach*—throughout their lives, in a variety of missions.

No matter which path those early students chose—two-year or four-year, certificate or bachelor's degree, lay woman or vowed religious—they all received a classical education. All students completed required classes in Latin, English, history, psychology, philosophy, religion, mathematics, science, and language. Classes beyond the core depended on the student's focus. By the 1930s, the college awarded three baccalaureate degrees: bachelor of arts, bachelor of science, and bachelor of music.

Then as now, students did not always know how long they would be able to stay in school. Dominican novices often went out to teach after only a semester or two; they completed the bachelor's degree over time, returning each spring for summer school. Some lay students did the same, if their parents ran out of money. Some two-year secretarial graduates returned later to complete a four-year degree. A few lucky ones were offered jobs to help pay for their education. The Cunningham twins both taught physical education in exchange for two years of tuition. "We will always be owing to the Dominican Sisters," Beatrice Cunningham Meyer '32 said gratefully at her sixtieth reunion.

The 1940s, 1950s, and 1960s.

As World War II began, Siena continued to offer a strong two-year secretarial program as well as four-year programs—now leading to six degrees: bachelor of arts, bachelor of philosophy, bachelor of music, bachelor of science, bachelor of science in home economics, and bachelor of science in commercial education. Now, however, only the bachelor of arts required Latin or Greek; students pursuing other degrees could substitute a "modern" language. All four-year degree candidates completed a major and two minors.

The required liberal arts core—four years each of theology, philosophy, and English; at least one year of a foreign language; a scattering of classes in science, history, and speech—remained unchanged through the 1960s. Graduation requirements remained much the same, except for this 1950s addition: every degree candidate "must also undergo a comprehensive examination in her major field."

By 1962, however, the curriculum reflected several key changes:

- The bachelor of music and bachelor of science in commercial education were no longer awarded. (Music majors earned a B.A. or B.Ph.)
- Secretarial science was no longer available as a four-year degree, but *was* offered as a minor and as a two-year certificate program.

In these years, the undergraduate curriculum was organized in five divisions:
- Religion and Philosophy (or Theology)
- Language and Literature
- Natural Science
- Science of Human Relations
- Fine Arts

FAME IN THE FIFTIES

1950: *Chemical Engineering News* reports that Siena Heights was fourth among all liberal arts colleges in the nation in contributions to the *Journal of the American Chemical Society* in 1942-45, and fifth for 1945-50.

1953: The January issue of *Mademoiselle* ranks Siena Heights College eighth in the nation among women's colleges producing top flight scholars—graduates who who go on to earn doctoral degrees.

1953: On July 19, *The New York Times* includes Siena Heights College among the nation's top twelve schools producing outstanding women scholars, along with Cornell University, Radcliffe College, and the University of Chicago.

Graduate Education:
  Meeting the Needs of a Working Population.

Siena Heights first offered graduate courses for the master of fine arts in 1951, adding the master of arts, master of science, and master of arts in teaching in 1957.

As noted in the 1962 catalogue, the expansion of graduate studies was prompted by "the shortage of properly qualified elementary, secondary and college teachers and administrative personnel;" the graduate division would meet the need for "highly trained personnel for the rapidly expanding public and parochial school systems." In building the program, Siena Heights made two decisions that foreshadowed future developments:

- *First, graduate education would be open to both men and women.* This only made sense, in light of the increasing number of men in the teaching ranks. It was, nonetheless, a significant departure from tradition; previously, only a handful of clergy and one or two local men needing specific coursework, had sat as students in Siena Heights classrooms. In 1960, the first two men graduated with master's degrees from Siena Heights: Albert Raloff and Paul Bolduc.
- *Second, class scheduling would accommodate the needs of working adults.* This, too, was a logical decision; teachers taught during the day and could not enroll during regular college hours. Thus, the 1962 catalogue noted, graduate classes would be scheduled during the summer—*and* in "late afternoon and evenings during the regular academic sessions."

Perhaps no one realized how this decision—to accommodate the needs of a new population of working adult students—would reshape the college in the coming decades.

ACADEMICS IN THE REAR VIEW MIRROR

Some of the strongest programs in the college's first fifty years did not last long after that.

Lost Languages.

Spanish is the only foreign language offered at Siena Heights in 2019, but for many years, the curriculum included classes in Latin, Greek, French, and German, with occasional offerings in Italian (and, in the 1990s, Japanese). But times change. . . .

When St. Joseph College was founded, most American high schools taught Latin. The young women who enrolled at the college knew they would take at least another year of Latin, plus a year of another language. Students could major in Latin, French, and Spanish; and minor in Greek and German, as well.

Founding faculty member Sister Regina Marie Lalonde, OP, taught at Siena Heights from 1922 to 1971, covering all of the languages except Greek, and the cultures related to each language, too. A pioneer in language teaching, she used post–World War II Army surplus materials to build two language listening booths at the back of Sacred Heart Hall 312. In the late 1950s, she installed a full-scale language laboratory in Room 307. "Interestingly, Sister Regina did all the mechanical and electrical connections for these herself," chemist-turned-archivist Helen Duggan, OP '41, reported.

Another giant of the faculty, Sister M. Laurine Neville, taught French, Spanish, Italian, and occasionally English from 1937 to 1966. The first person from Siena to reach out to the Spanish-speaking community in Adrian, she often involved her students, and Father Clarence Dorsey in the 1940s, in her outreach to migrant farm workers and their families. Sister Evangeline Davis, OP, followed Laurine as head of languages. Other pillars of the classical (Latin and Greek) language faculty included Sisters Mary (Patrick Jerome) Mullins, Ellen Vincent McClain, and Dorothy Folliard.

...continued on page 62

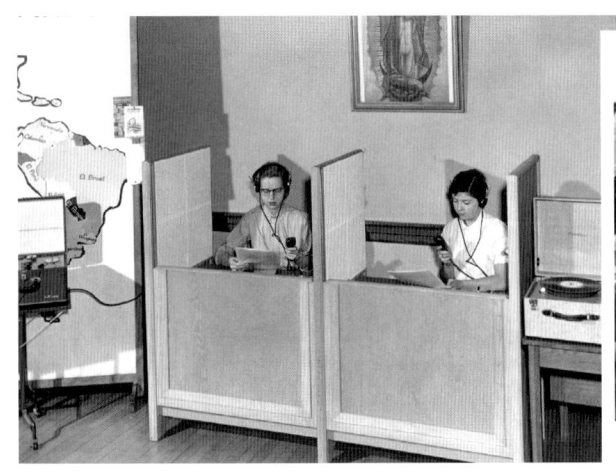

During her forty-nine years teaching languages at Siena Heights, Sister Regina Marie LaLonde, OP built one of the first recognized language labs out of Army surplus materials, a two-booth facility that she later replaced with a much larger lab, which she also built herself.

Continued from page 61...

During the 1960s, most public high schools stopped requiring Latin; students were not interested in what seemed a "dead" language. Colleges faced similar decisions. By the end of the decade, Siena Heights (like many others) had eliminated core requirements. Almost immediately, enrollment in language classes fell dramatically.

Language study is not required at Siena Heights in 2019, except for students majoring in humanities. No classical languages are taught (although, until his retirement in 2016, Anthony Scioly, chemistry professor, occasionally offered introductory Latin). The Spanish Department is alive and well, however, offering language, literature, and culture classes leading to a major or minor.

The Science of Home Economics.

When students today hear that Siena Heights once offered home economics, they are likely to laugh dismissively, filing the information with "easy and forgettable majors of the past." In fact, the bachelor of science in home economics was a rigorous degree, anything but easy, incorporating chemistry, biology, nutrition, psychology, management, consumer economics, and accounting. Oh, plus cookery, textiles, and clothing construction—which, in the years before fast food and cheap retail, were extremely useful.

The Home Arts Department, as it was called, prepared students for some of the more challenging careers then available to women. Some majors would teach; some, in the 1960s, entered retailing. But for many graduates, "home ec" was solid preparation for science-based careers in dietetics and nutrition—in schools, hospitals, and government offices.

In 1937, students remodeled a ten-room dwelling nearby as a so-called "practice house" which they dubbed Caleruega Cottage, for St. Dominic's birthplace in Spain. Home arts majors took two-week turns budgeting, marketing, planning and preparing meals, and managing general housekeeping—a "co-op" experience before the term was invented. Consumer education students engaged in research, such as testing the advertised durability of hosiery.

Home economics survived the turmoil of the 1970s to become, by 1978, part of the then-new management division, which also offered programs in fashion merchandising and food service/lodging/institutional management (later renamed hotel, restaurant, and institutional management). All three programs disappeared in the early 1990s.

Secretarial Science.

It is difficult today to grasp how few career options were available to women a century ago, and even through the middle of the twentieth century. But working as an office assistant *was* a possibility; and though there was little likelihood of advancement, a woman could become a core member of an office team. Secretarial science offered a legitimate career path, attainable in two (or four) years. Marie Bride Walsh, OP '43, was typical: "I took secretarial because I wasn't sure I was going to be able to finish my college education, and I wanted to be able to work." Jeanne Sheteron O'Reilly '47 did the same; and helped run her husband's company for several decades.

Sister Mary George Nolan, OP, treasurer and business manager of the college, was head of the secretarial program from 1935 to 1970. While teaching, she simultaneously managed many construction projects including the library addition, Ledwidge Hall, and Studio Angelico. Beloved by secretarial students, she demanded hard work, maintained high standards, and was interested in any new office tool that came along. She "would have embraced computers with enthusiasm," Jeanne O'Reilly said.

Through the 1950s, students could earn a bachelor's degree in secretarial science, as well as a two-year certificate. Like all alumnae of the time, secretarial graduates brought a solid liberal arts foundation to whatever work they went on to do. Many secretarial graduates had great success in business, their careers evolving as society evolved.

By the 1960s, secretarial science was available only as a two-year program. By 1978, it was offered only as a minor in the management division; and by 1980, it was replaced by a new program in office administration. A "secretarial science teaching minor," the last vestige of a once vital program, was gone a few years later. By then, women were earning business degrees with men. Eventually, computers would turn most people into their own secretaries.

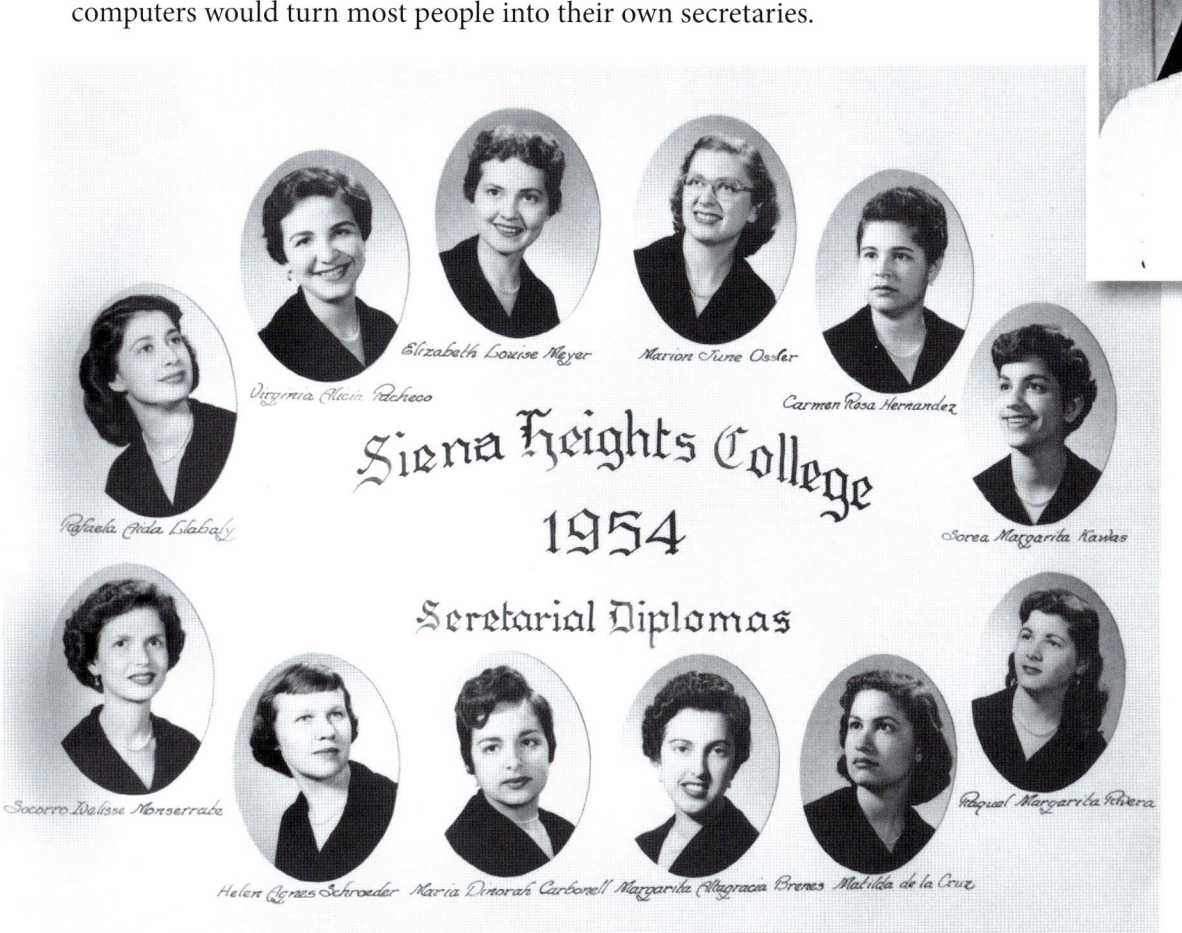

Sister Mary George Nolan, OP, simultaneously served as college business manager and treasurer, overseeing the building of many facilities, while also teaching the secretarial program from 1936 to 1970.

The First Fifty Years: A College for Valiant Women

Medical Technology.

Well into the twentieth century, women were not welcome at most medical schools. Although Donita Sullivan '52 successfully completed her M.D., and became a pioneer in the field of pediatric rheumatology, she was a rare success story—and Sister Miriam Michael Stimson, OP was quick to deter a student from her dreams if she believed the student unlikely to withstand the prejudice and isolation, not to mention the academic rigor, of medical school.

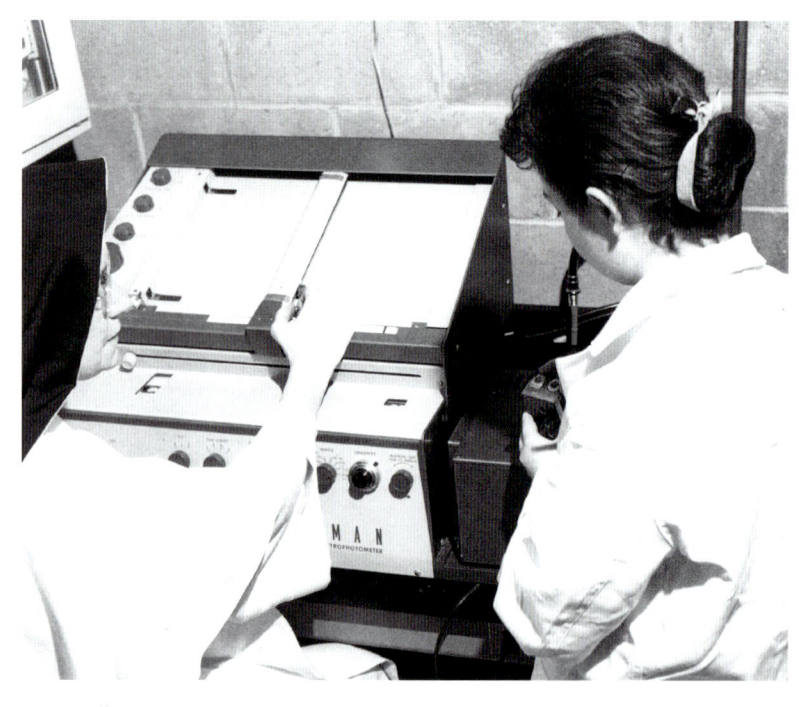

The field of medical technology, however, *was* open to women; and as early as the 1940s, Siena Heights offered a challenging curriculum where students took a heavy load of science for three years, then spent senior year working/studying full-time in a professional setting, most often Providence Hospital in Detroit. The program was rigorous—especially for students like Nancy Mason Erhardt '58, for example, who double-majored in medical technology and philosophy.

Medical technology was a significant and successful part of the science curriculum until community colleges began offering two-year programs for laboratory technicians. The Siena Heights medical technology program ended midway through the 1970s.

Diana Albera Luciani '58 served as Sister Miriam Michael's research assistant and won a Fulbright Scholarship for a year of postgraduate study.

MEDICAL TECHNOLOGY: NOT FOR THE FAINT-HEARTED!

Sister Miriam Michael Stimson, OP, ensured that the medical technology program was academically rigorous—but also that it was practical and hands-on, in some unusual ways, as remembered by Diana Albera Luciani '58:

"Sister Miriam Michael taught biochemistry and because the class was small, we often had lectures in her lab. She would even prepare her famous tea occasionally! Most of the students were studying for a degree in medical technology. This meant that some of the practical aspects of biochemistry would be applied in class. Two memorable lessons involved drawing blood and stomach pumping.

"Sister was the guinea pig for the blood, and all of the students had to draw blood from her once. Her theory was that if we could do it with her and then to each other, we could do it with anyone. You can imagine the nerves we all had on the appointed day.

"The stomach pumping was even worse, however. It meant that we had to swallow a tube, place the other end with the pouch into our lab coat pocket, and attend our morning classes in this state. Because it was a yearly ritual, the teachers were accustomed to seeing these poor creatures struggling to behave normally; the other students were another matter. But we all survived, and believe me, we knew exactly how it felt to have blood drawn and stomachs pumped. If it served to make us more sympathetic to the poor patient, then there was a method to Sister's madness!"

HAIL, SIENA! Siena Heights University

THE MYSTERY OF THE SACRED HEART

The life-sized statue of the sacred heart of Jesus that greets all who enter Sacred Heart Hall was a gift to the college at the building's dedication in 1922. Adrian Dominican historian Sister Mary Philip Ryan, OP, noted that, when the building opened, the sculpture stood "in the center of its spacious marble hall," where it still stands today, cherished by generations of SHU students. In intervening years, however, the statue—or a replica?—stood outdoors on a gently raised mound in front of Sacred Heart and Walsh Halls. Photos show the lobby in the 1960s, and outdoor views from 1925 and at the 1954 groundbreaking for the chapel. Beloved by students for generations, the statue also has been affectionately known, occasionally, as "touchdown Jesus."

Legends of the Faculty

DEANS THROUGH THE DECADES

1924
Sister Agnes Rita Paiement, OP

As dean of the college in its earliest years, Sister Agnes Rita (like all faculty) lived in a dorm room in Madden Hall. Her duties included supervising the four to eight girls who shared the room with her.

Sister Agnes Rita, left, the first dean, and Sister Ann Joachim.

1927
Sister Frances Joseph Wright, OP

Sister Francis Joseph made the ideal of the valiant woman seem attainable, said historian Sister Jeanne Lefebvre, OP '66. Early students "learned from her what it could mean to be 'clothed with strength and dignity' and to dare to 'laugh at the days to come.'"

1934
Sister Benedicta Marie Ledwidge, OP '29

A skilled writer and energetic administrator, Benedicta Marie was a friend to students, and much loved by them. After seventeen years as dean, she became vice president, then president of the college, also serving simultaneously as vicaress to Mother Gerald.

1951
Sister M. Kevin Campbell, OP

In addition to her duties as dean, Sister Kevin Campbell helped teach the "Cultured Woman" class in the 1950s, guiding students in the proper way to sit, stand, walk gracefully in heels, and make polite and enlightened conversation.

1957
Sister Dorothy Browne, OP

At this time, the deanship included responsibilities that were later divided between the academic dean and dean of students. Sister Anne Marie Brown assisted Sister Dorothy in the areas of admissions, advising, residential life, and Student Council.

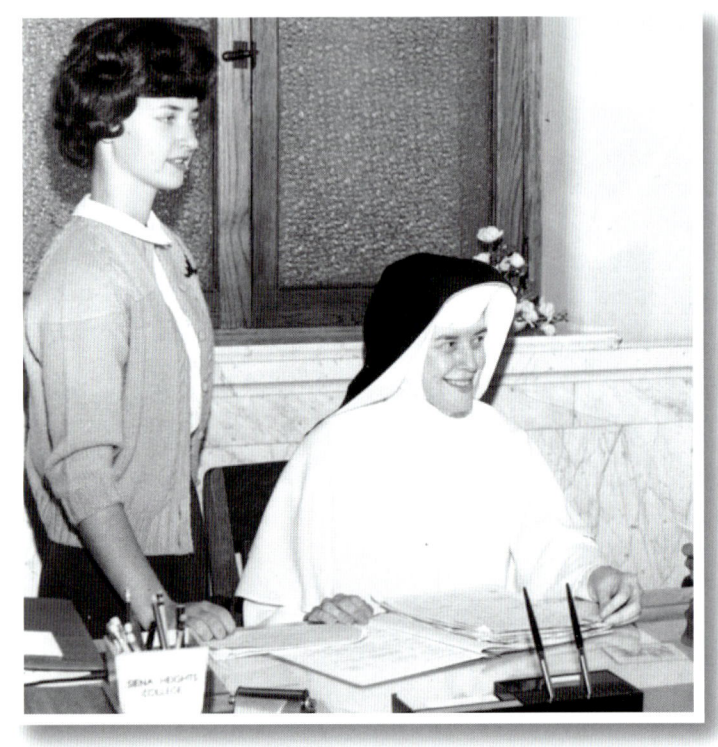

Dean Anne Marie (Rose Ellen) Brown, OP, meets with Patricia Mosesso McCardy '65.

1963
Sister Anne Marie (Rose Ellen) Brown, OP '40

The dean was responsible for both academics and student life until 1965, when Sister Irma Gerber, OP, was appointed dean of students. Sister Anne Marie also covered the president's office from November 1969 until January 1, 1970, when Richard Reaume became acting president. Art professor David Van Horn described Anne Marie as "very precise" and "a very lovely person."

1970
Sister Jean Fitzgerald, OP '49

Sister Jean was appointed dean of the college when Anne Marie Brown became director of admissions. "She really wanted to bring the college into a more contemporary swing of things. She had a feeling the college was a bit behind in its thinking," said Father David Van Horn of the Art Department. "Hugh Thompson and Jean Fitzgerald functioned very much as a team." Another person who figured into the leadership at this time was John Edgar Miller, dean of two-year programs, who also became an assistant to President Thompson.

HAIL, SIENA! Siena Heights University

1974
Sister Grace Ellen Minten, OP '42

Grace Ellen was acting academic dean for a year when Jean Fitzgerald became special assistant to Hugh Thompson. Grace Ellen "brought great compassion to that office," said Trudy McSorley of the theater faculty. "She kept us sane during the difficult times."

1975
Thomas Maher

After organizing a "Blue Sky" committee to brainstorm creative scholarly work that would complement the institution, Dean Maher secured a federal Fund for the Improvement of Post-Secondary Education (FIPSE) grant for faculty/college development. "I credit Tom Maher with our mission statement that was approved in 1976," said then-chemistry professor Sister Sharon Weber. "I remember him calling every Adrian Dominican who passed his office in to explain to him what the Dominican heritage and tradition meant. . . . [He] brought us back to recognizing that we needed to touch into those rites and to begin to reclaim our Catholic heritage."

Dean Tom Maher pours more coffee as trustee and benefactor Bob Sage lights his pipe.

1980
James A. Ebben

Hired by Tom Maher to direct the FIPSE grant, Jim became dean when Tom left. He also served as acting president in 1983–84, during the search that resulted in the hiring of Sister Cathleen Real. "Jim did a very fine job," recalled Sharon Weber, OP. He "held deeply the values of Catholic higher education."

1985
Sharon Weber, OP '69

Sister Sharon, an established member of the chemistry faculty, served as acting dean in 1985–86, while Jim Ebben was on sabbatical.

1986
John B. Bennett

John Bennett held the dual title of dean of the college and provost. "If ever there was a person who caused confusion in the ranks, it was John Bennett," said chemistry instructor Susan Mole. But, she added, "many of the things he espoused were just excellent."

1990
Robert Gordon

Having previously served as director of academic advising, chair of general studies, and assistant dean, Bob was associate provost to John Bennett before succeeding him as dean and provost. (The "provost" title was dropped in the mid-1990s.) Bob promoted faculty development, a rigorous liberal arts core, and a focus on Dominican values. He had "great reverence for the retired sisters" who served Siena, then-theater professor Trudy McSorley said, "and he is an intellectual. I cannot say enough for him." Bob mentored many faculty, added Mary Weeber, then director of freshman advising. "His stock advice to me was, 'Well, go ahead and try it; you might fail. But then you'll learn something, won't you.'" Mary called him "a wonderful dean," always "on the side of the faculty."

1996
Sharon Weber, OP '69

Returning to Siena Heights after six years in Adrian Dominican congregational leadership, Sister Sharon succeeded Bob Gordon as undergraduate academic dean when he became dean of graduate studies. In 2006, Sharon was named vice president for academic affairs—still serving as undergraduate dean while also overseeing the deans of the College for Professional Studies and the Graduate College. She continues as vice president, the university's highest academic officer, in 2019.

2011
Mark Schersten became dean of the College of Arts and Sciences, freeing Sharon Weber to focus on university-wide academic leadership. Mark brought twenty-seven years of faculty experience to the dean's office, having taught philosophy since 1984, simultaneously chairing the humanities division for much of that time.

2016
Matthew Draud is an ecologist with a strong interest in marine systems, especially coral reefs. Before becoming undergraduate dean at SHU, he spent thirteen years heading biology programs at Long Island University (NY) and Armstrong State University (GA).

The First Fifty Years: A College for Valiant Women

A Century of Study

1919–2019 SIENA HEIGHTS UNIVERSITY

SOCIAL SCIENCES

History, economics, secretarial science, and education were once considered social sciences at Siena Heights, but in the twenty-first century history falls in the humanities, economics is part of business, education is a stand-alone division, and secretarial science is no more. Today, the social sciences include social work, psychology, and political science (all offered to some degree from the beginning), plus criminal justice (added in the 1970s). In the 1980s, following a curriculum reorganization, all four programs were part of the same academic major—bachelor of arts in human services—each with a different concentration. Not so in 2019.

SOCIAL WORK:

The multitalented Ann Joachim, OP, handled some of the very early classes, but Sister Mary Therese Crimmins, OP, shaped the sociology and social work program from the 1940s into the 1960s. She also counseled teachers at the Girls Training School in Adrian, often taking students along to give them insights into the needs of neglected, delinquent, or orphaned girls. Before "internships" entered the college vocabulary, Sister Mary Therese placed social work students in agencies such as Catholic Charities, as far away as Chicago, to provide them with field work experience; that program eventually was discontinued, to Sister Mary Therese's regret. Field work was revived in the early 1970s by then chair Sister Ann Judith Provancher, OP, who also added classes in juvenile delinquency and anthropology. In the mid-1970s, Sister Molly Lorms, OP, initiated an effort to earn accreditation for a bachelor of social work (BSW) degree, but the effort was abandoned when the college opted to turn social work into a concentration within human services. In the early 1980s, Catherine "Kitty" Madden coordinated the "human services: social work" major. In the late 1990s, under the direction of Jo-Ann Lauderdale, the Social Work Department again sought, and this time gained, full accreditation to award the BSW. The many distinguished social work majors through the years included Evelyn Capoun '48 in Toledo, Ann Abrams '52 in Chicago, Cindy Doyle '72 in West Michigan, and Terry Beurer '80, at the Michigan Department of Human Services. **In 2019:** Dalila John directs the professional social work program, which includes 450 hours of field placement over two semesters. Sociology and anthropology, directed by Linda Easley, feature a distinctive emphasis on community based learning in local schools, the Boys and Girls Club, and the Daily Bread. Social work is not offered through the College for Professional Studies, but CPS students may complete the BA in community and human services.

During her tenure on the social work faculty, Kitty Madden helped initiate development of the hospice program in Adrian.

PSYCHOLOGY:

For the first few decades, the study of psychology was limited to two classes in educational psychology and a single course in "personality development and conduct" offered in the home and family life division. By 1962, adolescent psychology appeared in the education curriculum and the psychology of behavior problems was an offering in sociology (part of home and family life). Psychology emerged as an academic subject area in the 1970s before becoming a concentration in the human services major. New faculty Whit Hames (1978), Tom Radecki (1980) and Peggy Motsch (1981) were the first SHU teachers specifically focused on psychology. Whit Hames spearheaded the development of a two-year program in gerontology. Psychology became a separate department in the late 1990s, with Peggy Motsch as chair. Jeff Lindstrom joined the faculty in 2001. **In 2019:** Psychology has enjoyed a period of considerable growth. The annual Daily Bread food drive, coordinated by Jeff Lindstrom's social psychology class, has raised the profile of the department. Gerontology continues to be offered as a minor. Psychology is available to CPS students at Siena's Monroe Center.

Peggy Motsch congratulates Brandon Roof '14 as the outstanding psychology graduate of 2014 at the Siena Heights Monroe Center.

POLITICAL SCIENCE:

In her role as history professor, Sister Ann Joachim also taught political science in the early years of the college; and while Siena Heights offered no political science major, AJ provided a strong foundation for graduates who pursued public service careers, and for future law students like the Honorable Alice Robie Resnick '61, whose career included serving on the Ohio Supreme Court. Tim Leonard joined the faculty in 1976 and subsequently coordinated the human services: public administration program that lasted into the 1990s. By the end of that decade, the human services terminology was gone, political science was linked divisionally with criminal justice, and a political science minor was available to all students. A brilliant teacher especially interested in Middle Eastern

HAIL, SIENA! Siena Heights University

Tim Leonard.

history and politics, Tim chaired the social and behavioral sciences division, inspiring generations of students right up to his untimely death in 2010. **In 2019:** Eric Kos, previously an adjunct in philosophy, now teaches political science and presents the annual Constitution Day program on campus. Off-campus students may complete a degree in public service administration.

CRIMINAL JUSTICE:

The criminal justice program came about in the mid-1970s in response to a request from local law enforcement officers including Lawrence Richardson, Jr., the first black police officer in Adrian (and later Lenawee County sheriff), who enrolled in the first classes and graduated in 1976. Sister Beth Butler, OP '63, a veteran of prison work who called herself "the nun with a gun," directed criminal justice for its first five years, making it one of the largest programs on campus and earning Outstanding Teacher of the Year honors. "She was just such a remarkable teacher that she had a grand calling to students," colleague Whit Hames recalled. "Many police officers from the area still ask how Beth is doing." Through the 1990s, William Wise directed the program, adding a cooperative work experience requirement. Since 2005, Danielle "Elly" Teunion-Smith '89, a former State Police officer, has coordinated the bachelor of arts in criminal justice and added a focused program in probation, parole, and community corrections. **In 2019:** Criminal justice students have the opportunity to participate in "Criminal Justice: Fact and Fiction," a course taught inside Adrian's Gus Harrison Correctional Facility where half the students are "commuters" (from campus) and half are "residents" (inmates). Adjunct faculty and guest speakers from law enforcement and the judicial system enrich this and other courses in the department. Criminal justice is not offered through the College for Professional Studies, but many law enforcement professionals have earned the bachelor of applied science degree, coming to Siena Heights for the broadening influence of the liberal arts.

Whit Hames joined the Social Science Department in 1978, and introduced gerontology during his twenty-plus years on the faculty.

Sister Ann Joachim organized formal flag raising as an act of citizenship.

The First Fifty Years: A College for Valiant Women

A Century of Study

1919–2019 SIENA HEIGHTS UNIVERSITY 100

MATH AND SCIENCE

Mathematics and science, core elements of the founding curriculum, remain vigorous areas of student interest a century later.

All students in the earliest years completed at least two semesters of science and one of math. Sister Bertha Homminga, better known as the longtime registrar with the phenomenal memory, started both programs at St. Joseph's College in 1922 as one of the founding faculty; she was a one-woman math and science department, teaching at first in Room 201 of Sacred Heart Hall.

When Sister Miriam Stimson, OP '36, arrived as a college freshman in 1932, the biology and chemistry laboratories had been relocated to the fourth floor. Scientific supplies, however, were stored in the stairwell between the ground floor and the sub-basement. "That's where we kept our chemicals," Miriam said. There was no elevator yet, so "if you wanted anything, you went down five floors, and carried them up. We got our exercise that way."

When Miriam returned to teach at Siena Heights after graduate study, she established a research laboratory on the ground floor of Sacred Heart Hall, and involved serious students in her own grant-funded research.

Before computers, science and mathematics depended on the slide rule. Sister Ann Charles (Helen) Duggan, OP, kept her slide rule in this monogrammed leather case which she could hang from the belt of her habit. The circular slide rule was even more compact.

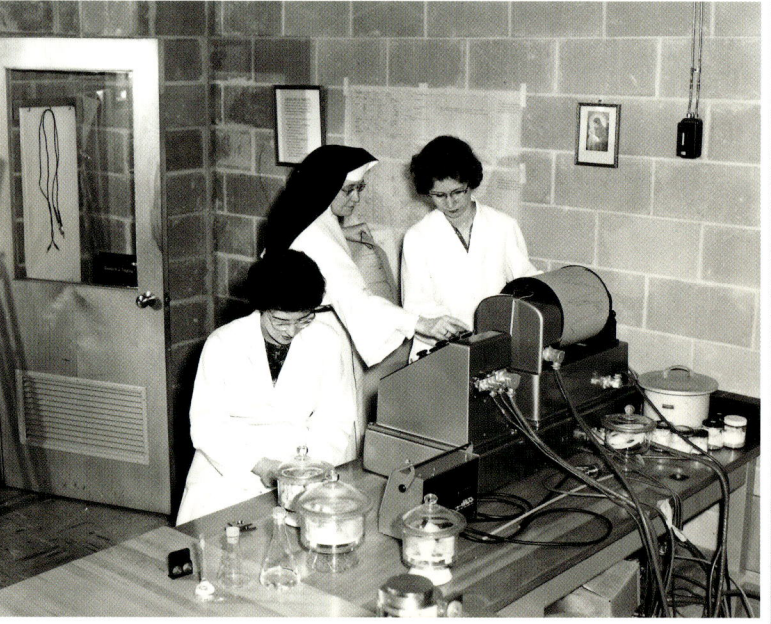

Science students from the 1920s into the 1950s had a good view from the fourth floor windows in Sacred Heart Hall whenever they looked up from their studies. By 1962, science faculty including Sister Miriam Michael did all their teaching three floors down in the new science wing.

70 HAIL, SIENA! Siena Heights University

FACILITIES CHANGES AND UPDATES

Until the mid-1950s, science classrooms remained on the fourth floor of Sacred Heart Hall, directly above the third-floor library. Students did research in the labs, Sister Miriam recalled, and "sometimes we had to have water dripping for twenty-four hours. If anything overflowed, the library would get flooded. It was a constant problem." In addition, there simply was not enough space for all the science being done. Diana Albera Luciani '58 remembered taking genetics and comparative anatomy in the basement of Archangelus Hall near the laundry room and kitchenette: "The area began to smell more and more of formaldehyde. It really was obnoxious to be ironing clothes or heating up a snack amid the odor."

When the college's accreditation with the North Central Association of Colleges and Schools was up for renewal, Siena Heights embarked on a building project to provide new facilities for science and the library. The new building, actually an addition onto the north side of Sacred Heart Hall, provided library space on the upper floor, and up-to-date labs and science classrooms on the lower floor, and additional classrooms and storage even lower. The new building was named Angelicus, but mostly was called the science building; and was further expanded in the 1980s.

In 2000, a renovation of the math and science area provided updated research equipment, computerized classrooms, and modern laboratory tables. Several years later, the science lecture hall received a complete make-over, becoming the Sister Miriam Michael Stimson, OP, Lecture Hall, thanks to support from the family of one of her protegees, distinguished dietician Sister Mary Alan Stuart, OP '62.

GROWTH OF THE DIVISION

Over the decades, the science faculty grew—from Sister Bertha's staff of one (or less than one, since she also taught math)—as a reflection of the curriculum and student interest:

- By 1946, there were two science professors: Sisters Agnita Reuter and Miriam Michael Stimson. With all students required to take two science classes—and medical technology majors advised to take sixteen!—those teachers must have been busy indeed.
- By the 1960s, there were five science faculty. In addition to Miriam Stimson, Sisters Irma Gerber, Helen (Ann Charles) Duggan, Jean Walter Hitzeman, and Eleanor (Paul Ellen) Stech were teaching. Through the 1950s and 1960s, doctors at Providence Hospital in Detroit also served as adjunct faculty, teaching the medical technology majors who spent senior year working at the hospital.
- The full-time science faculty fell to three during the 1970s, when core requirements were abandoned and enrollment in the sciences waned; one of those professors was chemist Sharon Weber, OP '69, who would be a lasting presence and guiding voice in the department. In the 1980s, Carl Kaster (biology) and Anthony Scioly (chemistry) joined the faculty, bringing energy and long-term commitment to the division.

. . . continued on page 72

Right, top to bottom: The 1970s and 1980s found faculty Gene Chapman working with biology students, Tim Husband engaging students in mathematics, and Sister Sharon Weber advising student chemists.

The First Fifty Years: A College for Valiant Women

MATH AND SCIENCE *continued from page 71...*

As the 1980s approached, the need for math faculty began to rise. A single professor had sufficed for years, but the computer age was coming. In 1977, a young Tim Husband was the sole mathematician on the faculty; by 1984 there were four. An adjunct, Sam Ewing, taught the first computer classes at Siena Heights; Bob Xeras joined the faculty and soon was teaching all computer classes. With Sam Abraham's arrival in 1986, computing had fully arrived. Soon, the division was renamed Computing, Mathematics, and the Sciences (CMS).

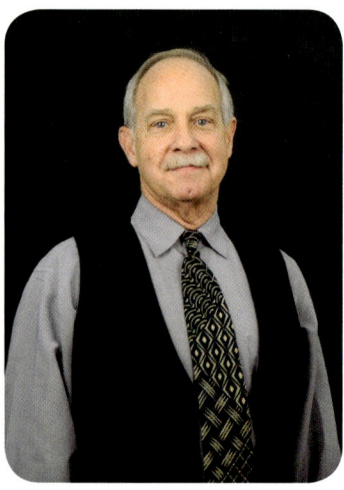

Legendary teaching: Carl Kaster, biology, and Tim Husband, mathematics, are the only three-time winners of the Outstanding Teaching Award at Siena Heights.

By the late 1980s, Siena Heights had reinstated core requirements, which proved to be a boon to the division in surprising ways. Previously, nearly all students in science classes planned to become doctors or researchers; they were eager to learn and easy to teach, Tim Husband recalled; but teaching non-science majors, who enrolled to fulfill a requirement, took more resourcefulness. "The effort made us better teachers," Tim said. The faculty became more innovative, "learning all the time, with the students.... That's the fun of it," he added. The revival of general education requirements "helped us teach better."

Responding to environmental concerns in the 1990s, the division made a "conscious and deliberate effort" to improve safety and modernize laboratory methods, recalled Susan Mole, a chemistry instructor at the time. "Now, for the same educational experience, (we) use much safer materials and we certainly reduced the volume of waste." Similarly, in 2018, professor Steven Wathen led the Chemistry Department to adopt the "green chemistry commitment," ensuring that student chemists gain skills aligned with the needs of the planet.

A TRADITION OF RESEARCH

Miriam Stimson's early involvement in research set the stage for an ongoing focus on original inquiry within the CMS division. Although teaching has always been the uppermost concern for faculty, professors in math and science continue to pursue research investigations, often involving students in their work. Biology professor Jun Tsuji, for example, coauthored research papers with eighteen students in the past two decades. In addition, all math and science majors complete a senior project that, in most cases, reflects original research conducted over several semesters.

The senior project requirement evolved out of a curriculum evaluation in the late 1970s. Science faculty of the time agreed their students needed problem-solving skills, the ability to write term papers as well as lab reports, the confidence to give oral reports, and awareness of ethical issues in science—as well as standard coursework. Based on those discussions, chemist and now vice president of academic affairs Sharon Weber, OP '69 recalled, the senior research project became a signature part of the program. In 2019, students and visitors alike stop in the science hallway to read senior posters reporting on students' research findings.

Math and science students often present their findings at professional meetings and conferences. Siena Heights is routinely represented at annual conventions of Beta Beta Beta, the national biological honor society, where twenty-eight SHU students have won Midwest Region research awards and two—Billy Houghteling '96 and Lauren Coe '12—have earned the national first-place award. Mathematics juniors and seniors have presented yearly at the Rose-Hulman Undergraduate Mathematics Conference since the mid-1980s. Teams of students also compete yearly in an international mathematical modeling competition where Siena Heights twice has received honorable mention rankings above larger nationally and internationally known institutions.

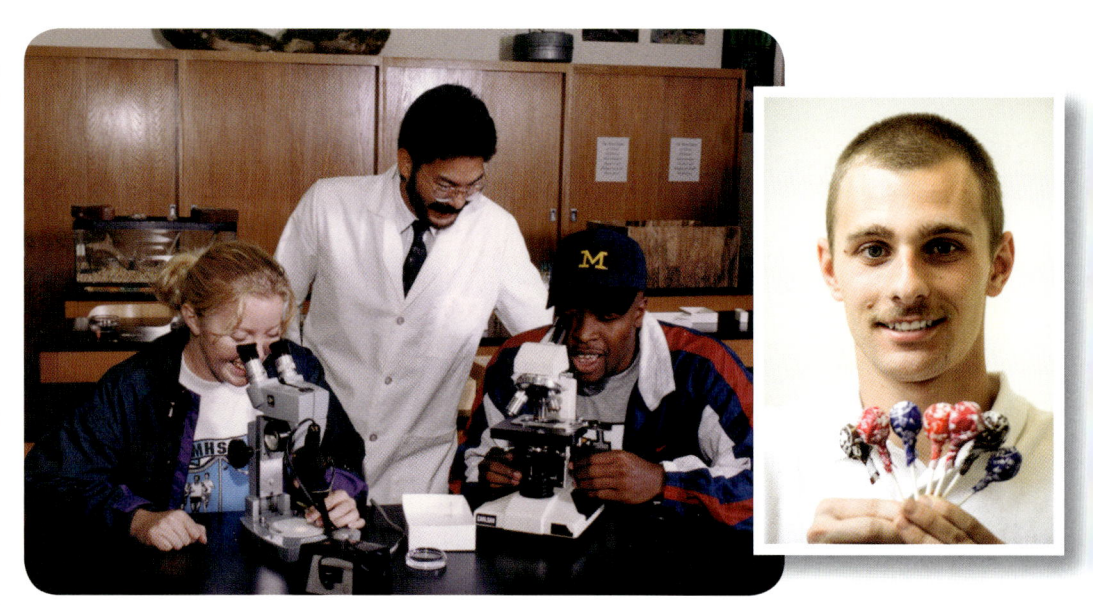

Since the mid-1990s, biologist Jun Tsuji has involved many biology students in his professional research and writing. Mathematics majors do independent research, too: Corey Heid '13 presented the results of his senior project at an international math meeting in San Diego—which led to an invitation to another conference in Canada and publication in an international journal. His topic: "How many licks does it take to get to the Tootsie Roll center of a Tootsie Pop?" (His statistical answer: 356.)

HAIL, SIENA! Siena Heights University

TWENTY-FIRST CENTURY SCIENCE ADDITIONS

Environmental Science: Environmental science was added to the CMS curriculum in 2006, headed by professor Heather Moody. Environmental science majors choose a biology, chemistry, or environmental management concentration; the environmental management option offers state, federal, and international environmental certifications. Environmental science students also gain hands-on experience volunteering with the River Raisin Watershed Association and other environmental groups. In 2018, the SHU environmental science program was recognized for excellence by Universities.com.

Nursing: One of Sister Peg Albert's first decisions as president was to start a nursing program at Siena Heights. The first students enrolled in 2008; eleven years later, nursing is thriving. Siena offers two routes to the bachelor of science in nursing:
- a traditional four-year pre-licensure program for main campus undergraduates, who are officially accepted into the program mid-way through sophomore year;
- an online RN-to-BSN program for registered nurses already in the workplace.

An innovative curriculum—plus high retention, graduation rates, and first-time pass rates on the licensing exam—earned the program an impressive ten-year accreditation in 2015 from the Commission on Collegiate Nursing Education. Distinctive elements of SHU nursing include a partnership with the Adrian Dominican Sisters (students are paired with sisters to learn empathy, communication, and interviewing skills); strong ties to area hospitals (clinical experience is included from the start); and innovative partnerships with other departments such as social work. In 2019, Siena Heights will introduce an online graduate program leading to the Master of Science in Nursing (MSN) degree.

Engineering: Since 2016, Siena Heights has offered students the possibility of earning two degrees in five years through a partnership between SHU and the University of North Dakota. By completing a bachelor's degree of the student's choice "on the ground" at Siena, and a bachelor of engineering science from UND through online coursework and two summer visits to that campus, program graduates bring an interdisciplinary education to the engineering workplace—where knowledge of business, computing, or communication is a competitive plus. The Siena part of the program, which kicked off with thirty students, emphasizes engineering design as well as technology and includes lab experience. Siena Heights also collaborates with the Lenawee Tech Center, providing opportunities for SHU engineering students to enrich upper-level online engineering with hands-on technical and mechanical experience.

A distinctive feature of the nursing program is the opportunity to get up close and personal with the operation and services of a Life Flight helicopter.

A (Half) Century of Study

1919–2019 • 100 • SIENA HEIGHTS UNIVERSITY

GRADUATE EDUCATION

Soon after graduate studies were introduced in the 1950s, the college began to focus heavily on graduate teacher education, reflecting Siena's long commitment to preparing quality teachers and school administrators. Counselor education was the second major emphasis. Then, during Sister Miriam Stimson's tenure as graduate studies director, an addiction counseling program, first offered in 1984, addressed the increase in drug addiction throughout society.

During her thirteen years as director, Miriam implemented a system of graduate committees, whereby each graduate student met monthly with his or her own committee of professionals, from campus and community, to discuss books the student chose. "Not education books, because you had already done that," Sister Anthonita Porta, OP remembered. "You would read books out of your field," then discuss them with the committee, and "all of a sudden we went from professor-student to 'we are together in this.'" The committee also would help the student think through an independent study topic; by graduation, the student and his or her committee had become colleagues. Although "a really fine process," Anthonita said, it was a victim of its own success, abandoned when faculty became overwhelmed by serving on too many committees at once.

In graduate studies as in undergraduate classrooms, quality teaching is paramount. Sister Miriam Stimson meets with a graduate class in the 1980s.

HAIL, SIENA! Siena Heights University

Until 2006, all master's degree candidates wrote a thesis. The thesis requirement ensured a high degree of intellectual rigor (Miriam Stimson denied graduation to students until the thesis met her exacting standards) and distinguished Siena Heights from less challenging programs. Eventually, however, the graduate marketplace changed enough that Siena Heights elected to drop the thesis requirement.

In 2002, graduate studies became the Graduate College at Siena Heights University. A few years later, the Graduate College introduced the master's program in leadership. For several years, the Graduate College also offered the Specialist of Arts in education, a degree higher than the master's but below the doctorate, of particular interest to school principals and administrators. In 2018, the Graduate College inaugurated its first totally online program: a master of business administration degree emphasizing ethics and sustainability.

> *In 2019:* The Graduate College is comprised of four main programs: teacher education (Adrian); clinical mental health counseling (Adrian, Southfield, and Lansing); leadership with concentrations in health care, higher education, and organizational leadership (Adrian and online), and business administration (online). Committed to serving working adults, and integrating theory with practice, the Graduate College continues to explore new opportunities, guided by Dominican values and the Siena Heights mission. In 2019, the Graduate College will launch an online master's degree program in nursing.

At a 2010 Metro Detroit Center graduation reception in Southfield, faculty and staff, from left, Gail Ryder, Linda Pettit, and Betsy Brooks congratulate Cydney Clayton, in pink, on completing her master's degree.

Proud graduate Anthony Bowen '17 flashes a jubilent smile upon receiving his master's degree in clinical mental health counseling from SHU president Sister Peg Albert.

Leadership of Graduate Education

Directors of Graduate Studies
Sister Mary DePaul Gillette, OP (1957–64)
Sister Claudia Hinds, OP (1964–74)
LeRoy Harvey (1974–76)
George Eppley (1976–78)
Sister Miriam Michael Stimson, OP '36 (1978–91)
Peggy Treece Myles (1992–96)

Deans of the Graduate College
Robert Gordon (1996–2006)
C. Patrick Palmer (2006–10)
Ann Hooghart (2010–12)
Linda Sandel Pettit (2013–15)
Cheri Betz (2015–present/2019)

The First Fifty Years: A College for Valiant Women

Part 3
Everything Changes!

Transition and Tumult in the 1970s

Education had changed. The workplace had changed. Women's roles had changed. Even the Catholic Church had changed. And after fifty years, Siena Heights had to change, too.

Archangelus Hall, and Ledwidge Hall behind it, provided the home base for incoming students at the start of the 1970s. Jeans, bare feet, and bandannas were part of the new look for students, as shown by Danita Binkowski '78 outdoors, and David Valentine '79 and friend indoors. As the decade passed, many new students would find *their* Siena Heights somewhere other than on the main campus.

NEW LEADERSHIP, NEW UNCERTAINTIES
Reading the Signs of the Times.

As the 1970s began, Siena Heights was overwhelmed by an institutional identity crisis. Despite a half-century of phenomenal success educating women, the college could not continue as it had existed for all those years. Almost everything in society was changing. The college had no choice but to change, too. And leading the change, with aggressive enthusiasm, was the new president, Dr. Hugh L. Thompson.

Dr. Thompson arrived just before the fall semester in 1971, the first non-Adrian Dominican, the first layperson, and the first male to lead the college. He also was not Catholic; he was Lutheran. A former athletic coach, he was ambitious, energetic, and pragmatic. He arrived ready to raise money, recruit students, and shake things up. He was a stocky man with a big personality. Sometimes he rubbed people the wrong way.

Hugh Thompson "saw his role as building the stability of the institution. And he saw everything growing from that," recalled then-trustee Willard Reagan. Academics and special programs were great, Reagan said, explaining the new president's attitude, but "only if you could keep the doors open." And keeping the doors open had become a real issue. Along with many small colleges at the time, especially Catholic women's colleges, Siena Heights was facing genuine threats to its future.

First, there was the cost of a changing workforce. For decades, Siena Heights had operated with a faculty and staff made up entirely of Adrian Dominican Sisters. The sisters took vows of poverty and embraced their work as a mission. Sister-faculty not only taught, they also supervised the dormitories, oversaw the dining room, cleaned the classrooms, and chaperoned outings. It was called "contributed service." But in the aftermath of Vatican II, sisters had more mission options, and many chose health care or social work instead of teaching. Vowed religious faculty were replaced, more often than not, by lay educators who required real marketplace salaries. Expenses went up. With the passage of time, more and more lay people joined the staff. Eventually, justice demanded that the sisters be paid at a rate equivalent to their lay colleagues. Costs went up more.

President Thompson welcomed trustees and spouses, including Mr. and Mrs. John Abraham and Mr. and Mrs. Donato Sarapo, to Siena Heights. "The charisma of Hugh was his ability to attract people to the institution and to involve them in its growth." *Sister Rita Gleason, OP '40, Director of Development 1973–83*

Hugh Thompson waved in a new era when he became president in 1971.

The 1970s also brought significant change to most religious communities. In an increasingly secular society, with opportunities for women opening up everywhere, fewer women chose vowed religious vocations. In addition, many nuns and sisters (and priests) left their orders, feeling called to lives of service as non-vowed and/or married citizens. For the Adrian Dominicans, the results were predictable: fewer sisters generating income meant fewer resources for supporting their members, their outreach causes, and their sponsored institutions.

Where once the congregation had supported Siena Heights entirely, now the college needed to generate its own financial support, through fundraising as well as tuition—and needed to increase both kinds of income. The small student populations that Siena Heights had nurtured for so many years—with graduating classes of sixty or fifty or fewer lay students—could not sustain the institution.

Sister Jeanne Lefebvre, OP '66, reflecting on this period, once described the situation this way: "The new college administration was struggling to keep a small-town church-related liberal arts college alive in an age more receptive to urban, secular, career-oriented institutions. This was a 'struggling-for-survival' and 'searching-for-a-new-identity' Siena."

Sometimes referred to as the snowflake or spider logo, the design was meant to visualize a student-centered college that was quality-oriented with contemporary goals. It is believed to have been designed by Sister Jeannine Klemm, OP.

Everything Changes! Transition and Tumult in the 1970s

Bucks, Budgets, and a Powerhouse Board.

Hugh Thompson's efforts to build stability at the college went in many directions. From the get-go, he emphasized strengthening the Board of Trustees and building the budget through aggressive fund-raising and student recruitment.

Sister Petronilla had begun the move toward independent governance by establishing a lay Advisory Board, which evolved into a six-member Board of Trustees prior to Thompson's selection as Petronilla's successor. Once installed as president, Dr. Thompson rapidly expanded the Board as a means of engaging influential business leaders in the life of the college. Within two years, he had recruited a core of successful, wealthy executives from Toledo and Detroit, and increased the Board to forty trustees.

He expanded the administration, too, especially in the areas of fundraising and recruitment. He expected the four members of the new development staff to make a combined forty fundraising calls a week, and charged each member of the admissions staff to visit four high schools a day. He held himself to similar standards. He announced his goal of keeping Siena's budget balanced—even with the increased costs of lay faculty, athletics, and an expanded staff—and was relentless in reaching out to trustees, businesses, and donors.

"Dr. Thompson was a real go-getter," recalled Sam Baughey '72, a Vietnam veteran whom Thompson hired to assist with corporate relations and athletics. The president was successful, too: "You could not say no to Hugh," observed Willard Reagan, who chaired the trustees during Thompson's years. "He was absolutely terrific at raising money and recruiting trustees."

In keeping with the increased business orientation of both the president and the Board, the college also adopted a new logo, intended to convey a contemporary corporate identity. The bold new design, informally called the "snowflake" or "spider" logo, was meant to visualize Siena's commitment to student-centered programming, and is believed to have been designed by the Art Department's Sister Jeannine Klemm, OP.

The new president was very persuasive with donors and trustees. "You could not say no to Hugh." *Trustee emeritus Willard Reagan*

PRESIDENTIAL PROFILE NO. 6

Dr. Hugh Lee Thompson

President of Siena Heights College: 1971–1977

*First Male President. Built the Board of Trustees.
Established Intercollegiate Athletics.
Promoted Career-Responsive Academics.*

Dr. Hugh Thompson, perhaps the most controversial person to hold the office of Siena Heights president, played a pivotal role in moving the college forward and ensuring its future in a time of great change. He, himself, represented complete change: he was not an Adrian Dominican, nor a vowed religious of any kind, nor even a Catholic (he was Lutheran). Energetic and outgoing, he was a vocational educator and former coach who could be both charmingly persuasive and abrasively direct. His presidency was marked by remarkable growth and creativity—but also by high anxiety, especially among the faculty. Under his leadership, however, the college made many changes that remain a key part of today's university.

During his six-year tenure, Dr. Thompson expanded the fundraising, public relations, admissions, and financial aid offices at Siena Heights. He increased enrollment from fewer than 500 mostly female students to more than 1,000—470 men, 592 women. He increased the Board of Trustees from six to forty members, recruiting powerhouse businessmen from throughout the region. He brought in corporate leaders such as Robert Sage and Kenneth Herrick as major benefactors. He secured a three-year federal grant to support academic initiatives. He established a vigorous intercollegiate athletic program, built Zollar Field for soccer and the Thomas Emmett Courts for tennis, and began fund raising for a fieldhouse. And he instilled the curriculum with a new attentiveness to student and community needs and career interests, setting the stage for Siena's pioneering outreach into degree completion for working adult students.

Near the end of Thompson's presidency, Siena Heights established the set of student and institutional goals that remain in the academic catalog today; and created a mission statement that articulated, for the first time, the college's intent "to assist people to become more competent, purposeful, and ethical."

After leaving Siena Heights, Dr. Thompson became president of Detroit Institute of Technology, held leadership positions at several other institutions, and served as chancellor of Indiana University–Kokomo from 1980 to 1990. He died in 2007.

> "He was not a teacher, not an academician, and he really did not understand people being preoccupied with academic things. And there was that split between him and faculty; the rapport never really grew. But I'm here to say, he did a lot we should give him credit for."
>
> *Father David Van Horn, Art Faculty 1970–97*

> "He brought a businessman's perspective to the school, which had its negative and positive aspects."
>
> *Theodora McKennan, OP '51, History Faculty 1962-63, 1970-76.*

Hugh and his wife, Patricia, had four daughters, one of whom graduated from Siena Heights: Cheryl Thompson Seneca '75.

> "His intentions were of the highest caliber, and he was an extremely hard worker who had the interest of the college at heart. But he seemed to lack a full understanding and appreciation of the dedicated commitment of a religious faculty."
>
> *Hilda Gelegan, OP '42, Faculty 1965–70, Director of Development 1970–73*

COEDUCATION: NEW LIFE ON CAMPUS
Are You Ready for a Brand New Beat?

As freshmen in the fall of 1968, Ruth LaFontaine '72 and her classmates did not wear uniforms, but they were required to choose "appropriate" clothing—and "we were checked to make sure we were dressed properly for class." By junior year, however, dress codes were gone completely, Ruth said: "We could wear jeans," and soon, everyone did. The sisters had a new look, too. Vatican II had loosened *their* dress code, and most Adrian Dominicans exchanged their long white habits, first for short habits, then for colorful secular clothing. By 1970, *all* the women of Siena Heights looked very different.

And in the fall of 1970, twelve males moved into Archangelus Hall.

In contrast to their faculty forebears, teachers in the 1970s cut a diverse pattern as shown by this foursome: from left, Sister Marie Gabriel "Gabe" Hungerman, IHM (philosophy), Sister Molly Lorms, OP (social work), Richard Reaume (education), and Sister Jane Farrell, IHM (history). Some sisters chose a more traditional look; but Sister Carmelia "Carmie" O'Connor, OP (religious studies), did not hesitate to put an athletic windbreaker over her modified white habit.

"Students Love Those Jeans! Blue jeans. Students strolling into classrooms throughout the nation are clad in jeans. Bell-bottom jeans, straight-legged jeans, blue, brown, green, and white jeans, all covered with multitudinous decorative or necessity patches, are THE college wardrobe for male and female students." *Reflection,* Siena's General Newsletter, (Vol. 1, No. 1) September 1972

Before then, a handful of men had enrolled but most were commuters; one or two had lived in rooms at the back of Benincasa, well separated from the female population. The arrival *in the dorm* of the so-called "dirty dozen" marked the start of full participation for men in all aspects of college life. "We took over a dead-end hallway of Archangelus, fourth floor, northwest wing: locked doors on either end, four sisters guarding the entrances," Doug Miller '74 recalled.

"We were louder than the rest of the residents. And we were messier," he added. Men were not allowed to use the elevator, either. "We walked up the four flights from the old smoker."

A new decade was underway.

The mid-1970s admissions staff, led by Anne Marie Brown, OP, *front left*, included a young Fred Smith, *front second from right*. "We each visited four schools a day, four days a week, made so many phone calls—no questions asked. These reports went straight to the president. He could slam his fist on the table, but he could turn on the charm very well. He was directly involved . . . how to get the numbers, how to plan the territory. He could be a tough guy to deal with, but Sister Anne Marie handled him pretty well." *Fred Smith, Admissions then Athletic Staff, 1970s 2019.*

Veterans and Cannonballers:
Men, Women, War, and Sports.

Siena Heights opened its doors to men in the middle of the Vietnam war. Some early men came to Siena to avoid the draft; college enrollment provided an automatic deferral. Others, like Lee Benish '72 and Sam Baughey '72, came as veterans, recently returned from Southeast Asia. A few, like Bill Small '73, came because Siena Heights was Catholic, nearby, and had done well by an older sister. Still others enrolled when vocational training turned out to be an insufficient credential for career advancement.

However those early men arrived, President Thompson wanted to keep them at Siena Heights—and recruit more. As a former coach, he was convinced that intercollegiate athletics would help to build male enrollment. By the spring of his second year, Thompson had hired the college's first athletic director, Harvey Jackson, and established its first men's team: baseball. The Siena Heights "Cannonballers" chose their name in honor of Sister Ann Joachim's battle to save the Wabash Cannonball. On April 23, 1973, the Siena Heights Cannonballers took on the Adrian College Bulldogs, in the first ever athletic contest between the two schools. Siena lost, 8-4, but athletics won. The era of the student-athlete was here to stay.

By fall 1974, as Siena began its second full year of intercollegiate competition, Siena Heights offered four varsity sports for men (golf, tennis, cross country, baseball) and three for women (volleyball, tennis, basketball). Sister Mary Alice Murnen, OP was women's athletic director. And the college had its highest-ever enrollment, with more than 1,150 students—up 30 percent from the previous year. A total of 420 new freshmen and transfers joined the student body.

With men and women both competing for Siena Heights, the teams adopted a new name, too. No longer the Cannonballers, they were the Saints!

By spring of 1975, the Saints had added men's wrestling and women's bowling. Siena's female athletes had won the 1974–75 All-Sports Trophy from the Southeastern Women's Athletic Conference. And men's basketball (previously a city-league intramural activity) was set to begin its first varsity season in the fall.

Hugh Thompson's instincts were right. Athletics attracted more students—both male and female. Although many of the early athletes did not graduate from Siena Heights, eventually, as President Thompson had hoped, athletics did keep those student-athletes enrolled through graduation. With 212 students earning diplomas in the spring of 1975, Siena Heights was on track to a successful future.

Athletics appealed to women as much as to men. Lisa Binkowski '75 played basketball all four years, adding volleyball, tennis, and bowling during her senior year. After graduation, she stayed on as an assistant to coach Mary Alice Murnen, OP.

This baseball team made Siena Heights history as the college's first intercollegiate men's athletic team. Before long, they would be Saints, but in 1973 these athletes were the Cannonballers: *standing from left*—Joe Antonazzo '75, John Woodson, Ron Shannon '75, Mike Prebish '77, Tom Coleman '76, Bob Locke, coach Pete Sedello; *kneeling from left*—John Angelo '75, Gary McCullough '75, Chuck Harrigan, Pat Filipek '76, and Gary Cottrell.

HAIL, SIENA! Siena Heights University

Legends of the Faculty

Father David J. Van Horn, C.PP.S.

Father David Van Horn arrived at Siena Heights in the fall of 1970, when everything was changing. One of the first men to join the fulltime teaching staff, he was an artist, teacher, and priest who walked with the community through change for twenty-seven years.

"It was a zoo," he said of Siena in 1970. The college was dealing with coeducation, Vatican II, Vietnam, and post-sixties culture. Richard Reaume was interim president, the first male ever to be in charge on campus—and Hugh Thompson came soon after, shaking things up even more. A "zoo," perhaps; "but what a stunning experiment it turned out to be," Father Van Horn reflected.

Amidst the changes, Sister Jeannine Klemm, OP, was leading the Art Department into a period of dynamic growth. She hired David to teach art appreciation, but instead he built an entire art history curriculum. "Jeannine let me start all those classes," he recalled appreciatively. "She never questioned what I wanted to do," so he initiated courses from medieval art to modern, from Italian to Oriental, African, and Native American art.

He was a brilliant teacher whose passion brought art history to life. "With a sweep of his arm, the whole classroom" was taken back to the Italian Renaissance, Lisa Wilkie once observed; the discussion that followed was so vivid, she said, the artists of the period "could just as well be in the room, talking themselves about one another's work." In addition to art history, he taught design, and especially enjoyed teaching students of all majors in the senior core class known then as GEN 401. He could "awaken questions and a desire for learning" in his students, helping them think in new ways, Donna Milbauer '89 said. Honored as the Outstanding Teacher of the Year at Siena Heights in 1981, he was named Michigan Professor of the Year, and one of the top ten educators in the country, by the Council for Advancement and Support of Education in 1988.

He was also a practicing artist, a gifted ceramist who held degrees from the Dayton Art Institute and the Art Institute of Chicago and had studied in Italy on a Fulbright Scholarship.

A priest of the Missionaries of the Precious Blood, Father Van Horn often said Mass at Siena Heights, drawing faculty, staff, and students to Ledwidge Hall or Studio Angelico for his homilies. A scholar on St. Catherine of Siena (he read her 400 letters in the original Italian), he often worked Catherine's ideas into his message and his conversation. A deeply spiritual man who loved gardening and exploring other cultures, who played the flute around campus, and who lived without telephone or television, Father Van Horn was a favorite of Siena students and performed many alumni weddings, later baptizing the children of these marriages.

Father Van Horn retired in the spring of 1997 and died two years later. The David J. Van Horn Memorial Garden, designed and built outside Studio Angelico by colleagues John Wittersheim and Jamie Goode '87, was dedicated in October 2000.

Everything Changes! Transition and Tumult in the 1970s

From Walsh Hall to Sage Union:
A New Center of Student Life.

Since its opening in 1968, Ledwidge Hall had been the focus of student activities. Ledwidge Ballroom was a much-loved gathering space—and a popular venue for wedding receptions for early-1970s graduates. The bookstore was on the lower level of Ledwidge, along with a common room called "Beta Rho" featuring pinball, a pool table, and vending machines. Archangelus Ballroom was another much-used space, large enough for dances, but furnished with a piano and small seating areas for meetings or poetry readings.

But President Thompson planned to increase enrollment, and aimed to recruit more men and more commuter students. He began looking for space—not in the residence halls—to accommodate a broader range of student activities. The opening in the early 1970s of Francoeur Theater, and the Verheyden Performing Arts Center that surrounded it, provided the solution.

With music and theater relocating to the new facilities, Walsh Hall could be repurposed as a student union. Musicians and thespians mourned the loss of Walsh's outstanding acoustics, but students in general were thrilled with the possibilities Walsh would provide when the main floor was leveled and the auditorium seats removed.

A new sign welcomed visitors to campus. Ledwidge Hall was a new residential showplace that included a social area called "Beta Rho" equipped with pool tables and lively décor.

86   HAIL, SIENA! Siena Heights University

In the fall of 1972, students helped complete the interior renovation of Walsh Hall which, as Sage College Union (named for benefactor Bob Sage), became the hub of student life.

Renovation was supposed to be finished by the fall of 1972. But it wasn't. Students returned to find the work still in progress, with no timetable for completion. In that era of activism, Student Senate president Thom Miller '74 (the first male and first commuter to hold the office) took action. Meeting with President Thompson, he proposed that student volunteers could help move the project along. Thompson accepted the offer. Student teams began cleaning, polishing, and painting—generating rare praise from the president: "As you know, I am not one to pass out accolades," Thompson admitted, before commending the students for their help transforming Walsh into Sage College Union, in a letter to the student newspaper.

The building, renamed to honor the Sage Foundation for its support of the renovation, became the new heart of student life. In that pre-computer, pre-cell-phone era, students visited Sage daily to peer through mailbox windows, looking for letters from family, friends, and distant loves. Sage's main floor became an all-purpose event space, perfect for rock bands, talent shows, dances, toga parties, and the famous (to alumni of a certain era) "wapatoola" gatherings. Sage's nooks and crannies provided meeting spaces and offices for student organizations and student life staff, and lockers and a lounge for commuter students. The basement gymnasium remained, at first, but already there were rumors of a new athletic facility.

Everything Changes! Transition and Tumult in the 1970s

Pranks and Protest.

Sister Eugenia Clare Kiefer, OP '35, who taught at Siena Heights from 1964 into the new decade, lived through the transition from an all-women's school to a fully coeducational college. With men in the dorms, she recalled, life took on a new rhythm, punctuated by heavier footsteps and the thumps of basketballs being dribbled down the halls.

Sister Eugenia Clare and a few other faculty still lived in the residence halls, but no longer patrolled as they had in the past. There was a "change in responsibility for discipline," she said. By 1970, "we had no more responsibility for checking the students in at night and seeing they turned out their lights and were in the rooms. We'd hear their radios on the windows at 5:00 in the morning; they were just going to bed when we were getting up!"

Sister Theodora "Teddy" McKennan, OP '51, taught history in the early 1960s, then returned to the faculty in 1970, living at first in Archangelus Hall. She remembered the "ethereal music" that had drifted from the stairwell one early morning before Christmas in 1962; choral students had sung Christmas carols, then slipped noiselessly to the next floor. Eight years later, she "was surprised and delighted all over again to hear the carols, but with the masculine voices and more of a wild shuffling up and down the stairs! But it was the same spirit, and it was wonderful."

Pranks became more common with a coeducational student body. Many a night, sisters and students woke from sleep to the sound of the fire alarm. "Sister Alice Monica Dibley received a fur coat from her sister when she died, and she saved that for fire alarms," Sister Teddy recalled. "I don't think they ever discovered who was setting off the alarms. Maybe it was only one student. But at two or three in the morning, in the cold of winter, we were being routed out of bed. And only Alice Monica was warm!"

Protest came to campus, too. Like college students across the country, Siena Heights students were debating the Vietnam War, calling for civil rights, listening to new music, and exploring new futures. In the spring of 1971, students drove to Detroit to participate in the first Earth Day. "Students were very passionate," Ruth LaFontaine '72 recalled. In the evenings, students gathered in Archangelus Ballroom to sing folk songs, with Father John Keefer playing guitar.

The Clarion Call of a Student Strike:
"The Library is the Heart of the College!"

Following Thom Miller's "first commuter" presidency, the Butler brothers of Adrian, Les '75 and Leo '75, broke the mold again for student leadership: first African-American president (Les), first African-American vice president (Leo), first twins to simultaneously hold the top two positions in student senate. Les and Leo "were very vocal and had strong leadership skills," recalled Gail Clark '76. "They had the capacity to get people together on issues."

Twins Leo '75 and Les '75 Butler brought energy and drive to Student Government, where they served as president and vice president respectively and organized a student strike to protest closing the library on Sunday evenings, among other concerns. At left, Leo meets with students informally. Leo and Les were the first of several Butler siblings to attend Siena Heights.

The library was a popular study location for on-campus students in the 1970s.

The Butlers famously got students, and many faculty, together for what is widely believed to be Siena Heights' only student strike in its first one hundred years. "We had a list of ten concerns," Gail Clark remembered. "We encouraged students who believed in this list to not go to class that day. It was quite a radical move." Supportive faculty assigned no homework for that day, she said, and brought coffee and rolls to the students gathered on the lawn in front of Sacred Heart Hall. It was a peaceful protest, "nothing violent," she added. "We were just discussing the issues, hoping to draw attention to the issues, and that did happen."

Concerns at the time included a lack of minority faculty, lack of periodicals and other resources dealing with minority issues, and objections to a budget-driven proposal to close the library on Sunday nights. Then-chemistry professor Sharon Weber, OP '69, recalled, with some admiration, the students outside chanting, "The library is the heart of the college!" The strike accomplished at least one of its purposes: the library stayed open on Sunday nights. President Thompson willingly met with the Senate Executive Board to address their other concerns, though some would persist for several more decades.

Academic Energy!

Upon his arrival, President Thompson had gone right to work looking for ways to reshape the curriculum to attract more new students. Many of his initiatives seemed to threaten long-standing liberal arts programs, generating anxiety in the faculty ranks. In the midst of the tumult, however, there was great vitality in academic life. Faculty were not always happy with the nature or speed of change, but history professor Sister Jane Farrell, IHM remembered 1970 to 1976 as "the best six years, I think, of my professional life. The people on the faculty were exceptional, and I think the mission—particularly to the east side of Adrian and the up-and-coming migrant workers, the poorer side of Adrian—stood out."

...continued on page 88

Continued from page 87...

Sister Patricia Siemen, OP '72 (who in 2016 became prioress of the Adrian Dominican Sisters) recalled her senior year at Siena Heights as "one of the most pivotal years in my life." Studying Third World history with Sister Teddy McKennan, as well as Black history and Latin American history, "my consciousness just expanded," Pat recalled. Studying prison literature with Sister Mary Louise Hall, OP, she encountered readings from Aristotle in ancient Greece to the Soledad brothers in 1969. "And I had Sister Carmie (Carmelia O'Connor, OP) for independent study in liberation theology. All those concepts absolutely opened my mind."

Pat Siemen also was one of a dozen or so students—including Thom Miller '74, Les '75 and Leo '75 Butler, Colleen Sheridan Kaltz '72, and Barbara Riesterer Lawrence '74—who participated in Siena's Model United Nations teams in the early 1970s. Pat's delegation represented Canada and had to take the Canadian position on issues of apartheid, which was "the first time I really knew about apartheid." That year, the Siena team won the regional Model U.N. competition and went on to nationals at Harvard University, where Siena Heights was cited as one of the top four programs, along with Georgetown, Princeton, and University of Utah, Pat said. "Now that was a big deal!"

"We knew there was some transition going on" at the college in 1971–72, Pat added, "but whatever was going on, I just know that the faculty interacted well with the students, and there was real quality of presence and care—that personal interest, knowing the students, knowing how they are along the way."

This mid-1970s Pops Ensemble exudes energy, kicking as they sing, perhaps practicing for one of the several Disney World trips the group made in the 1970s. The weather was considerably colder in December 1974 as these students headed to the airport for a spring semester in Italy: *from left*—Shirley Martin Van Benschoten '75 (*back*), Kathie DeMeo, Patty Kamper (*back*), Sonya Jenkins, Jim Stout '75, John Warner '76, John Schneider '74, Carol Bachelder Steck '75, and Jeff Scott.

A Century of Study

SUMMER SCHOOL: ANOTHER SIDE OF SIENA

FOR FIFTY YEARS, A CAMPUS FULL OF TEACHERS.

For decades, the college was full to overflowing each summer as young Adrian Dominicans came "home" from their teaching jobs. The sisters were Siena's first working adult students: teachers eager to be back in school themselves. In the years before certification, Adrian Dominican novices, even postulants, began teaching in Catholic schools long before earning a degree, then returned, summer after summer, to finish the degree.

In 1939, when Siena Heights had just received its new name, the summer school catalogue listed twelve time slots for daily classes, with ten offerings in the 8–9 a.m. slot, and eighteen in the 10–11:30 slot. Altogether, seventy classes, plus five Studio Angelico workshops, were scheduled to begin on June 26. Every building would be in use. The campus would be buzzing!

Not every summer student was a sister. Local teachers enrolled. So did lay students like Mary "Parl" Solem, who came to Siena in 1945 but withdrew after two years when her father ran out of money; she went to work, teaching in a one-room school near her Illinois home, but returned for five summers, earning her degree in 1952. Other students took summer classes to graduate *early*. One of Parl Solem's roommates was Paula Harrington Carroll, a gifted musician who graduated in 1952, a year before the freshmen she started with.

Alumnae have warm memories of those summer days. "Sister Miriam Stimson would bring in fruit—a few raspberries that were ripe or some strawberries from her garden—to get us started in the morning," said Sharon Weber, OP, recalling summers studying chemistry, after teaching elementary students all year. One summer, she and her classmates paraphrased songs to prepare for exams: "Find an electron, and it goes 'round, 'round, 'round. . . ."

THEOLOGICAL DEBATE IN THE 1970S.

By the late 1960s, fewer sisters were entering the congregation and teachers needed degrees before teaching. The focus of summer school changed. In the aftermath of Vatican II, summers in the 1970s became famous for a series of Theology Institutes coordinated by Sister Carmelia "Carmie" O'Connor, OP of Siena's religious studies faculty. Carmie "wrote letters to the world famous, inviting them to Siena," Sister Jeanne Lefebvre, OP '66 remembered. "Incredibly, many responded, and once they had met Carmie, they came again."

Co-sponsored by Siena Heights and the Adrian Dominican Congregation, the summer theology institutes were ecumenical, interdisciplinary seminars that attracted women and men, lay and religious, students and teachers from across the United States and around the world. The seminars were legendary for lively dialogue and exciting exploration of new theological concepts such as liberation theology. Institute participants "still marvel at the spirit of community and empowerment that seemed intrinsic to the experience," Sister Jeanne said. "Many of them had been directly involved in the civil rights and antiwar movements of the 1960s, and they were actively involved in the emerging peace and justice movements of the 1970s."

The institutes influenced Siena's academic-year community, too. A handful of September-to-May faculty and students participated each summer, and "there was a catalytic reaction," Jeanne said, between the "struggling-for-survival and searching-for-new-identity Siena" of the academic year and the empowering spirit that flourished in the summer.

DIFFERENT DRUMMERS IN THE TWENTY-FIRST CENTURY

In summer 2018, a few professors offered summer classes, but classrooms were mostly empty—or being painted or repaired. Inside offices, though, administrators, staff, and faculty preparing new syllabi worked to the beat of a different drummer. Literally. Marching bands and drum-lines practiced indoors and out during band-camp season. Cheer teams clapped and called out rhythmic chants. Sports teams ran energetic drills to the whistle calls of encouraging coaches. And youth of many ages hustled noisily from arts or drama or sports activities to lunch in the University Center, calling out to friends and checking cell phones. On weekends, the wedding march floated from St. Dominic Chapel (formerly Lumen Ecclesiae) and receptions rocked the walls of Benincasa. The campus was busy, but in a different way.

Still, listening carefully, a visitor might hear whispers of the past behind the modern soundtrack: the chattering of a young sister, the accent of an Irish theologian, or the melody of an old study song. *"Find an electron, and it goes 'round, 'round, 'round. . . ."*

Everything Changes! Transition and Tumult in the 1970s

A New Approach to Campus Ministry.

What did it mean to be a Catholic college? What if many of your faculty—or students—were not Catholic? Should a Catholic college be different? *And this:* Was being Catholic an obstacle to recruiting more students? Such questions were discussed, argued, and wondered about in the late 1960s and early 1970s. No one was sure of the answers. No one knew exactly what Siena Heights was or should be in the post–Vatican II world. (Notices advertising the position of president after Sister Petronilla's resignation barely mentioned a Catholic connection.)

Fortunately, Father John M. Keefer, OP, came to campus as chaplain in 1969. Father Keefer, who served for nine years before leaving to work in Appalachia, was an influential presence guiding the Siena Heights community into a new kind of campus ministry.

A creative spiritual leader, he played the guitar, acted in Theatre Siena productions, and earned a fine arts degree in ceramics in addition to engaging students and faculty in the liturgical life of Lumen Ecclesiae Chapel. He welcomed the voices of Bill Marshall '78, Brenda Young Waters '79, and other student musicians as they brought modern music to Mass. He embraced the new spirit of the church wholeheartedly, and was known to rearrange pews, or decorate the chapel with white spray-painted tree branches, to create what he thought would be the most meaningful setting for a particular Mass or celebration. He wrote a column for the campus newspaper, reminding students to make time for faith and spirituality. And he modeled the idea of faith as service and social justice. "He made the liturgy come alive for the students of his day," said Sister Therese Craig, OP, of the theater faculty, "and urged them to read the signs of the times and answer with their time and their energy."

Sister Therese recalled Father Keefer leading days of fasting and prayer, food drives, work within the community, and soup and prayer events. "Social justice was a living activity for John," she said, calling him "a model for today in the tradition of St. Dominic."

Before he left Siena Heights, John Keefer received an honorary doctorate from the college, for being "a teacher, a preacher, and a celebrator" and for guiding the community "through times exhilarating and disappointing." The citation acknowledged that Father Keefer "created for us a climate of hope and helped us achieve a sense of shared purpose."

The college may have wrestled administratively with what it meant to be a Catholic institution, but many students—now alumni—of the 1970s remember a powerful and uncomplicated message of Dominican faith, hospitality, and service.

Father John Keefer was a powerful presence on campus in the post–Vatican II period. A dynamic preacher, creative artist, sensitive counselor, and active participant in campus life, he is shown here assisting President Vaccaro at the opening ceremonies of the second annual Renaissance Faire and Honors Day in April 1978. The Renaissance Faire, a lively tradition for several years, commemorated the feast of St. Catherine of Siena.

NEW TEACHING AND LEARNING
Flexibility and a Career-Conscious Curriculum.

Even before President Thompson's arrival, the faculty had begun rethinking old approaches to education; and in 1971 had eliminated core requirements, opting instead for maximum flexibility for each student. Siena's tradition of required liberal arts classes was abandoned in favor of an "academic advisement model," according to Sister Eleanor Stech, OP, a biology teacher at the time. In this new model, also called "guided free choice," each student, with his or her advisor, would craft the path of study most appropriate to the student's goals. One result of the change, Sister Eleanor remembered, was an immediate drop in enrollment for less popular classes, including foreign languages and "anything students thought of as hard." Students wanted "something practical," she said, something leading to a career.

Thompson embraced the concept of individualized education and took it to a whole new level, often to the discomfort of the faculty. His frequently articulated goal was to make Siena Heights responsive to community needs and contemporary student interests, but when he began to focus on occupational programs and two-year associate degrees, many faculty suspected him of trying to turn Siena Heights into a community college. Norm Bukwaz, however, who joined the sociology faculty in 1974, recalled it as just the opposite. "Dr. Thompson really had a strong feeling that Siena Heights could continue to do the liberal arts kinds of things," Bukwaz explained, "but he had to ward off the possibility of a community college being built in Lenawee County." Community colleges were popping up everywhere, Bukwaz explained, and the president wanted to "demonstrate that a community college wasn't needed" here because Siena Heights could meet that need.

Thompson's outreach led to a partnership with the Lenawee County Vocational-Technical Center by the start of his second year in office. Siena Heights agreed to develop thirteen two-year degrees in specific areas of interest to current Vo-Tech students, including such fields as accounting and fashion merchandising. Some of these programs would thrive, becoming established elements of the curriculum; others, such as aviation, would fly quickly into obscurity. But the concept of career-responsive education was here to stay.

Not surprisingly, Thompson also began pushing for a new business major. Siena's longtime secretarial program had been declining, and the president suggested that business would attract male students. "Everyone felt the pressure that Hugh began to put on business," recalled history professor Sister Jane Farrell, IHM. "That was going to be our savior. We were going to become this great big business school."

...continued on page 92

The Magnolia center in Southfield hosted the college's first off-campus degree completion program. For the adult students who enrolled, this converted elementary school *was* Siena Heights. Chuck Hakes was one of the first Siena Heights professors to teach there.

Everything Changes! Transition and Tumult in the 1970s

Continued from page 91..

"Siena Heights College is in the midst of an academic and economic boom," President Thompson said as the 1973–74 school year began. "Our success is directly attributable to the fact that we are not afraid to change our educational philosophy." A year later, in fall 1974, new programs at Siena Heights included:

- food service management, offered as a certificate, two-year, or four-year degree program;
- criminal justice, which had been requested by local police officers and enrolled thirty-three area law enforcement professionals that fall;
- a two-year electronics technology degree combining electronics courses at Vo-Tech with liberal arts classes at Siena Heights; and
- a general studies program providing "a broad liberal education" for students of any age who had started a degree sometime, somewhere, but had not yet finished it.

The structure of the curriculum changed, too. Academic programs were organized into four new divisions: Social Sciences and Humanities, Performing and Visual Arts, Natural Sciences, and—largest of all—Applied Science.

A reaccreditation team from the North Central Association (NCA) of Colleges and Secondary Schools had visited the previous year and issued its final report as the 1974 fall semester approached:

"This College is very much alive and stirring. While the increase in student enrollment, the introduction of new programs, and the faculty concern that things may be moving too fast are areas which need continual attention, they are also evidence of institutional vitality. The evaluating team considers this institutional vitality to be a significant strength."
—*NCA Final Report*

A New Kind of Student.

Hugh Thompson oversaw several more innovative developments. Perhaps most important for the future of Siena Heights was the decision to reach out to a new type of student—working adults, most of whom could not attend day-time classes, some of whom might not be able to come to campus at all, because they were too far away. This was an extension of the recently established "General Studies" program which had begun welcoming adults to campus to finish their degrees.

In fact, Siena Heights already had a proud history of educating working adults, starting in the 1920s with Adrian Dominican Sisters who taught school around the country during the year but came "home" to Adrian for summer school, to work toward their degrees. The working adult students of the 1970s, however, were not teachers; they were firefighters and factory workers, technicians and tradespeople, military veterans and business leaders. They had goals and backgrounds different from any students Siena Heights had previously enrolled.

As the curriculum became more sensitive to the career interests of both "traditional" students (those who came to college more or less straight from high school) and the new "non-trads" (older, probably working, perhaps with some college experience in the past), Siena Heights experimented with a variety of new educational ventures.

Starting in 1975, the college accepted invitations from area businesses, such as Westinghouse Corporation in Detroit, to offer course work for employees on-site. In addition, Siena Heights faculty traveled further afield, offering specialized weekend courses for industrial workers in Maryland, corporate employees in Wisconsin, and nurses in California.

Legends of the Faculty

1919–2019 SIENA HEIGHTS UNIVERSITY

Sister Eileen K. Rice, OP '68

When Dr. Eileen Rice died of breast cancer in 1994 at the age of forty-nine, the entire Siena Heights community mourned the loss of a master educator—a teacher's teacher, a fearless advocate for students, and a lifelong learner of remarkable intellect. She was a woman of boundless energy, too: a multitasker before the term existed. Faithfully cheering the Saints from the bleachers, she simultaneously graded papers, wrote lesson plans, read books, and talked with friends. She was a "teaching genius" who "gave her life to her students," then-dean Robert Gordon said, a woman of faith and "the quarterback of our faculty."

Sister Eileen joined the Siena Heights teacher education faculty in 1975 (after two years as principal of St. Joseph Academy) and chaired the department until her passing. For much of that time, she directed both the undergraduate and graduate education programs. Committed to the idea that everyone teaches, everyone learns, she answered her phone, "Teaching and learning!"

Eileen was famous for her long days, advising students in her office at 6:30 a.m., teaching all day, and returning phone calls after her last evening class, according to Melissa Durbin Tsuji '90, who added that she earned the affectionate nickname "Attila the Nun" because "she expected the very best from her students."

Sister Eileen with one of her beloved cats: PDQ Bach, familiarly called Petey, or PD.

A voracious reader with the mind of a mathematician, Eileen introduced "Idea Tasting" (subsequently, "History and Philosophy of Ideas") as a required course for graduate students, arguing that "this ability to have, consider, and cherish ideas . . . is the criterion of human specificity." She often quoted Oliver Wendell Holmes: "Once a mind has been stretched by new ideas, it never goes back to its original dimensions."

A tremendous supporter of the liberal arts, Sister Eileen also had a great interest in and support for vocational education. Perhaps not surprisingly, when she served as president of the Siena Heights Alumni Association in the late 1980s, she was energetic in reaching out to graduates of the college's new off-campus programs and organized the first event to engage nontraditional alumni: a graduation picnic at the Southfield center.

In 1980, Eileen Rice was the first person to receive the Outstanding Teaching Award; in 1989, she was honored a second time. Shortly before her death, she spoke of living each day to the fullest—and continued teaching energetically to the end. After her death, the prestigious teaching award was renamed the Eileen K. Rice, OP Award for Outstanding Teaching.

At Honors Convocation in spring 1980, Sister Eileen (left) received the college's first Outstanding Teaching Award, while graduating senior Kendra Goetz was honored by the division of communication arts and education.

Everything Changes! Transition and Tumult in the 1970s

A New Degree of Outreach.

The boldest academic venture of the 1970s was the decision to craft a new type of degree for the new nontraditional students. The bachelor of applied science (BAS), approved in 1975, paired a technical major, comprised largely of a student's prior vocational certification, training, and experience, with a solid block of liberal arts classes from Siena Heights. Whereas traditional students explored the liberal arts first, finding their interests and choosing a subject to study in-depth, BAS students would do the opposite, coming to Siena with a "major" in hand and broadening their studies with such classes as philosophy, ethics, communication, and history. Because of this reverse approach, the BAS was described as an "inverted major."

Norm Bukwaz helped lead these developments. After joining the faculty as a sociology instructor, he had moved to coordinating student co-op experiences, then directing general studies. Through all of this, he realized the potential value of enrolling adult students along with the traditional students Siena had always served, and became aware of a new market.

"In the mid-1970s, people with technical training had no options" for earning a bachelor's degree without starting out just like any other freshman, Bukwaz said, and few mid-career workers could afford that, in time or money. But the workplace was changing. Where once a worker could advance strictly on the basis of job performance, now that same worker needed a bachelor's degree to move up. Siena's BAS provided a way for mid-career adults to build on what they already knew and dramatically cut down the time needed to earn the degree.

Partnerships and Satellite Programs.

With the BAS in place, the college initiated two other pioneering efforts:

- First was the notion of partnering with technical training schools. In the 1970s, many trade schools realized their graduates would need the credential of a bachelor's degree to succeed beyond entry level. Siena Heights negotiated partnerships with such programs, offering a smooth path for their graduates to enroll in a four-year degree program. The first such partnership was with the RETS Electronics School in Detroit in 1975. Since then, Siena Heights has established similar cooperative arrangements with dozens of specialized schools that train professionals in broadcasting, radiologic technology, sign language interpreting, and massage therapy (to mention only a few)—and with community colleges offering a variety of two-year vocational degrees.

- The second BAS-facilitated development was the establishment of satellite locations where working adult students could attend classes on a regular basis—without taking time off from work or driving to Adrian. The off-campus sites offered evening and weekend classes in convenient locations. Siena's longest-running off-campus center is the Metropolitan Detroit Program in Southfield, established in 1977 in the former Magnolia Elementary School. The Southfield center, now known as the Metropolitan Detroit Program, operated at the Magnolia Center for many years, and has since been headquartered in several different corporate buildings. Also in 1977, Siena began a similar program in Sylvania, Ohio, on the campus of Lourdes College; that program ran until 1985, when Lourdes began offering its own four-year degrees.

At first, faculty and students on the main campus remained largely unaware of the off-campus operations. Four decades later, it is hard to imagine Siena Heights without the College for Professional Studies, which operates in eight on-the-ground locations across Southern Michigan and online through the Distance Learning Program. In the 1970s, however, when Hugh Thompson introduced these changes, many people considered him a threatening disruptor rather than a creative innovator. Few realized how important these decisions would prove to be, and how they would shape the vigorous future of Siena Heights.

A MISSION FOR THE AGES
The Valiant Woman.

Perhaps it was corporate leaders on the Board of Trustees who pushed the idea of a mission statement. Maybe Hugh Thompson's own business sense prompted the discussion. However the move began, faculty, administrators, and trustees worked together in the mid-1970s to craft a new—a *first*—"mission statement" for Siena Heights College. But in a sense, everything old was new again, because the college had always operated with a mission in mind.

For five decades, the college lived by a statement of "Aims and Ideals" which began, "The Siena Heights graduate is expected to be *a valiant woman* and *to put out her hand to strong things.*" Beyond that, the college identified nine specific goals, which included:

- developing "the intellectual powers of the young women in its care,"
- developing each student's "dignity as a woman,"
- providing "consistent training in the fine art of home-making and in the application of the fundamental principles underlying Christian family life," and
- providing the student "with the ability to gain a livelihood."

A modern reader might assume, wrongly, that those were the goals of a charm school, not a top-flight academic institution. The "valiant woman" in Proverbs 31:10–31 reflected the strong Dominican belief that women had intellects and identities of their own, and that developing those gifts was a duty and responsibility. Those ideals undergirded a rigorous academic enterprise that launched the careers of many pioneering women, including:

- Miriam Michael Stimson, OP '36, whose research played a key role in unraveling the structure of DNA,
- Connie Berube Binsfeld '45, the first woman to be elected to serve in the local, state, and executive branches of Michigan state government;
- Dr. Donita Sullivan '52, who helped found the medical field of pediatric rheumatology,
- Justice Alice Robie Resnick '61, the second woman elected to the Ohio Supreme Court.

...continued on page 96

This 1946 yearbook was one of several named for the Siena Heights ideal of the valiant woman. From the mid-1970s to the present, the watchwords have been *competent, purposeful,* and *ethical.*

Everything Changes! Transition and Tumult in the 1970s

Continued from page 95...

In the Adrian Dominican view, the fact that most Catholic girls would marry and raise families never conflicted with the expectation that those same young women would aspire to and achieve at the highest levels of academic excellence. A graduate of Siena Heights was expected to be strong, smart, humble, and compassionate; and to take on the challenges of her world, whether she was Miss, Ms., Mrs., Dr., or Sister.

A New Ideal: Competent, Purposeful, and Ethical.

By 1970, though, the original "Aims" were outdated. The college was coeducational and the old words, however well-intended, did not resonate with contemporary students. Young men and women did not see themselves as being in the college's "care," nor did they want to follow the paths of their parents.

First, the college emblazoned its stationery with a new slogan—"Siena Heights—Where we believe you can change the world"—and included a new "purpose" in the catalogue: "to provide an environment in which the students and faculty may critically discover, examine, preserve, and share a record of the knowledge, wisdom, and values of the present and past."

Then, near the end of Hugh Thompson's presidency, Siena Heights replaced the "Aims and Ideals" with a new statement. The college sought many of the same things—to help students achieve intellectually, live unselfishly, and find fulfillment—but the words in the 1976 catalog were new:

> *The mission of Siena Heights College is to assist people to become more **competent**, **purposeful**, and **ethical**. The college, therefore, provides an educational process which challenges individuals to identify, to refine, and to achieve their personal goals. Through this process, Siena expects to engage each of its students in the development of a personal philosophy of life.*

These 1945 alumnae—from left, Connie Berube Binsfeld, Michelena DeRose, and Peg Crowley—appear happy to be back for their thirtieth reunion in 1975. But not all alumni were pleased. At their tenth reunion in 1974, members of the Class of 1964 "did not recognize" the college and "were very taken aback," recalled Patricia Molly Pacquette '64. "I saw it as, 'What happened to the Siena I knew?'" Ten years later, when she was a graduate student and her son an undergraduate, she recognized the 1970s as a metamorphosis the college "had to go through. . . . If Siena had stayed an all-women's school, it would have died. Today it is flourishing."

The mission was followed by detailed student and institutional goals which have remained virtually unchanged for forty years.

It was then-trustee Sister Jeanne O'Laughlin, OP '58, who first proposed the trio of qualities that became unforgettable bywords for Siena students: *Competent. Purposeful. Ethical.* And twenty years later, when the mission statement was revised in the mid-1990s under the leadership of President Rick Artman, it would retain the familiar triad in this more concise statement:

> *The mission of Siena Heights, a Catholic university founded and sponsored by the Adrian Dominican Sisters, is to assist people to become more competent, purposeful, and ethical through a teaching and learning environment which respects the dignity of all.*

They may have graduated decades ago, but chances are good that Siena's valiant women alumnae were competent, purposeful, and ethical, too.

HAIL, SIENA! Siena Heights University

A Century of Study

1919–2019 SIENA HEIGHTS UNIVERSITY

MEMORABLE COURSES THROUGH THE YEARS

In every generation, some courses stand out in memory!

PARLIAMENTARY PROCEDURE

Students in the early years seemed universally unhappy about taking this famous class with the demanding Sister Ann Joachim. And yet: alumnae of the era said it turned out to be remarkably useful, empowering them to become effective leaders in careers as well as church and civic life. "We all had to take parliamentary procedure from Ann Joachim. We all hated it," Margaret Vaughn said, remembering the 1940s, but "it was probably one of the best courses I ever took. I have certainly used it over the years."

THE CULTURED WOMAN

Students in the 1930s met occasionally with Sister Fidelis Duncan for what they called "charm classes." By the 1940s and 1950s, "The Cultured Woman" (privately called "Cultured Vulture") was a weekly class in etiquette, mandatory for freshmen. Thursdays, students came to dinner wearing heels, hats, and white gloves. "Sister Robert Louise was there admonishing our table manners and exhorting us to be ladies of dignity and charm and not to spill the blueberry pie on the white tablecloths," remembered Henriette Nagle '59. After dinner, they trooped to Walsh Hall, where Sister Kevin Campbell "taught us how to stand and sit noiselessly, how to walk across a stage to a podium and then walk down the stairs—in three-inch heels—without tripping and making fools of ourselves. We learned how to make introductions and respond with polite remarks." As students, they rolled their eyes; as alumnae, they were grateful!

VALUES I, II, III

In the 1970s and 1980s, this series of religious studies classes, coordinated by Sister Donna Kustusch, OP '63, focused on Society and Faith, Ethics and Institutions, and Christ and Vision. Values I became a wildly popular elective, attracting twenty-six students in its first offering, and sixty-two the next semester. Colleen Mikin DeVito '92, who took all three courses, remembered that Values I involved a lot of self-reflection and "increased my awareness of myself and . . . my role in society." In II and III, she studied liberation and feminist theologies, and worked with Mexican immigrants. Colleen majored in psychology and humanities, but called the Values classes "the most significant" of her college career.

DILEMMAS AND DECISIONS

Created by Dean Tom Maher in the mid-1970s, first offered by professors Bob Gordon and Tim Husband, "D & D" was a one-credit course for freshmen that impacted student "for years to come," according to Robin Wagner '87. The class was not required, and was limited to four sections of no more than fifteen students; but it was ground-breaking as the college's first attempt to boost student success by focusing on study habits, actions and consequences, and the link between today's choices and tomorrow's possibilities. Forty-plus years later, all freshmen enroll in a 21st century version of the class called First Year Experience.

IDEA TASTING

Introduced by Sister Eileen Rice, OP '68, this graduate-level class once was required for all master's degree candidates. Its light-hearted title belied a rigorous content that guided students through the origin, analysis, and appreciation of great ideas. Patricia Molly Paquette '64, who returned to Siena for a master's degree in the 1980s, loved the class: Sister Eileen, she said, forced her "to do a lot of soul-searching and mind stretching. It was at that point I realized that *that* was part of the Dominican tradition." Eventually, Professor Mark Schersten took over the class. Today, renamed History and Philosophy of Ideas, the class is still required for graduate students in education.

THE ADULT LEARNER

Established in the 1970s by then-academic dean Tom Maher and first Southfield center director Peter Bouvier, this class was designed to help working adults return successfully to the classroom. The course aimed to enhance critical thinking and communication skills while introducing Siena's mission, values and expectations. Bachelor of Applied Science students, transitioning from technical study to liberal arts learning, were able to polish writing, speaking, and research skills, while exploring (often for the first time) the idea of open intellectual inquiry. In 2019, The Adult Learner remains a vital part of the curriculum, required for all students in the College for Professional Studies. For many CPS alumni, it is a highlight of their education.

CULINARY CHEMISTRY

Professor Julius Nagy first served up this intro-level chemistry course in 2014, offering an alternative laboratory science experience for non-science students. While studying the physical and chemical properties of ingredients and the chemical reactions of food preparation, students also venture into history, economics, and the effects of food on the brain. The immediate success of the class led to its permanent inclusion in the curriculum. (Faculty and staff in Sacred Heart Hall enjoy tasting the results of class experiments in pickling, browning, grilling, and baking.)

Everything Changes! Transition and Tumult in the 1970s

THE END OF THE SEVENTIES
Goodbye. Hello. Game On!

In spring 1977, President Thompson announced his resignation. Some faculty and more than a few sisters were, perhaps, relieved at the prospect of more collegial, less abrasive leadership in the future. But Thompson had left his mark on the college.

Betty Dolan, OP '46, then a member of the advancement staff, wrote this letter of thanks to the departing president for the June 1977 issue of *Reflection*: "Your determination and effort to make Siena the growing place it is today has richly paid off, for indeed, it has grown up and out from the small college so many of us loved dearly, to an institution that is well recognized, highly esteemed, and capable of meeting the challenges of higher education."

The seventh president, Dr. Louis Vaccaro, arrived at Siena Heights a few months later, shortly before the start of school in the fall. Almost immediately, trustee Willard Reagan recalled, the trustees cornered Dr. Vaccaro to ask, "Do we need an athletic facility?"

Before his departure, President Thompson had been fundraising for a new building to provide athletic offices, an indoor track, and a regulation-size basketball court. The building, Thompson had argued, would help tremendously in recruiting male students interested in athletics. With Thompson gone, the Board wanted to know, before moving forward, if the new president agreed.

As the 1970s began (top aerial), Ledwidge Hall and Studio Angelico were the new buildings on campus; but by the end of the decade, (below) Verhyden Performing Arts Center and the Student Activities Center (now called the Fieldhouse), had expanded the campus even more.

HAIL, SIENA! Siena Heights University

"Absolutely," Dr. Vaccaro replied. The facility, he said, would "pay for itself in students."

A $50,000 challenge grant from the Kresge Foundation helped generate the support still needed for the project, and Vaccaro presided at the groundbreaking on October 8, 1977, in his first semester as president.

The Fieldhouse—then known as the Activity Center—opened to great celebration the next fall, a legacy to both the sixth and seventh presidents of the college. Now Siena Heights teams played "at home" instead of in town at the Piotter Center. Student fans, few of whom had been willing to trek the two miles to Piotter, filled the home bleachers. Practices, which had been scheduled late into the night at Piotter, now took place on campus at reasonable hours. And between athletic events, the Activity Center hosted student events from circuses to rock concerts.

In the spring 1979 *Reflections* (the first issue to be named *Reflections* plural!), student sports-writer Larry Sands '79 reported that "the new Activities Center and outstanding fan support were important ingredients in the success of the women's and men's teams" in the 1978–79 season. "Women's coach Sister Mary Alice Murnen noted that improved recruiting and convenient practices were two of the many ways the new building benefited the athletic program."

FIELDHOUSE DEDICATION: A HISTORIC OCCASION
(But who really won?!)

"In October 1978, when President Vaccaro was here, we dedicated the Fieldhouse during Alumni Weekend with a cross country race against Findlay College (now University) that was to end in the Fieldhouse," recalled longtime basketball coach Fred Smith. "We had a band playing and we ran a five-mile course around campus and on country roads."

The Findlay coach was a guy named Pat Palmer. Michael Miron '81 (now a SHU faculty member) was Siena's student men's cross country coach at the time. Mike pulled in two basketball players—Al Sandifer '82 (now a SHU coach) and Tyrone Wilson '84—to make sure Siena had a cross-country team that day, then ran hard himself, feeling "all kinds of pressure to win," Fred said. Everyone wanted a Siena Heights student athlete to win the race that would dedicate the building.

Alas, it was a pair of Findlay teammates, one named Tim Bauer, who crossed the finish line first and broke the ribbon.

In the end, though, Siena Heights came out a winner: Pat Palmer left Findlay in the spring and came to Siena as a coach and athletic director. Tim Bauer left Findlay, too, following Pat to Siena, graduating in 1982, and becoming the legendary coach who still trains Saints cross country teams in 2019. It all began that October day in 1978! "Coach Bauer remembers it well, as do I," said Fred, who organized the event as interim athletic director.

Above: Flag-bearer David Valentine '79 leads the parade celebrating the dedication of the Student Activities Center (aka, the Fieldhouse) in October 1978, with a high school band following.

Left: Findlay College won the Fieldhouse dedication cross country race; but a year later, when Pat Palmer left Findlay to coach for Siena Heights, dedication-day-champ Tim Bauer came, too, the fourth runner from Coach Palmer in this line of Saints runners. Four decades later, Tim is still focused on SHU cross country.

Everything Changes! Transition and Tumult in the 1970s

A (Half) Century of Study

THE BACHELOR OF APPLIED SCIENCE

The introduction of the BAS—the bachelor of applied Science degree—in the mid-1970s transformed the academic landscape at Siena Heights.

No other institution in Michigan (and few, if any, nationally) offered the BAS when Siena's trustees gave final approval to the program in May 1975, just in time for the first few graduates to receive their degrees. Pushed through by President Hugh Thompson in the face of considerable faculty skepticism, the BAS was an experiment that proved wildly successful, opening Siena's doors to an entirely new student market: men and women already working as occupational professionals. Since 1975, nearly eight thousand alumni have earned this unique degree that blends in-depth vocational study with the broadening influence of liberal arts education.

Beginning in the 1960s, the growth of community colleges provided an alternative path to higher education for high school graduates, many of whom opted to complete their core requirements in two years at a (usually less expensive) community college, earning an associate of arts or science degree before transferring to a four-year college to complete a major and a bachelor's degree. Siena Heights welcomed these transfers, whose goals were not so different from traditional students, and even added two-year programs to compete with the community colleges.

But there was another student population out there: vocational professionals who needed a bachelor's degree for career advancement. These were successful men and women with past vocational training (ordinarily an associate of applied science degree from a community college) and on-the-job experience. Once, that was enough for a career; but by the 1970s, employees often needed four-year degrees to move up the ladder. Most colleges rejected vocational credentials, requiring these mid-career workers to start at the beginning, like any freshman, and follow the usual four-year plan (which, for someone working full-time, could take fourteen—or many more—years).

What these practicing professionals needed was a "pull everything together" degree program, then-head of off-campus programs Norm Bukwaz recalled. Enter Siena Heights and the BAS.

Designed for occupational professionals in technical, health care, and other specialized fields, the BAS allowed students to receive credit not only for community college coursework but also for "college-level learning attained in noncollegiate settings" such as the military, corporate training, or field certification, Bukwaz explained. Using an "inverted major" concept, BAS students transferred in with their "majors" complete, and focused their Siena studies on liberal arts learning, communication, management, and advanced analysis and evaluation skills. Evening and weekend courses accommodated full-time work schedules.

The BAS was first offered to electronics technicians through a partnership with RETS Electronics School in Detroit. Since then, the BAS has provided a degree path for professionals from radiologic technologists and respiratory therapists to broadcasters, sign language interpreters, nurse anesthetists, police officers, firefighters, nuclear technologists, massage therapists, and more.

In the most recent survey of Siena's BAS graduates, conducted by an outside research group and released in 2015:

- More than 80 percent reported the degree helped them professionally, improved their communication skills, and broadened their perspectives.
- Half reported that, because of the degree, at least one of these things occurred: they got a promotion, obtained a new job, increased their earnings, or moved into a new field.
- Nearly three-quarters said the BAS improved their leadership or management skills.
- More than 90 percent said the program improved their personal and family lives.

All in all, "the BAS degree works for them," Bukwaz said.

The first BAS recipients graduated in the 1970s.

It has worked for the university, too. Nearly 30 percent of all bachelor degrees ever awarded by Siena Heights are BAS degrees. And while these nontraditional alumni followed a long (or very long) route from high school to college, they graduated from Siena Heights committed to life-long learning; one out of five BAS alumni has pursued graduate study, Bukwaz said.

Ironically, in the years immediately following Hugh Thompson's departure from Siena Heights, there was some discussion of eliminating the BAS that he had fought to establish. As Norm Bukwaz recalled, the community was "torn between the market opportunities the BAS presented" and Siena's history as a classical liberal arts institution. In the end, it was a classical liberal arts professor, Sister Eileen Rice, OP, who influenced the decision to keep the BAS: as it turned out, Eileen—the great promoter of "idea tasting" to explore our liberal arts heritage—was also a strong proponent of vocationally linked education.

Meet two of Siena's BAS graduates: Cindy Birdwell '06 (above), SHU director of public safety and the daughter of a nontraditional student who earned his degree at age forty-five, was a seasoned professional when she graduated. State trooper Harold Love (below) completed his degree in 2008; since then, he earned a master's degree and began a new career in counseling.

An Academic "Blueprint" and Curriculum Reform. Again.

When President Thompson left, the college was nearing completion of a major curriculum overhaul. Thompson had charged academic dean Dr. Thomas Maher, who had arrived in 1975, with dramatically reducing the number of majors. Sisters Sharon Weber, OP, in chemistry and Eileen Rice, OP, in education were among the faculty who worked with Dean Maher to develop what was called the "Academic Blueprint."

"We developed eleven majors with some concentrations," Sister Sharon (now academic vice president in 2019) recalled. The plan was not widely popular, she said, because it involved cutting some majors, but it also introduced the concept of an "embedded core" whereby departments "looked at things you wanted students to be able to do and you made sure that somehow all of that got done within your major or within the courses required by your major." The science division, for example, required philosophy as an underpinning for discussion of ethical issues in the sciences, and rhetoric to ensure students could write well.

Soon after arriving, President Vaccaro engaged the faculty in a review of the proposed "blueprint" *and* a reconsideration of general education—the "core requirements" that had been abandoned a few years earlier. "After lengthy debate," Vaccaro reported, the faculty adopted a "two-tiered approach to the question of the college core," voting to implement both the embedded core in the majors and a 12-semester-hour core required of all students, regardless of major.

The pendulum had swung back toward the middle.

Everything Changes! Transition and Tumult in the 1970s

A New Internationalism.

Siena Heights had often welcomed students from faraway places. In earlier decades, young women from Puerto Rico and the Dominican Republic often came to the college after meeting Adrian Dominicans as teachers in their home high schools. Other students had come to campus from Jamaica, Thailand, Guam, and the Philippines.

But President Vaccaro brought new energy to international recruiting, deliberately seeking to enrich the diversity of the student community as a reflection of an increasingly global society. In his third year as president, Vaccaro boasted increases in full-time undergraduate enrollment of 10 percent in the fall and 16 percent in the spring, compared to the previous year. As reported in *The President's Report 1979–80*, that year's total enrollment of fifteen hundred included new students from eleven U.S. states, Puerto Rico—and sixteen other countries: Iran, Nigeria, Lebanon, Bangladesh, Ecuador, Brazil, Venezuela, Panama, Pakistan, Taiwan, Eastern Caroline Islands, Japan, Iraq, Jamaica, Mexico, and Trinidad.

The college's international student population in the late 1970s represented South America and the Far East, as well as Europe and the Middle East.

PRESIDENTIAL PROFILE NO. 7

Dr. Louis C. Vaccaro

President of Siena Heights College: 1977–1983

Modernized Admissions Efforts.
Increased International Student Enrollment.
Led First Capital Campaign.

Dr. Louis Vaccaro arrived on campus in August 1977, driving with his family from New Hampshire where he had served as president of Colby-Sawyer College. With his ready smile and outgoing personality, he was warmly welcomed, especially when he donned apron and chef's hat to prepare his signature spaghetti and meatballs for the students in Benincasa.

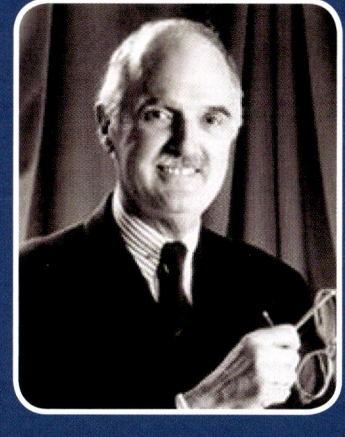

Dr. Vaccaro focused immediately on enrollment, with a special emphasis on recruiting international students. During his presidency, undergraduate enrollment grew from about one thousand full- and part-time students to more than fourteen hundred in 1982–83, including eighty-four international students from twenty-six countries. He also worked to spread public awareness and "keep Siena in the forefront of vital, exciting colleges." Promoting athletics was an important part of both recruitment and awareness-building. The Student Activities Center (now the Fieldhouse) opened in 1978, generating increased excitement for Saints athletics.

Vaccaro also oversaw Siena's first full-scale capital campaign, raising $6.5 million for renovations, endowment, and a major expansion of the library (adding three floors to the back of the existing facility). During his tenure, general education requirements were reinstituted, organized around the theme "Work, Money, and the Human Condition," and technology entered the curriculum with the addition of a minor in computer and information systems. He also is credited with modernizing Siena's admissions and financial aid operations, using computer technology to create a more efficient model of enrollment management.

In 1983, the Board of Trustees "accepted with regret" President Vaccaro's resignation. The alumni magazine *Reflections* listed "sharply improved alumni relations" among the "remarkable achievements" of his presidency. He left Siena to lead the College of Saint Rose in Albany, New York. He continues to promote internationalism in higher education.

In 2004, Dr. Vaccaro was inducted into the Siena Heights Athletic Hall of Fame in recognition of his support for athletics as president. In 2016, he received the Alumni Association's Honorary Alumni Award in recognition of his sustained involvement and support for Siena Heights.

> **"Lou was a charmer. His strength was a little different from Hugh Thompson's, and his approach was different. Dr. Vaccaro's view was that you make a lot more money by increasing enrollment than you do by recruiting people to give money. So his goal was to build up enrollment."**
>
> *Willard Reagan, Trustee Emeritus*

President Vaccaro and his wife, Linda, enjoyed cooking together and serving Italian spaghetti and meatballs to students in Benincasa.

> **"Lou did a lot to expand the name recognition of the college."**
> *Dr. Robert Gordon, Professor Emeritus and former Dean, Provost*

> **"When you say 'Vaccaro,' you just think flamboyant."**
> *Mary Griffin, Child Development Faculty*

One snowy winter—perhaps the blizzard of '78—the residence life staff sponsored a snow sculpture competition. In an effort to build community, residence hallways had been designated "houses" and given Greek letter names. Members of the NU house, also shown with their hallway banner, built an impressive snow fort in Trinity Garden. (Whether or not they won the competition is unknown!)

106 HAIL, SIENA! Siena Heights University

THE SEVENTIES: WHAT A DECADE!

When the last year of a tumultuous decade ended, Siena Heights had adjusted to its new identity as a coeducational college with international flair, dynamic athletics, a career-conscious curriculum, sensitivity to nontraditional students, and a groundbreaking degree-completion program for working adults. As the 1970s slipped into the 1980s, Siena Heights was a vibrant and "happening" place:

- Twenty-six students were studying overseas in Studio Angelico's fourth semester-long Art Study Program in Italy.

- Susan Matych-Hager directed the first of what would be twenty-five annual Madrigal Dinner Concerts. Through the years, Faculty Tim Husband, Pat Palmer, and Spencer Bennett would serve as court jesters.

- The Chi sisters, Margaret and Jane, arrived on campus from the People's Republic of China, ready to pursue master's degrees, three decades after China's Cultural Revolution prevented Margaret from accepting a Siena Heights scholarship the first time.

...continued on page 108

Margaret and Jane Chi came to Siena Heights from the People's Republic of China as graduate students in 1979, thirty-one years after Margaret was offered a scholarship she was prevented from accepting because of Mao's Cultural Revolution. When President Vaccaro met the sisters on a trip to China, he offered to honor the scholarship belatedly. The sisters' nephews, Maurice and Jacob Chi, also became Siena Heights students in the 1980s.

Everything Changes! Transition and Tumult in the 1970s

Continued from page 107...

- Philosophy professor Barbara Wall, OP led forty students, faculty, staff, and alumni on a nine-day trip to Russia.

- Cross country runner Jim Miller (left) became the first All-American in Saints athletic history.

- Coach Mary Alice Murnen's women's basketball team finished its regular season with a perfect 23-0 record, ending postseason play at 27-2.

- Coach Ben Braun's men's basketball team posted its finest season yet with a 23-7 record behind co-captains Cleo Hayes and John Dillard.

- Cleo Hayes '80 (right) ended his basketball career with 1,249 points; coach Ben Braun called him "one of the best passers I've ever seen."

- Women's basketball (below), coached by Sister Mary Alice Murnen, OP (*standing right*) relied on a strong nucleus of freshmen to compile a perfect season.

108   HAIL, SIENA! Siena Heights University

- Students and faculty commemorated the feast of St. Catherine of Siena with their third annual Renaissance Faire, donning costumes and raising scholarship funds.

- Celebrities Steve Allen and Jayne Meadows received honorary degrees for their work on the PBS series *Meeting of Minds*. Eileen Rice, OP, organized and Bob Gordon hosted a Siena Heights *Meeting of Minds* featuring St. Thomas Aquinas (Dr. Barbara Wall, OP), Emily Dickinson (Dr. Mary Louise Hall, OP), Ezra Pound (Dr. James McDonald), St. Raymond of Capua (Father David Van Horn, CPPS), and William Shakespeare (Glenn Crane).

- Campus newcomers, whose names would be embedded in the college's future, included John Wittersheim (art), William Blackerby (business), Patricia Hogan, OP (philosophy), Patrick Palmer (athletics), and Amy Lillywhite (president's office), to name a few.

- As the '70s ended, Siena Heights was poised to undertake its first major fundraising initiative, a $6.5 million campaign to raise capital, endowment, and operating dollars. The 1980s would kick off with a "Commitment to Excellence."

- Nontraditional students (below) were a key part of Siena Heights by 1979, enriching the college with a new group of enthusiastic alumni.

Everything Changes! Transition and Tumult in the 1970s

A Century of Study

ART

In the earliest years of St. Joseph's College, art was offered only as an "extra" to students, who could take private drawing lessons if they were able to pay the additional fee. In Mother Camilla's mind, art was something of an "ornament," rather than an essential element of a broad education. Mother Gerald's decision to send Sister Helene O'Connor, OP '34, to Italy, to study art, changed the future of art at the college.

Upon returning from her studies in 1938, Sister Helene founded the Art Department as we know it, naming the program Studio Angelico after the Dominican Renaissance painter, Fra Angelico. After initially setting up shop in Room 112 of Sacred Heart Hall, Helene moved Studio Angelico to the fifth floor of Sacred Heart Hall, transforming the former attic into professional studio space for painting, sculpture, calligraphy, metal work, weaving, and ecclesiastic art. Visiting artists such as Ade Bethune, Melville Steinfels, and Joseph O'Connell enhanced the faculty, mentored the students, and contributed lasting art to the hallways of the college. Bethune produced the Catherine frescoes outside Benincasa. Steinfels painted the St. Albert fresco in the Science Building, and designed the altar mosaics and Stations of the Cross in Lumen Ecclesiae (now St. Dominic) Chapel. O'Connell created the wrought-iron wall-sculpture of Mary that hangs in the Science Building.

Beloved by art majors, feared by many others, Sister Helene organized Studio Angelico on the guild system, and made sure all art students knew her definition of art as "the right making of that which needs to be made." Helene involved her most serious students in the design and production of religious cards, statues, ceramic objects, and hand-woven items—to be sold in the studio shop or shipped across the country. Helene guided Studio Angelico to national stature as a renowned resource for artists and a center for high-quality liturgical art.

Sister Jeannine Klemm, OP '44, already a member of the art faculty, succeeded Helene as chair in 1956; over the next three decades, she further enhanced Studio Angelico's reputation while putting her own distinctive stamp on the department. She guided the design and construction of the current Studio Angelico building in 1969, and directed the students who moved the department from Sacred Heart Hall into the new facility. Jeannine also professionalized the art program, first by establishing the bachelor of fine arts (BFA) degree and then by gaining accreditation from the National Association of Schools of Art and Design. She also insisted that every BFA candidate "have their own private exhibition. Now that was unheard of," Father David Van Horn, another legendary member of the faculty, recalled. Decades later, the "senior show" remains a key element of the BFA program.

Under Jeannine's leadership, Studio Angelico expanded its curriculum to include photography and graphic design. With her sister and colleague, Sister Jean Agnes Klemm, OP '44, she also initiated the "Semester in Italy" program; over two decades starting in 1973, Jean Agnes and other faculty led ten groups of art students to Florence, Italy, for a full term of art, cultural studies, and exploration. Upon Jeannine's retirement in 1988, the exhibition space in Studio Angelico, previously known as the Little Gallery, was renamed Klemm Gallery, in honor of Jeannine's "300 years of hard work, which she certainly did," Father Van Horn observed!

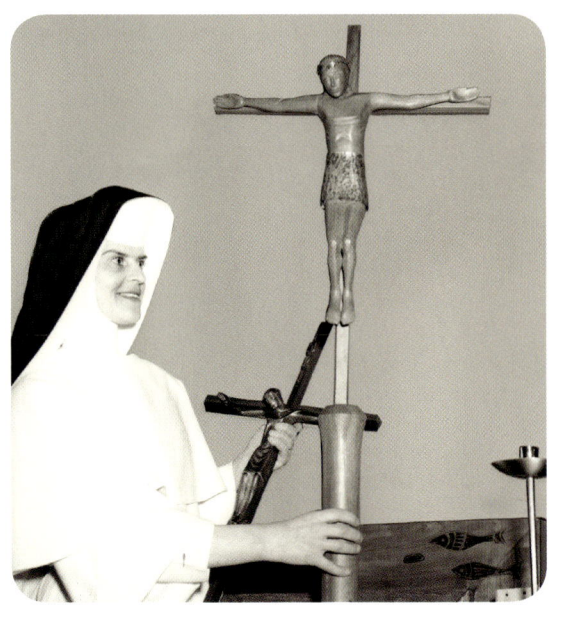

Sisters Helene and Jeannine both emphasized the art of calligraphy. Here Alyce Stapleton Hallman '58 and Denise Kimball Dursum '58 work on projects.

Sister Helene O'Connor (with clay) established the Art Department, gave it its name, and ran Studio Angelico on the fifth floor of Sacred Heart Hall for twenty years. Sister Jeannine Klemm (with crucifix) directed the program for the next thirty years and built the Studio Angelico facility in use today.

Printing and ceramics were popular in early decades. Students in the 1950s print shop may have been working on religious cards to be sold in the Studio Angelico shop. Donna Rich Palko '64 and Mary Jo Embach Mapes '64 focus on details of their ceramic projects beneath the fifth floor rafters of Studio Angelico.

In the twenty-first century curriculum, painting and photography live side by side with computer-generated graphics and animation.

Over the years, Siena Heights students have studied with many memorable faculty. Early graduates remember, the guidance of Sister Mary Joannes O'Connor, OP (youngest sister of the legendary Helene), Tom Burke, Father John Keefer, Dave Mulligan, Frank Mannarino, and others. The Father David Van Horn Memorial Garden outside Studio Angelico pays tribute to Studio Angelico's founding art historian. The John Wittersheim Sculpture Garden, which places outdoor sculpture on campus each year, honors the creative force behind the metals studio for thirty-four years. Sister Barbara Cervenka, OP, Tom Venner, Lois DeMots, Joe Bergman, Christine Reising, Deb Danielson—and current faculty—have all maintained the high standards of teaching and creativity that defined the department from the beginning.

The department's tradition of excellent social gatherings also continues. From Sister Jeannine's famous Italian *Befana* dinners before Christmas (an attraction of which was "the witch who passed out goodies to the guests," according to Jean Agnes), to pig roasts next to the outdoor kilns behind Studio Angelico, to recent Halloween festivities, and Homecoming tailgates featuring a baroque culinary concoction known as "the exorcism," the Art Department nurtures creative goodwill, as well as fine art.

In 2019: Today's art students major in painting, ceramics, sculpture, photography, digital media, graphic design, printmaking/book arts, and art history. Studio Angelico in the twenty-first century includes not only easels, potters' wheels, and assorted work tables—but also computers!

During his three decades on the faculty, John Wittersheim maintained a quirky mix of religious imagery and fire power in the metalsmithing studio.

Contemporary ceramics include indoor and outdoor kilns. Here, Tom Venner, of the 1980s/90s art faculty, removes fired work from a kiln.

Everything Changes! Transition and Tumult in the 1970s

A Century of Study

TEACHER EDUCATION

Teacher education was at the heart of St. Joseph College on day one, a century ago. Decades later, the college would debate the role of career preparation in liberal arts education, and would pioneer a "new" movement to help working adults earn degrees; *but both of those ideas were here from the beginning.* At a time when teaching was one of the only careers open to women, and Catholic schools everywhere needed sister-teachers, Siena recognized that, in those earliest years, most lay students and virtually all sister-students would teach after graduation, even if only for a short time. The founders embraced the job of training those future (and sometimes current) teachers. Through the decades, teacher education would be shaped, and reshaped, by changing state regulations and a changing society.

In 1924, St. Joseph College was approved to issue limited teaching certificates and to prepare programs leading to a baccalaureate degree. Then, teacher education was a certification program, not a major: students majored in a subject of their choice, completed all other requirements for the degree, and took additional courses in how to teach.

Sister Ambrose Collins, one of the earliest education teachers, was a monumental figure in Siena's early years. By the 1930s, she also was deeply involved with the Girls Training School in Adrian, advocating for more humane and compassionate treatment for the girls. She frequently took education students to the Training School with her, to prepare them for teaching pupils whose backgrounds might be very different from their own.

In those years, students could qualify for a teaching certificate long before completing a degree. Many sisters entered Catholic school classrooms as novices, with just a certificate; some entered as postulants, without even that much training. They returned to campus after each school year, enrolling in summer school as long as it took to complete their degrees. Master teachers offered classroom demonstrations each summer, mentoring the beginners.

When Michigan began requiring all teachers to have bachelor's degrees, seasoned educators returned to college, many enrolling at Siena. Katherine Blake of Blissfield was one of those returnees. She had attended St. Joseph Academy as an elementary student, and began teaching in the late 1920s with a certificate from the Normal School (later Eastern Michigan University). Barely out of her teens, she taught forty-four K-8 students in a one-room schoolhouse south of Riga; her contract stipulated that she arrive early enough to break the ice in the well, and start the fire in the stove, before the school day began. About thirty years later, she enrolled at Siena Heights, graduating in 1962 with the degree she now needed to teach much smaller classes—with no ice-chipping or fire-building required!

Sister Alice Joseph Moore, OP '39, taught on the education faculty from 1956 to 1965, and started the college's first job placement office (focused on placing new teachers, of course). She also helped start the graduate program in education, which was prompted by new requirements that teachers continue improving their skills.

Sister Claudia Hinds, OP, joined the education faculty in 1963, teaching undergraduate and graduate classes, supervising student teachers, and succeeding Alice Joseph as department head in 1965. During her tenure, which lasted until 1974, Sister Claudia also became head of graduate studies, and started a reading clinic for local youth.

Social changes brought change to the curriculum in the 1970s. Mary Griffin '69, a graduate of the then-new "reading specialist" master's program, joined the department and soon developed a new program in early childhood development "to meet the needs of society," she said. Previously, infant and toddler care were not part of any education program because out-of-home child care was unheard of when all children stayed at home "with Auntie or Mom or Grandma," Mary explained. As women entered the work force, the need for quality child care exploded. Siena's child development program soon expanded to include both a two-year associate degree and a four-year bachelor's degree.

In 2019: Siena Heights maintains rigorous teacher education requirements, including an abundance of classroom clinical field experience (more than 250 clock hours for the bachelor's degree and initial certification), continuous self-assessment, and a philosophy that sees teaching as both an art and a science. Certification programs within the division of education require both state and national accreditation. Teacher education is offered only on the main campus.

- *Undergraduate Level:* Students seeking elementary or secondary certification complete significant education coursework on top of a major in an approved content area (including special education in cognitive impairment or learning disabilities); students also may complete a minor as an additional endorsement. Students focusing on early childhood education may choose a Montessori concentration or elementary certification.

- *Graduate Level:* Siena Heights offers the MA in education with concentrations in: early childhood education, early childhood education/Montessori, special education/cognitive impairment, and special education/learning disabilities.

Montessori education was another response to changing times. Sister Anthonita Porta, OP '63, studied with the innovative educator Maria Montessori before joining the graduate education faculty. The Montessori method—stressing development of initiative and self-reliance in young children—was not well known when Anthonita established the Montessori Children's House at St. Joseph Academy in 1971. Siena Heights developed "a wonderful alliance" with the academy, she said, enabling education students to observe and student-teach at the pre-school. Some students opted for further Montessori training elsewhere, transferring their credits to Siena. In 1992, Sister Anthonita opened the Montessori Teacher Training Institute at the academy, attracting students from across the country—and next door.

Sister Eileen Rice, OP '68, was a dominant figure in teacher education from 1975 until her death in 1994. Under her direction, education flourished at both the bachelor's and master's degree levels. Education was linked organizationally with the visual and performing arts in those years, and education students also were encouraged to participate in the arts, especially child drama.

Dee Crane '87, a master's graduate of Siena Heights, joined the faculty in 1991, eventually chairing the program. During her years, in response to national demographic changes, "urban education" was added to the curriculum, to provide students with inner-city classroom experience.

Teacher education continues to be a dynamic program at Siena Heights. According to Carrie Mitchell, director of undergraduate and graduate education, "hot programs" in 2019 include music education ("many Siena band and choir members are music ed majors"), special education, and early childhood with elementary certification. The division remains vitally attentive to changing regulations at state and federal levels—and to cultural changes that affect both students and teachers.

Clockwise from above: Committed faculty and plenty of in-class observation and student teaching are longstanding hallmarks of teacher education at Siena Heights. Professor Mary Griffin counsels a student. Student teacher Barbara Laberge Seebaldt '63 welcomes elementary students to her desk. In an earlier decade, education students observe a master teacher in a Catholic elementary classroom.

Everything Changes! Transition and Tumult in the 1970s

PART 4

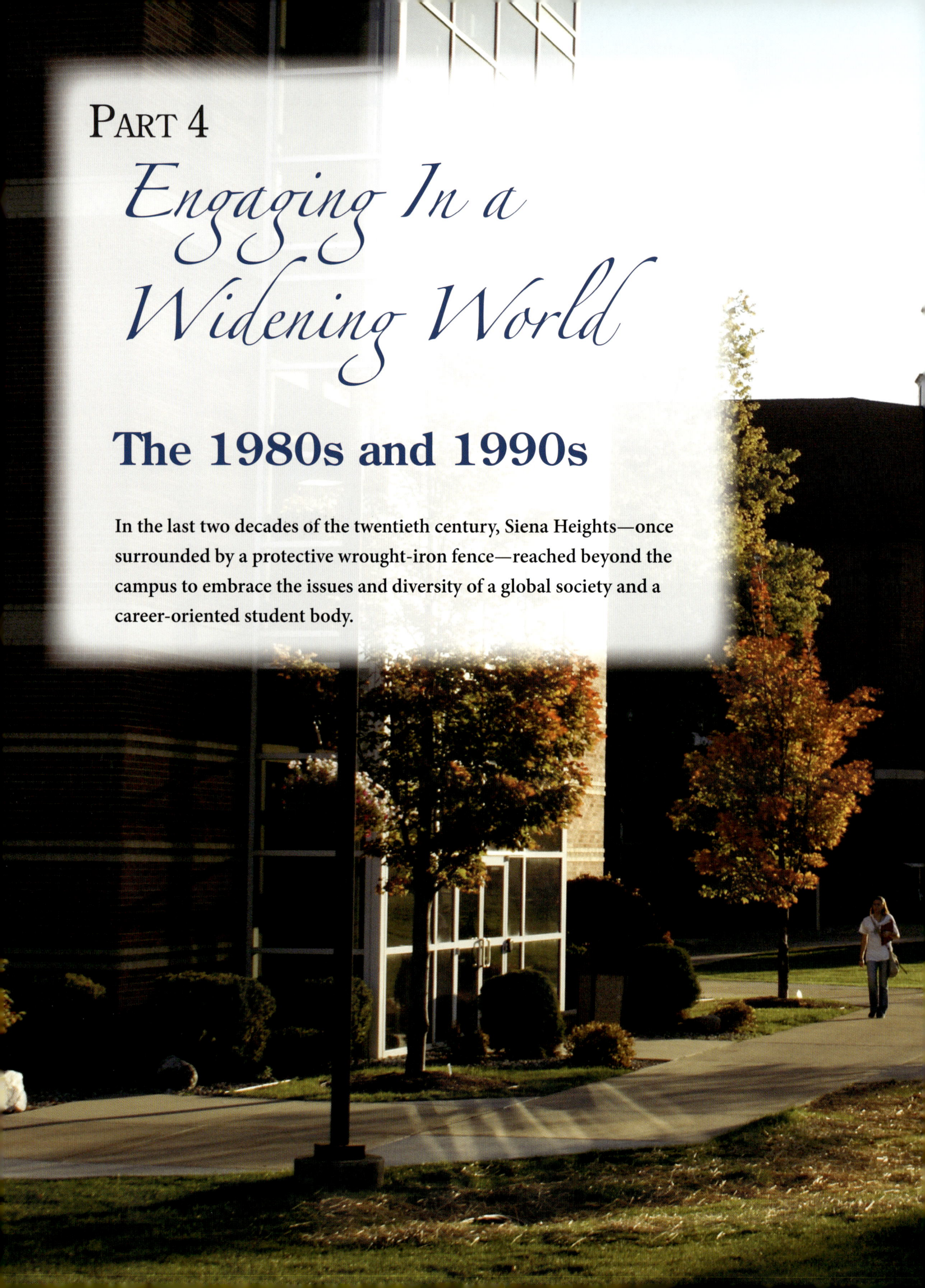

Engaging In a Widening World

The 1980s and 1990s

In the last two decades of the twentieth century, Siena Heights—once surrounded by a protective wrought-iron fence—reached beyond the campus to embrace the issues and diversity of a global society and a career-oriented student body.

An early-'80s expansion of the science/library wing added valuable library and classroom space, but the changes were invisible to passersby. The 1990s, however, changed the face of the campus with the addition of Dominican Hall, a three-story classroom-conference-and-computer facility, shown left and inset.

THE CHALLENGE OF CHANGING DEMOGRAPHICS

For Siena's first fifty years, students at siena Heights had looked pretty much the same. Things began changing in the 1970s. By 1980, the change was significant.

Sister Petronilla had welcomed coeducation, but the graduates in her years were nearly all women in their early twenties who had walked the same halls to class and shared the same campus traditions. Hugh Thompson furthered the change, with athletics and a new curriculum; in his time, there were men among the graduates, though most were still women. There were commuters, too, but everyone still knew their way around campus.

By 1980, though, when President Louis Vaccaro presided over his third commencement, the graduates were men and women of many ages—and more than a third of them were strangers on the Adrian campus: they had studied in Southfield, Michigan, or Sylvania, Ohio (on the campus of what was then Lourdes Junior College).

Over the next two decades, the make-up of graduating classes would become ever more diverse as Siena Heights embraced a dual role as both a traditional educator of high school graduates on the Adrian campus and a pioneer educator of working adults at off-campus locations. At the same time, like colleges everywhere, Siena Heights faced a decline in the number of high school graduates nationally, the result of baby boomers having fewer children.

President Vaccaro responded to the declining eighteen-year-old population by modernizing Siena's admissions and financial aid offices, with strong results for the main campus. At a growing network of degree-completion centers, Siena welcomed an eager population of nontraditional students in their twenties, thirties, forties, even fifties and older. But "non-trads" did not enroll only at the satellite sites; they came to Adrian, too.

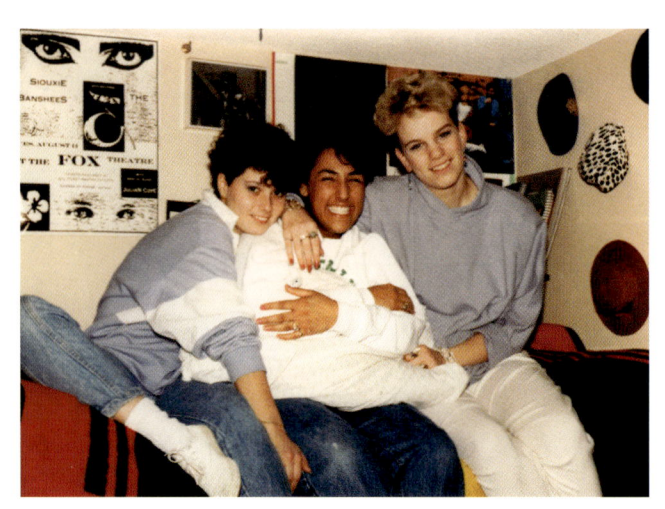

Above: On campus, the traditional-aged student body included young women like, *from left*, Lisa Leverington Loiacano '91, Dana Friedel '89, and Peggy Kerr '91, seen here as freshmen in the fall of 1987; and young men like these in the dining hall with residence hall assistant Michael Griffin '80, *fourth from right*. **Right:** Nontraditional students were studying not only at degree completion sites across the state, but also on campus—where working adults like business executive Tracy Church '93, *in black jacket*, took classes with eighteen to twenty-year-olds.

116 HAIL, SIENA! Siena Heights University

The rapid change in the student population was both energizing and challenging.

In the classroom, the impact was nearly always positive. In Adrian, working adult students brought a level of experience and dedication to class that was welcomed by professors and inspiring for traditional students. At the off-campus centers, classes of non-trads became lively communities of career networking and idea sharing for students who could put their lessons to work immediately.

The changing student population prompted new approaches to scheduling, advising, and traditional teaching formats. Evening and weekend classes were the norm off-campus, and soon appeared on the Adrian schedule, too. The biggest change was the addition, at the off campus sites, of an accelerated, eight-week course format; initiated in the late 1970s, it became the norm in Siena's bachelor's degree completion program. By end of the 1990s, with seven off-campus sites in operation, some Adrian faculty—Tom Radecki, Bill Blackerby, and Donna Baker, among others—spent hours every week driving to Southfield, Monroe, Lansing, Jackson, the Kellogg Center in Battle Creek, the Lake Michigan Center in Benton Harbor, or the various locations of the Theological Studies Program offered in conjunction with the Lansing Diocese. (The Sylvania program ended in 1985 when Lourdes College began offering its own four-year degrees.)

Like recent high school graduates, older students often began their Siena Heights studies with fear and uncertainty. Traditional freshmen worried about stepping up to the higher demands of college, but non-trads worried about their ability to go back to school at all. By graduation, however, there was no difference. Crossing the stage to receive their diplomas, nontraditional students (and their families) were just as excited as traditional students (and their parents). Like their twenty-two-year-old counterparts, nontraditional graduates were proud of their accomplishments, grateful to their professors, excited to be alumni, and ready for the future. Surveys would show, again and again, that off-campus graduates had exceptionally positive views of Siena Heights, and credited the faculty with changing their lives for the better.

For Siena Heights, however, off-campus education presented a different challenge after graduation—because off-campus alumni had no cherished memories of Trinity Garden or Sacred Heart Hall, no shared experience of dorm life or meals in Benincasa, no connections with sports teams or theater productions, or even with a specific graduating class. In short, off-campus graduates had none of the traditional ties that had always brought people back to Adrian for reunions or special events—and had turned proud graduates into generous alumni, happy to support their *alma mater*.

With such a dynamic student mix—a blend of youth and experience, full-time and part-time, teenager, grandparent, and mid-career executive—Siena Heights ended the 1990s with no "typical" student—nor any "typical" alumni. Finding new ways to engage with *all* graduates after commencement would be an ongoing challenge in the decades ahead.

In addition to being a home for athletics, the new Student Activities Center (Fieldhouse) provided a venue for entertainment of all sorts, from circuses to jazzfests to concerts including this memorable appearance by rocker John Cougar in 1981.

Engaging in a Widening World: The 1980s and 1990s

LIBERAL ARTS AND CAREER PREPARATION: FOES NO MORE

Following the 1970s, when the college dropped all core requirements, Siena Heights in 1980 began to reassert the primacy of the liberal arts. Students would now complete a limited core of classes exploring the theme "Work, Money, and the Human Condition," choosing from a menu of electives to fulfill the twelve-credit-hour requirement. A few years later, the requirement was increased to eighteen credit-hours; and by the end of the 1980s, the college had returned the core to about 30 semester hours. Bob Gordon, associate dean at the time, said the increased general education requirement "makes the college a stronger college." The revived liberal arts core lasted, with modifications, for twenty-five years.

In her first state-of-the-college address as president in 1984, Sister Cathleen Real articulated a dual goal of ensuring students a strong liberal arts foundation, while also preparing them for careers. Career-oriented academic programs such as business and criminal justice already were popular with students. New programs in the 1980s and 1990s included gerontology, computer and information systems, sport management (an immediate hit with students interested in the business side of athletics), graphic design, and other workplace-related majors.

At the off-campus centers—which in the mid-1990s adopted the tagline "Education That Works"—scores of students elected the bachelor of applied science (BAS) degree, combining workplace experience and certification as a major and coming to Siena for the broadening influence of history, philosophy, literature, and communication. Commencement programs from the 1980s on listed BAS graduates with career majors such as electronics and allied health.

By the end of the 1990s, conflict between the liberal arts and career preparation had pretty much disappeared in an overall focus on education that assisted people to be competent, purposeful, and ethical, whatever career they chose.

The library continued to offer solitude for study and reading—and research assistance from librarians like Jean Baker.

PRESIDENTIAL PROFILE NO. 8

Sister Cathleen C. Real, C.H.M.

President of Siena Heights College: 1984–1993

Concentrated on Diversity and Community Relations. Supported Athletics through NAIA Service.

Sister Cathleen Real came to Adrian in July 1984 from the College of St. Mary in Omaha, Nebraska, where she was acting president and had been academic vice president for a decade.

Her years as president of Siena Heights were marked by an increase in academic standards, growth in non-traditional enrollment on and off campus, increased attention to racial and cultural diversity, and new attention to technology. Gracious and personable, more comfortable with one-on-one meetings than public speaking, she became a strong presence in the community and a leader in the National Association of Intercollegiate Athletics (NAIA).

Her tenure also saw a rapidly diminishing presence of Adrian Dominicans on campus. As one step in reclaiming the college's institutional roots, she adopted a new logo incorporating the college shield and the founding date of 1919.

Sister Cathleen initiated a tradition of long-range planning with a Five-Year Plan for 1988–93, aimed at improving academics and upgrading facilities, and led Siena Heights into the $12.2 million *Vision 2000* campaign. The centerpiece of the campaign was a new building that would provide an impressive new computer center, high-tech classrooms and auditorium, conference space, and a spacious atrium for special events. Dominican Hall was near completion in 1993 when Sister Cathleen left Siena Heights for an assignment with her order.

Sister Cathleen now serves her congregation and community in Davenport, Iowa. The Sister Cathleen Real Scholarships continue to support nontraditional female students at Siena Heights.

"Sister Cathleen brought a type of grace to that office that we needed and a vision that we were happy to have."

Trudy McSorley '70, Theater Faculty/Dean for Students Emerita

"She brought a sense of stability to this place."

Fred Smith, Athletic Director

"She was a mature woman with good sound judgment."

Willard Reagan, Trustee Emeritus

INNOVATIVE PARTNERSHIPS: BUILDING A FAR-REACHING PROFILE

Building on the success of off-campus programs begun in Southfield and Sylvania in 1977, Siena Heights looked further afield, trying two new degree-completion operations in the 1980s:

- The first initiative—and most influential in the long run—was a pioneering partnership in 1982 with Lake Michigan College, a two-year institution in Benton Harbor in southwest Michigan. This program, with Siena Heights maintaining offices on the host institution's campus, established the model Siena would follow into the twenty-first century, partnering with community colleges across the state.
- The second initiative, in 1985, duplicated the RETS program started in Detroit in 1975, but took it to Baltimore, Maryland. Siena Heights professors, such as Bob Gordon, drove repeatedly to the East Coast to teach intensive weekend seminars for electronics engineers interested in earning the BAS degree but unable to attend weekday (or night) classes. The same willingness to provide education in an unconventional manner had inspired a program several years earlier, for nurses in Southern California. Both programs were short-lived, but that commitment—to finding creative ways to meet the needs of a specific group of learners—prompted Siena's first on-line option in the early 2000s: providing degree completion within the unpredictable scheduling constraints of nuclear power workers in Southwest Michigan, a program offered through the Lake Michigan Center.

Presidents Cathleen Real and Rick Artman both oversaw the development of a dynamic network of degree-completion centers across southern Michigan. In addition to Southfield and Benton Harbor, Siena Heights opened five new off-campus programs in the 1990s.

Left: As president of the Alumni Association, Sister Eileen Rice, at right, organized the first alumni outreach event in Southfield, a graduation picnic for new off-campus grads. **Below:** A decade later, the Southfield program moved into new offices in a nearby business center; celebrating the move are, *from left*, faculty and staff Sister Pat McDonald, Jack Bologna, Anthony Rana, Carl Mannino, and Steve Goddard.

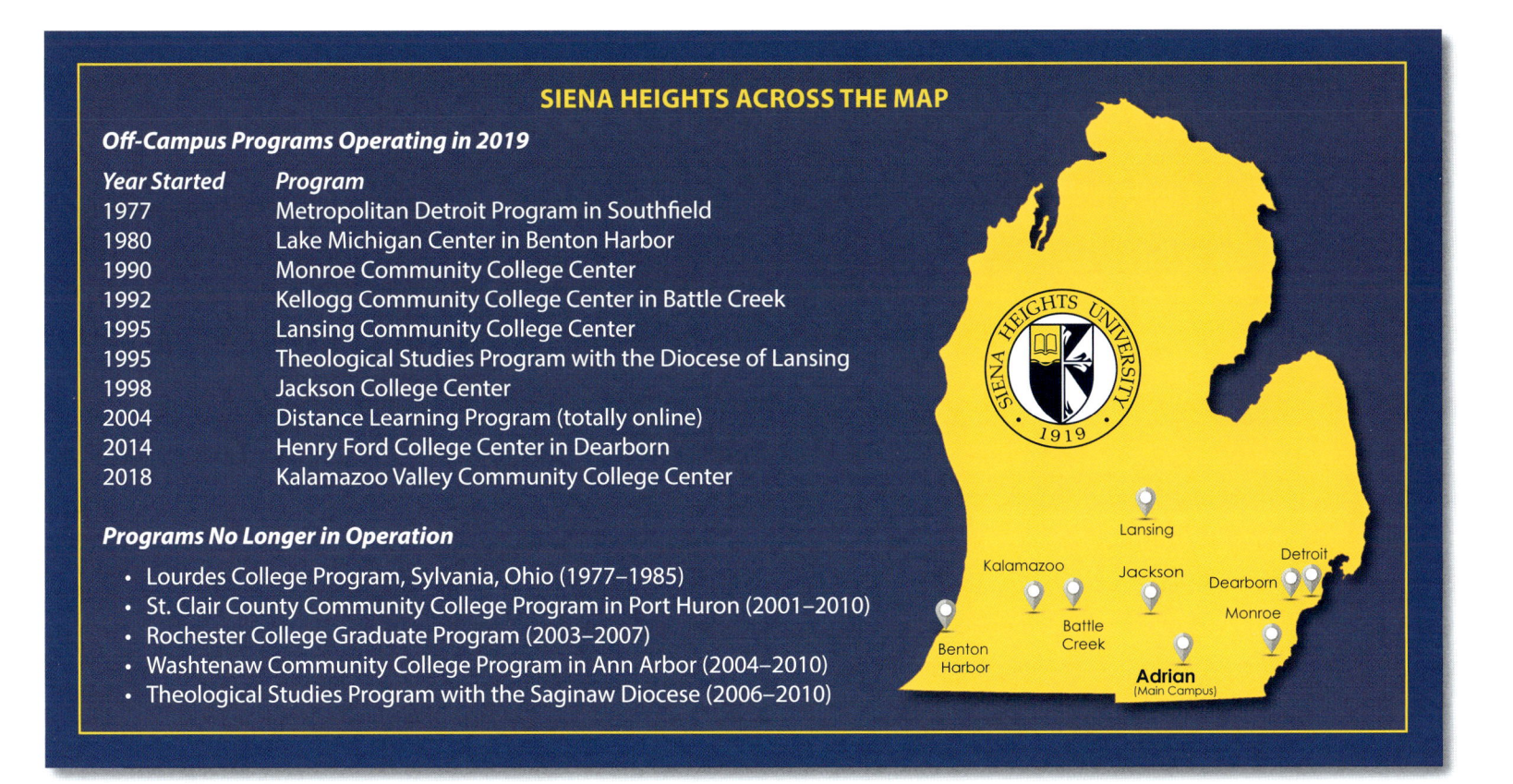

SIENA HEIGHTS ACROSS THE MAP

Off-Campus Programs Operating in 2019

Year Started	Program
1977	Metropolitan Detroit Program in Southfield
1980	Lake Michigan Center in Benton Harbor
1990	Monroe Community College Center
1992	Kellogg Community College Center in Battle Creek
1995	Lansing Community College Center
1995	Theological Studies Program with the Diocese of Lansing
1998	Jackson College Center
2004	Distance Learning Program (totally online)
2014	Henry Ford College Center in Dearborn
2018	Kalamazoo Valley Community College Center

Programs No Longer in Operation

- Lourdes College Program, Sylvania, Ohio (1977–1985)
- St. Clair County Community College Program in Port Huron (2001–2010)
- Rochester College Graduate Program (2003–2007)
- Washtenaw Community College Program in Ann Arbor (2004–2010)
- Theological Studies Program with the Saginaw Diocese (2006–2010)

Right: A Siena Heights communications class at the Jackson center takes a break on the Jackson College campus. **Below:** The Siena Heights flag has flown outside the University Center on the campus of Lansing Community College since 1995.

REFLECTING THE REAL WORLD: THE DRIVE FOR DIVERSITY

Graduating classes in the 1940s and 1950s often included students from Puerto Rico, the Dominican Republic, even Guam; but Jeanne Whitlow Mosley '59 was the first African-American graduate of Siena Heights. Others followed—Sheila Finch '68, the Butler brothers and Debra Parish in the 1970s—but students of color remained a rarity.

By the 1980s, however, Siena had both the Southfield program, where the student population reflected the ethnic diversity of metropolitan Detroit, and the Lake Michigan program in Benton Harbor, where the student body reflected local diversity and an international business community. In Adrian, the issue of diversity—rather, the lack of it—soon moved front and center. Through the 1980s and 1990s, presidents Louis Vaccaro, Cathleen Real, and Rick Artman all worked to foster a more culturally diverse campus community.

President Vaccaro sought diversity through internationalism. He took particular pride in increasing international enrollment from one student when he arrived in 1977, to one hundred students from thirty-three countries when he left in 1983. He also established an English as a Second Language Institute for students whose language skills were not yet up to the challenge of college work; and encouraged international travel. The Upward Bound program, started during Hugh Thompson's presidency, engaged many Hispanic teens from local neighborhoods in high school enrichment and college preparation. Athletics also helped attract students of color to the college.

In her years as president, Sister Cathleen Real worked to make Siena Heights more supportive of Hispanic and African-American students. In particular, she sought to address the low level of Hispanic enrollment on a campus located virtually next door to a significant Hispanic community. A succession of black and Hispanic advisory groups, committees, and task forces addressed student and faculty concerns, which included student recruitment, faculty and staff hiring, and multicultural course offerings. Dionardo Pizana '90 in admissions and Idali Feliciano '93/M.A. in advising worked to strengthen outreach to and support for Hispanic students. A major grant from the Eli Lilly Foundation provided funding for multicultural campus workshops and related projects. Sister Cathleen's Five-Year Plan for 1988–93 included a goal of developing academic programs responding to national issues surrounding minorities and a growing aged population.

...continued on page 124

Nurturing Diversity: Upward Bound
Upward Bound was the first of three federal TRIO programs that have encouraged diversity and achievement on the Adrian campus. **Above:** Karen Glaser, at right, and Annita Galnares Aranda '87, between them, led Upward Bound for many of the program's forty-three years, starting in 1974, preparing local high school students (left) for success in college.

HAIL, SIENA! Siena Heights University

Legends of the Faculty

1919–2019 SIENA HEIGHTS UNIVERSITY

William R. Blackerby

Bill Blackerby left a banking career to teach at Siena Heights, arriving in 1979 as the college was developing the business administration program. He has stayed in the classroom for forty years, continuing to teach a few courses each year well after retiring from fulltime work. But in a faculty where sustained dedication is not uncommon (think Tim Husband, Linda Easley, and Carl Kaster, just as examples), Bill stands out as the professor most committed to teaching *both* traditional and nontraditional students. For four decades, he has willingly traveled across the state, teaching wherever and whenever (nights, weekends, weekdays) needed. In his distinctive style—restrained, occasionally mysterious, often perplexing, wryly funny—he has challenged and mentored hundreds of students, the young and the not-so-young, and still hears from alumni who seek him out for guidance, golf, or a good laugh.

Bill grew up in Pontiac, avidly following the Detroit music scene as a teenager (he remains an ace on rock and blues history). He began his working life in the automotive industry and his education at Lawrence Institute of Technology. When his interests changed, he earned a master's in business at Wayne State, then found success in banking and finance in Michigan's "thumb" area. When teaching other employees became more satisfying than the rest of the job, he began looking. Then Siena Heights (specifically, business chair Chuck Milliken) called. . . .

Right from the start, Bill taught off campus—at Siena's new degree completion programs in Southfield and at Lourdes College in Sylvania, Ohio—as well as in Adrian. He helped develop the business program in Benton Harbor, cementing the partnership with Lake Michigan College by working with the LMC faculty. As Siena's off-campus network expanded, Bill "secured adjunct business faculty for us all over the state," then off-campus dean Norm Bukwaz recalled. "He kept the College for Professional Studies on its toes in regard to academic quality and service" and was involved in all CPS faculty searches, Bukwaz added. "And he is an academic advisor without equal, one for the ages." Bill eventually taught at almost every CPS center, and assisted the Graduate College on occasion. His signature courses include managerial finance, strategic management, and organizational behavior.

In Adrian, Bill also chaired the management division, headed the admissions office for an interim period, received the Outstanding Teaching Award, and was a longtime faculty representative to athletics. (Few if any faculty or staff can match Bill for attendance at Saints sporting events. He is not a loud voice in the stands, but he misses nothing!)

An unwavering commitment to students underlies Bill's entire history at Siena Heights. Students probably never knew, but he revised his syllabi every summer, seeking new business cases to capture their interest, new data to challenge their thinking, new technology to bring it all to life. Advisees like Iqbal Roshd '88 remember the succinct guidance from "Mr. Blackerby" that led them to career success. Those who mistakenly took him for a softie discovered too late Bill's iron backbone, when they met the consequences of a lapse in effort—or worse, in ethics.

In 2019, Bill still teaches one class, still sits in the bleachers for basketball and the stadium for football, and still cheers the success of four decades of graduates, traditional *and* nontraditional.

Bill Blackerby through the years: *from the top,* at the blackboard in 1980; with his son at Tim's 1996 graduation; and at a recent Siena Scholarship Summer Spectacular.

Engaging in a Widening World: The 1980s and 1990s

Nurturing Diversity: Student Support Services and the McNair Scholars Program
Above left: The McNair Scholars Program matches students like Chitranjan Greer-Travis '03 with faculty mentors like philosopher Mark Schersten for research projects and professional development. **Above right**: The Student Support Services program assists students like these three, including Kermit Williams '05, at right, to gain study skills and success strategies. Like Upward Bound, both programs are part of the federal TRIO program. Created after the Challenger disaster, the McNair Program provides undergraduates with the skills and experience to go on for advanced degrees. In 2019, Student Support Services and the McNair Program continue to enrich educational opportunities at Siena Heights.

Continued from page 122...

Student life reflected similar issues and concerns. Students in HFE—Hispanics for Education—worked to bring farm worker activist Cesar Chavez to campus. The student group WAMS—We Are Minority Students—provided support for students of color; by 1993, the group had reorganized as SHAAKA, the Siena Heights African-American Knowledge Association. Working with a college task force, members of SHAAKA helped organize the first Martin Luther King, Jr. Day activity, and the first presentation of Kente stoles to graduating African-American seniors. Students and staff together mounted the first celebrations of Black History Month, Hispanic History Month, and Women's History Month.

With additional support from the Lilly Endowment, President Artman promoted diversity in college programming. Exhibits in Klemm Gallery explored the Holocaust, Native American expression, and Afro-Brazilian art. Francoeur Theater productions included *A Shayna Maidel,* exploring anti-Semitism after World War II, and August Wilson's *Fences,* featuring the first all-black cast at Siena. A cross-cultural business project linked Siena's business management division, the Mexico study program, and the Students in Free Enterprise group.

Throughout these years, Siena's federally-funded TRIO programs, designed to help low-income, first-generation college students succeed in higher education, also supported diversity efforts. Upward Bound (established in the 1970s) assisted high school teens with college preparation. Student Support Services (established in the early 1980s) helped enrolled students make the transition to college. Beginning in the early 1990s, the McNair Scholars Program helped students from under-represented populations prepare for success in postgraduate education.

The quest for diversity, and for "a teaching and learning environment that respects the dignity of all," continues in 2019. HFE and SHAAKA have evolved into multiple organizations celebrating diversity of many kinds; but the activities begun two and three decades ago continue. Siena Heights still celebrates Martin Luther King, Jr. Day and still recognizes Black History, Hispanic History, and Women's History months. Siena Heights alumni continue to present Kente stoles to graduates of color, inspiring those who follow to persist to graduation. Student Support Services and the McNair Scholars Program continue enriching the campus community.

RECLAIMING RELIGIOUS ROOTS

By the mid-1980s, the number of Adrian Dominicans teaching and working on campus had declined steadily for almost twenty years. In addition, during Hugh Thompson's presidency, the college had deliberately suppressed its Dominican heritage, in the belief that prospective students might be "turned off" by a Catholic college. (The story is told of a new trustee in the 1970s who, while attending his first Board meeting, turned suddenly to President Thompson and said, "You never told me this was a Catholic college!") Thompson's successor, Louis Vaccaro, was a strong Catholic by faith; his selection as president signaled the first return to the college's religious foundations. But the number of sisters on campus continued to shrink. Where once students could not help but learn about Dominican values from their teachers and advisors, it now seemed possible they could graduate without knowing anything at all about Dominican thought.

The appointment of Sister Cathleen Real, CHM, as president in 1984—not an Adrian Dominican, but a vowed religious of the Congregation of the Humility of Mary—was another step in regaining the college's spiritual footing. Then, in 1990–91, the deaths within twelve months of three sisters—founding faculty member Regina Marie Lalonde, OP, and beloved professors Jeannine Klemm and Pat (John Mary) Hogan—threw into sharp focus the need to highlight the Dominican charism in deliberate ways on campus. Sister Cathleen may have had this in mind when she articulated her goal of seeking a "common understanding of our mission."

Dr. Richard B. Artman moved into the president's office in August 1994 and immediately turned his attention to Siena's Catholic identity. At his inauguration, he asked everyone to remember "what we are called to do, and to be, as a Catholic college, as a Dominican college." Under his leadership, Siena Heights revised its mission statement—which since the 1970s had held no mention of religion—to include the words, "a Catholic college founded and sponsored by the Adrian Dominican Sisters."

In response to Pope John Paul II's apostolic constitution *Ex corde Ecclesiae*, Artman appointed a committee to draft a document articulating elements of the Catholic intellectual tradition (a search for truth informed by the conviction that faith and reason are not contradictory but mutually informative) and the Adrian Dominican tradition (commitment to justice, service, and the ongoing interaction between reflection and action)—and identifying the ways Siena Heights expressed those traditions.

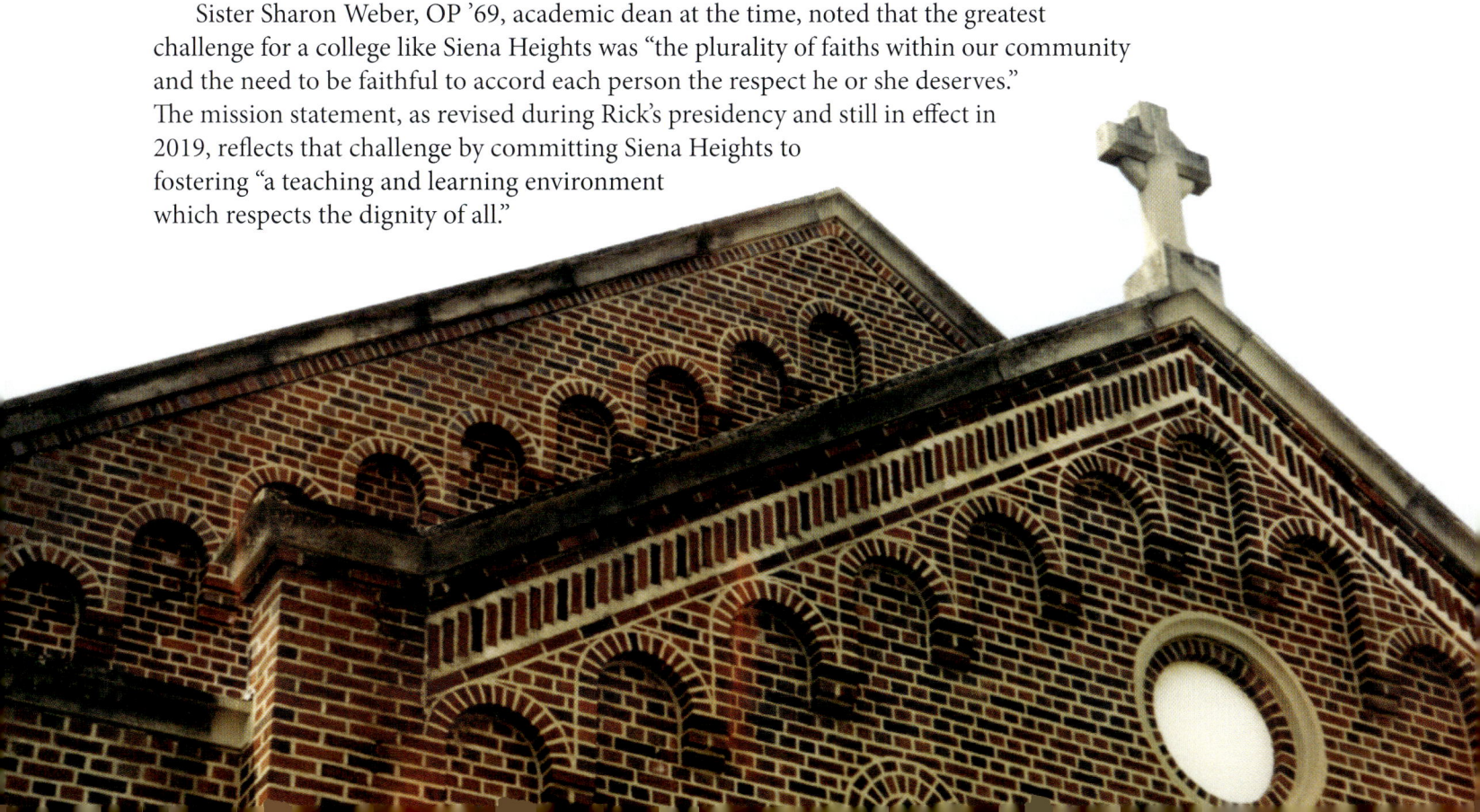

Sister Sharon Weber, OP '69, academic dean at the time, noted that the greatest challenge for a college like Siena Heights was "the plurality of faiths within our community and the need to be faithful to accord each person the respect he or she deserves." The mission statement, as revised during Rick's presidency and still in effect in 2019, reflects that challenge by committing Siena Heights to fostering "a teaching and learning environment which respects the dignity of all."

Changing Styles! On the main campus, Joni Warner '83 and Terry Beurer '80 kicked off the 1980s with formal attire, while Marty Dwyer Frew '99 wrapped up the next decade more casually.

NO "TYPICAL" STUDENT!

In the 1980s and 1990s, on campus and across the state, Siena Heights welcomed a student community increasingly diverse in age and experience. There was no *typical* student.

Mary Weeber '83, a new nontraditional student in 1980, was immediately impressed by the faculty—"Peggy Burns, Pat Hogan, Martha Manheim, Mary Louise Hall, David Van Horn, Tim Leonard"—and by the camaraderie she found with other non-trads: "We were all going through changes in our lives." The non-trads became good friends with Siena's international students, too. "We would invite them into our homes," Mary said, remembering one dinner where many students cooked their native foods and the eating began after midnight. "We were all sitting around together, eating this wonderful food. We had Christians and Communists, Arabs and Palestinians. We had Sunni and Shiite Muslims; people from Bangladesh, China, Japan, and Puerto Rico. One Iranian student looked at me and said, 'You know, if there's a God, he's at this table.'" Mary later joined the English faculty, and still teaches as an adjunct in 2019.

Terry Lewis '83 was drafted into the Army in 1969. After two years as a medic, he reenlisted, enrolling in the Army's then-new physician assistant program. While stationed in Mt. Clemens, Michigan, he decided to earn a bachelor's degree, and found Siena Heights—the only school, he said, that recognized the intense medical training he'd had as a physician assistant. Enrolling at the Southfield center, Terry gained tolerance and curiosity about other cultures while earning a BAS, which subsequently "opened many doors" for him. After a distinguished Army career, he became a college teacher; on an office wall covered with diplomas, his Siena degree held the center spot because "Siena Heights was the only school more interested in meeting *my* needs than making me fit theirs."

Patrick Irwin '86 grew up in southwest Detroit, son of a steelworker. With the steel mill near bankruptcy and no high school graduates in the family, Pat was poised for poverty when his principal, Sister Margaret Mary McGill, OP, and counselor, Grace DeLisle Hajdu '73, both said, "Go to Siena Heights. They care about people." Pat arrived with no money (like Siena girls in the '20s and '30s, he swiped fruit from nearby orchards when he was hungry); Sister Irene Morence, OP, in the financial aid office "was the sole reason I made it through that first year," he said. Sister Carmie gave him a rosary, to remind him of his faith. Running cross-country and track for the Saints kept him focused on school. Helping to found the Pi Lambda Phi fraternity confirmed his belief that everyone is "created free and equal." Since graduating, Pat has "given back" as an award-winning volunteer coach, founder of the Cesar Chavez Academy charter school, youth mentor, and community activist in Detroit—all while becoming vice president of human resources for Henry Ford Hospital.

...continued on page 128

PRESIDENTIAL PROFILE NO. 9

Dr. Richard B. Artman

President of Siena Heights College/University: 1994–2006

Led College to University Status.
Oversaw Off-Campus Program Growth.

Coming to Siena Heights from a career in student development, Dr. Richard Artman brought empathy and a strong student focus to the president's office. A native of Pittsburgh and a three-degree graduate of the University of Miami in Florida, Rick and his wife Joan moved to Michigan in 1994 from Nebraska, where he had served twelve years as vice president for student affairs at Nebraska Wesleyan University.

His immediate goal at Siena Heights was to "raise the spirits and release the potential" of the community, which had been rocked by a variety of challenges prior to his arrival. Faculty and staff union drives had proved unsuccessful, but divisive. A just-ended capital campaign had produced an impressive new building—Dominican Hall—but insufficient funds to pay for it, putting the college into debt for the first time. Personnel issues had ignited some unrest in the ranks. When Rick and Joan arrived, their enthusiasm, optimism, and upbeat personalities were an immediate tonic for spirits in need of raising.

At his inauguration in 1995, President Artman announced that Siena Heights was in "the business of betterment." In his "virtual slideshow" that day, he pictured a college becoming "better than imagined," and introduced many of the goals he would go on to achieve during his tenure: updated technology, a curriculum-wide emphasis on ethics, an ethics lecture series, a softball field, facilities renovations, scholarships, and a new name—Siena Heights *University.* Another of his accomplishments was to spotlight Siena's Catholic identity and highlight the ways Catholic values informed teaching and learning.

Rick maintained close ties with the main campus student body, rolling up his sleeves each fall to help students move into the residence halls, and, with Joan, hosting student groups at their home. A loyal fan of the Saints, he was a driving force behind starting the Athletic Hall of Fame.

President Artman established merit scholarships to attract high-achieving students to the Adrian campus, and initiated development of the Campus Village residential apartment complex. He was a strong supporter of the off-campus centers, too, and encouraged the development of online education. Traveling around the country together, Rick and Joan also revitalized connections with many alumni.

In 2006, Rick and Joan left Siena Heights for LaCrosse, Wisconsin, where he became president of Viterbo University. He retired in December 2016.

Supporting and encouraging students was a priority for President Artman.

Rick and Joan Artman worked as a team throughout his presidency.

Rick worked closely with trustee chairman Doug Kapnick and his wife, Mary, and Adrian Dominican Prioress Pat Walter, OP '66.

Go, Saints! Michael Morgan '83 (*top row left*) came to Siena Heights sight unseen from his Connecticut home, and became the college's first male cheerleader, renowned for his cartwheels (aka, Flounder Flops) across the basketball court. Fellow cheerleaders included Donna Kisner Baker '84 (*middle row right*) and Kathy Bennett '85 (*middle row left*); thirty years later, Michael, Donna, and Kathy returned to cheer the football Saints. In 2013, Michael received the Outstanding Alumni Award.

Continued from page 126...

Ila Hill '87 was a skeet shooting champion in her fifties when she enrolled for classes at the Southfield Center. A nurse anesthetist, she had taken up target shooting as a hobby at age forty, because she was bored and didn't like golf. It turned out she was a natural. A member of the U.S. shooting team from 1973 to 1981, she dominated women's shooting, nationally and internationally. When she stopped shooting competitively, she turned her attention to her career, and went looking for a college where she could build on her associate degree and nursing experience. Siena's BAS degree was just right for her.

Jamie Richardson '87 was one of many students who came to the main campus from small towns in rural Michigan. "Money was tight," he recalled. "If it wasn't for the work study opportunities, academic scholarships, and student loans Siena helped me procure, I might have had to drop out." Instead, he kept his car together with bondo and duct tape, ran cross country and track as a Saint, and began developing a world view in classes like Sister Peggy Burns' American Political Values. Several decades after graduation, Jamie, a successful executive with White Castle, reflected that, "More than anything, Siena Heights awakened in me the simple notion that we need God."

...continued on page 130

80s honors! In 1987, graduating seniors Michele Lourim and Jamie Richardson received outstanding student honors; English professor Dr. Martha Manheim received professor emerita status upon her retirement; and business professor Jack Bologna received the Outstanding Teaching Award. Twenty-three years later, Jamie was honored again with the Outstanding Alumni Award.

128 HAIL, SIENA! Siena Heights University

What ho! The Madrigal Dinner and Concert (above) was an annual highlight in the 1980s and 1990s. Music professor Susan Matych-Hager '68 orchestrated the production with help from hordes of students. "She was strict," recalled Claire Meli Urban '84, who was stage manager one year; but she "got excellent results." The event featured a procession with a real boar's head on a platter, and once, Claire admitted, "we placed lit cigarettes in the [boar's] nostrils . . . and processed it through the audience like a fire-breathing dragon!"

Music maestro! Jacob Chi '85 was an accomplished conductor in China before he came to the United States—and to Siena Heights—to earn a degree. As a student, he became conductor of the college's youth symphony, which included several adult musicians along with area young people. (Nontraditional student Linda Deatrick '93, *front row left* with French horn, took over for Jacob when he went on to graduate study and a professional conducting career.) Jacob was honored with the 2009 Outstanding Alumni Award.

Engaging in a Widening World: The 1980s and 1990s   129

Multitalented! Jacqueline Battalora '88 was a humanities major and peace studies minor, Student Senate president, active volunteer, and charter women's soccer player. After succeeding professionally as a Chicago police officer, attorney, author, and college professor, she received the Alumni Association's Outstanding Alumni Award in 2016.

Poetic Justice! Tod Marshall came to college with few goals, but Siena Heights turned him into a poet. He received the Outstanding Alumni Award in 2009.

Continued from page 128...

Iqbal Roshd '87 was raised in Bangladesh but lived in Canada when a personal letter from President Vaccaro was the deciding factor in his choice to come to Siena Heights. Outgoing and gregarious, Iggy became a resident assistant, a spirited member of the so-called Beautiful Losers, and a business major. Following the advice of his mentor, Bill Blackerby, he sought a career working with people. Today, a Siena Heights trustee and proprietor of a dozen Tim Horton's franchises, he is a proud Saint who attributes his success to his alma mater.

Tod Marshall '90 left a delinquent past in Kansas and came to Siena Heights with his belongings in a couple of trash bags, counting on soccer to help him start a new life. He was not a great student at first, but coach Doug Mello and philosophy professor Sister Pat Hogan turned him around. Siena, he said, "was transformative." Tod graduated with degrees in English and philosophy, earned an M.F.A. and a Ph.D., and today is an award-winning English professor at Gonzaga University and past poet laureate of the state of Washington.

Emma Gene Peters '91, known as Gene (though most people thought it was Jean), completed her degree in four years, but she was a fifty-two-year-old freshman when she began. Mother of six grown children, she commuted from Blissfield—but jumped into college life with both feet, joining committees and clubs, serving on Student Senate, eating in Benincasa, even spending summers working on the campus paint crew to earn money for tuition. "I walked into my first class scared to death," she said, "but Sister Pat Schnapp straightened me out real quick!" Raised Methodist, Gene was very comfortable at Siena Heights: "There is an openness about religion at this college that you do not find in a lot of other places." After graduation, she earned a master's and a Ph.D., becoming a college professor in her sixties.

Jim '91 and Tina DiGiorgio '93 Forsythe found friends, careers—and love—at Siena Heights. They were attracted by two of the college's most popular programs in the 1980s: art and education. Jim has maintained his interest in art, while working in inventory control for Ford Motor Company. Tina became a teacher, then an administrator, and now principal of a Catholic school. Enthusiastic alumni, they are parents of two Siena Heights students and one prospective Saint.

Jimalatice "JT" Thomas Gilbert '92 transferred to Siena and ran into the record books, becoming "the greatest sprinter" in SHU track and field history, according to coach Tim Bauer. A seven-time National Association of Intercollegiate Athletics All-American, JT earned a degree in human services: social work, helped organize the Siena Heights African-American Knowledge Association (SHAAKA), and founded the annual Kente celebration, providing Kente stoles to African-American seniors to wear at graduation, inspiring underclassmen of color to follow in their footsteps. A Saints Hall of Famer, JT said that, as an athlete and student leader, she gained experience dealing with diversity, personality differences, conflict resolution, leadership, and disappointment—all of which prepared her for a successful career in labor relations.

SHAAKA SHU Alumni of Color Reunion

Speaking Out! Leslie Love '93 helped establish the kente ceremony, honoring graduates of color, in the 1990s, and continues to support the program more than twenty-five years later. After careers as a stand-up comedian and a college professor, in 2019 she is a dynamic member of the Michigan House of Representatives.

Tracy Church '93 came to the main campus after earning a journeyman's card and an associate degree. He took one class at a time, from the late 1970s into the 1990s. For many of those years, he was vice president of a local manufacturing firm, going straight from work to the library to study before class. He graduated *magna cum laude,* twenty-seven years after finishing high school. The degree was not likely to change his career, he said, "but it changed the way I felt about myself."

...continued on page 133

Baby Saint! For his 1995 inauguration, President Rick Artman chose track athletes Don Jackson '96, an English major, and Delachaise Roosevelt '97, a child development major, and their son, Leonard, to carry the flags.

Engaging in a Widening World: The 1980s and 1990s   131

A Century of Study

1919–2019 SIENA HEIGHTS UNIVERSITY

BUSINESS

Through most of the first fifty years, "business" at Siena Heights meant secretarial studies. This was a significant program, offered in both two-year certificate and four-year baccalaureate formats (see *Academics in the Rear View Mirror*); but it reflected a time when the "glass ceiling" for women was well below where it is now. In the 1970s, three factors led to a sea change in the approach to business education. One was coeducation; male students were unlikely to aspire to "secretarial" careers. The second was women's liberation, bringing new opportunities for women in the workplace. The third factor was President Hugh Thompson, who recognized that graduates educated for business *administration* and *management* would become successful alumni well-positioned to help support Siena in the future.

Although the two-year secretarial science degree still attracted strong enrollment in the early 1970s, new business tracks in fashion merchandising and hotel/restaurant management were gaining popularity. Professor Marilee Purse joined the faculty in 1975 as coordinator of the hotel/restaurant (later "hospitality") management program. Under her direction, the program hosted international dinners in Benincasa and Science Hall, and prepared many alumni for successful careers. Fashion merchandising was renowned for its annual fashion show on the main campus. However, both programs disappeared from the curriculum in the early 1990s.

Professors Chuck Milliken and William "Buzz" Walzem joined the business faculty in the mid-1970s, ready to redesign and invigorate the management curriculum. "My goal was to do everything I could to make our Business Department as good as anybody's, anywhere," Chuck Milliken recalled. Between 1976 and 1980, "we cracked down on the standards and expectations," he said, and initiated a challenging "case study" approach to upper-level management classes. After an initial drop in enrollment, "we had meteoric growth in the department." When accounting was added to the curriculum, Don Hoyt coordinated the new program; later, Gerald Kruse, Donna Kisner Baker '84, and Carliene Palmer joined the accounting ranks.

Longtime business professor Bill Blackerby came to Siena in 1979 as the department moved into banking and finance.

Although Hugh Thompson had introduced—and pushed—business as a means of attracting male students, Milliken noted that the program also attracted women, right from the start. Before long, on a campus where female students still outnumbered males, women were the majority in many business classrooms.

In the 1980s, business became a leader in bridging the distance between Siena's main campus and its growing network of off-campus programs. John Hounker established the connection when he left the business faculty in Adrian to help William McDermott start the Southfield center. Jack Bologna, who joined the business faculty in 1984, strengthened the link between the on-campus department and the off-campus programs; eventually, Jack taught three of his four regular courses in Southfield, and one in Adrian, where he was particularly sought out by nontraditional students.

Two faculty who have had lasting impact on business administration students and alumni are Bill Blackerby *(in vest at blackboard)* and Chuck Milliken *(blackboard close-up)*. Professor Blackerby taught at almost every Siena Heights site, from 1979 through 2019. Professor Milliken joined the faculty in 1976 to help start the business program; he influenced graduates through the 1990s.

HAIL, SIENA! Siena Heights University

Business became a popular major among both traditional and nontraditional students at all SHU locations. Professors Blackerby, Kruse, and Baker crisscrossed the state through the 1990s, teaching Siena students from coast to coast. "I've sometimes had accountants for major corporations in my classes" at the off-campus centers, Kruse recalled in 1999. "It's as much fun learning from these people as it is teaching the course."

Claudia Blanchard, who joined the faculty in 1997, helped lead the business division from a bachelor of arts (BA) curriculum into the more professional bachelor of business administration (BBA) program. The BBA was a popular success immediately with career-minded students and prospective students.

In 2001, Siena Heights introduced a new business track in sport management, combining a strong business core with a specialized focus on sport, from historical and sociological dimensions to legal and economic considerations.

Graduate offerings in business began in the 1990s with a master's in human resource development, which evolved over time into the master of arts in organizational leadership. In January 2018, the university added the master of business administration to its graduate offerings; the distinctive MBA curriculum focuses on ethical and sustainable business practices. The program aims to graduate "ethical business leaders who can leverage the markets in a manner consistent with our Dominican values," Dr. Cheri Betz, dean for graduate and professional studies, explained.

In 2019: The Division of Business and Management offers the BBA on the main campus and at selected sites in the College for Professional Studies in the areas of accounting, business administration, management, marketing, and sport management. Concentrations are available in accounting, digital marketing, economics, entrepreneurship, finance, health care management, information technology management, international business, management, and marketing. The online BBA in accounting, business administration, management, and marketing is available through the Distance Learning Program. The Graduate College offers both the master of arts in organizational leadership and the totally online MBA.

Continued from page 131...
Seyed-Jalal Hosseini '96, a native of Iran, experienced the Iranian revolution firsthand, seeing things his Siena Heights classmates could barely imagine. As a student, he was active in student government and excelled in the classroom. After graduation, he earned a master's degree and went to work for the Harvard University School of Public Health, working to prevent the spread of AIDS through global education. Recipient of Siena's Recent Graduate Award in 2006, he gave the keynote address at that year's Common Dialogue Day, speaking passionately about "Distorted Morality: Finding God but Abandoning Love and Tolerance."

Ida Ronaszegis '99 was born and raised in Hungary, but left as a political refugee with her husband, finally immigrating to southwest Michigan from Germany in the mid-1980s. When her three children were in school, she returned to school herself; having earned an associate degree, she enrolled at Siena's Lake Michigan center and earned a BAS *summa cum laude*. She missed graduation in order to volunteer in Germany helping refugees of the Kosovo conflict. "So many people helped us," she said. "I want to help out."

Keith Rusie '99, like many Siena Heights students, was the first person in his family to graduate—first from high school, then from college, eventually from graduate school. At Siena, he carried a fulltime course load as a management major, worked half-time at an off-campus job, plus extra hours as a Siena Heights security guard, and, as a senior, served as president of Student Senate. After earning a master's in business administration, he went on to build a successful career in management with General Motors—a "dream job" for this grandson of a Detroit auto worker.

Engaging in a Widening World: The 1980s and 1990s

MY COLLEGE. MY UNIVERSITY. *MY SIENA!*

On July 1, 1998, Siena Heights College—by then a school with a main campus, six degree-completion sites, a graduate program, and a theological certificate program with the Lansing Diocese—officially became Siena Heights University. Sister Miriam Michael Stimson, OP '36, unveiled the new sign. President Artman and student Heather Buku '01 introduced the new logo. Blue and yellow balloons danced in the breeze. Everyone attending the ceremony cheered.

Two years after SHC became SHU, "college" came back into the vocabulary in a new way. President Artman proposed that Siena would operate more efficiently, and serve students more effectively, if its administrative structure reflected the complex institution it had become. Siena Heights became a university made up of three colleges:

- The College of Arts and Science (CAS) comprised all undergraduate degree programs on the Adrian campus.
- The College for Professional Studies (CPS) included undergraduate degree programs at all locations other than Adrian.
- The Graduate College (GC) encompassed all graduate degree programs, on-campus and off-campus.

Not everyone was happy with these changes. Some alumni worried that the small college they had known was becoming a mega-university. But before long, "Siena Heights University" flowed off the tongues of even fiftieth and sixtieth reunion alumnae as easily as "Siena Heights College" had. Soon, most people understood that "my Siena," whichever one they claimed, really was still "my Siena!"

Members of the Phi Sigma Sigma sorority—from left, Erin Fuller Marcero '05, Janine Golatka Neal '04, Allison Bays Face '05, and Joy Ackroyd '06—promote the university logo, with the light of truth beaming from the cross embedded in Siena's name.

Legends of the Faculty

1919–2019 SIENA HEIGHTS UNIVERSITY

Dedicated Adjuncts: A Siena Special

A distinctive feature of Siena Heights has been its ability to recruit and retain—often for decades—a talented cadre of dedicated part-time faculty. In higher education, these men and women are called adjuncts, and most institutions downplay their role, and even their existence on the faculty. Beginning in the 1970s, however, when the curriculum expanded into career-related fields, Siena Heights began relying more broadly on the expertise of working professionals whose first job was not "college professor." Through the years, many adjuncts have proven to be as committed and inspiring as their fulltime counterparts, teaching one or two classes a semester for many years. Such loyalty among part-timers is nearly unheard of in higher education. What has kept them teaching at Siena? "It's never the money," former College for Professional Studies dean Deb Carter said. "It's the relationship. And our values."

Meet a few of Siena's remarkable adjuncts:

DR. ROBERT BRADY (GRADUATE COLLEGE)

Licensed psychologist in Ohio and Michigan with an active private practice. Respected consultant to rehabilitation, disabilities, and pain clinics. Author of several books. An expert in career and vocational testing. Bob Brady was all that; but he considered himself, first and foremost, a teacher and mentor. He was a beloved adjunct in the Siena Heights graduate counseling program for more than thirty years, eventually teaching nearly every course in the counseling curriculum. "Siena Heights has a good understanding of what adjuncts can bring to the academic community," he said. Bob and his wife, Linda Brewster, also a SHU counseling adjunct, hosted weekend seminars that are legendary among counseling alumni. Upon his retirement, Siena Heights took the unprecedented step of honoring this adjunct teacher with Professor Emeritus status. Bob died in 2018. *Graduate alumni have benefited from many such dedicated part-time faculty.*

THE JUDGES OF LENAWEE COUNTY (COLLEGE OF ARTS AND SCIENCES)

Siena Heights students have received a lot of education "from the bench." The late Lenawee County District Court Judge James Sheridan taught at Siena for nearly forty years, almost from the beginning of the criminal justice program in the 1970s until his death in 2015. District Court Judge Laura J. Schaedler and Circuit Court Judge Margaret Scholz Noe '75 also have taught extensively for Siena Heights. Both as occasional guest speakers and as full-course teachers, the judges have brought experience, insights, and more than a few cautionary tales to SHU classrooms. *Criminal justice is just one of many Adrian undergraduate programs enriched by the talents of top-quality adjunct teachers.*

LAKE MICHIGAN LEGENDS (COLLEGE FOR PROFESSIONAL STUDIES)

For many years, the Siena Heights Lake Michigan Center in Benton Harbor held its own small graduation, where each graduate had a moment to speak. Mostly, they said thanks, mentioning family, friends, God—and faculty like Bob Badra, David Maysick, Bob Schodorf, Therese Lynch, and John Wallenfang. All were adjuncts. All had other fulltime jobs. All taught at Siena Heights for decades. Dr. Maysick guided students through statistics, Dr. Schodorf through biology. Professor Lynch, a lawyer committed to Catholic social teaching, drove from Chicago to teach weekend classes, and initiated a course in the philosophy of criminal justice. Dr. Wallenfang originated a political science class in civil rights and civil liberties. And Bob Badra inspired hundreds of students with his classes in religious studies and philosophy; at his 2018 retirement, Siena alumni called him brilliant, thought-provoking, challenging, and "the standard by which all other instructors should be measured." *All SHU off-campus sites claim similarly talented adjuncts who have been the face of Siena Heights for generations of nontraditional students.*

Longtime Lake Michigan Center adjunct professor Peter Sagala, left, regularly attends Commencement in Adrian, where he assists in hooding the new College for Professional Studies graduates as they receive their degrees.

Engaging in a Widening World: The 1980s and 1990s

THE CAMPAIGN TRAIL

In the earliest years, when the sisters were in need, they hitched the horse Dolly to a cart and went on "begging trips" through the countryside, seeking produce, grain, or a goat or chicken. By the time the college was founded in 1919, Mother Camilla could usually count on the generosity of sisters' families for donations and sometimes estate gifts.

By the 1980s, however, advancement—also called fundraising or development—was an established part of college operations. Gone were the days when the congregation could provide all that was needed. Gone, too, was the time when the energy of one person, Hugh Thompson, and the resources of a generous Board of Trustees, were *enough* to balance the budget. The president and trustees would continue to lead the way; but when Louis Vaccaro launched the $6.5 million *Commitment to Excellence* program in 1980—to expand the library, add classrooms, and build the endowment—the age of major fundraising was here to stay. From then on, no president would, or could, lead Siena Heights without mounting a significant development campaign.

Sister Cathleen Real announced *Vision 2000* in 1990. The centerpiece of that campaign was a new academic building that would reflect the increasing importance of technology in education. Dominican Hall would house classrooms, conference space and event facilities equipped with the latest audio-visual electronics.

By the late 1990s, colleges everywhere understood that staying abreast of social and technological change required steady development on campus—and the dollars to support it. In 1998, four years after his arrival, President Rick Artman initiated the "silent phase" of *The Campaign for Siena Heights University: Education with a Mission.* The campaign would fund endowment, computers, a fieldhouse addition, an endowed lecture series, and major renovations to residence halls, the chapel, and science and mathematics facilities.

> **SEEMS LIKE ANCIENT HISTORY!**
> **Technology on the Cusp of Change**
>
> In 1995, Siena Heights still had a telephone system that grouped multiple offices on a party line and required operator assistance to place a long-distance call. Only some faculty and staff had desktop computers. And the question of whether or not Siena Heights needed a website involved a debate on whether the worldwide web was a passing fad or here to stay.
>
> It would not be long before those old ways seemed very old, indeed. One of President Artman's first campus improvements was replacing the telephone system in 1996. One of his first fundraising goals was computers for the faculty. And one of the new public relations director's early projects was an official website for Siena Heights College.

A Century of Study

THE HUMANITIES

The academic areas collectively called the humanities historically constituted a large part of liberal arts education; and in the early decades of the college, students completed more than 40 semester hours in required religion, philosophy, English, and language courses. Today's requirements are considerably different: twenty-first century bachelor's degree candidates complete, at a minimum, three semester hours (generally one course) each in English and religious studies, plus a common thirteen-hour "Liberal Arts Studies" sequence that begins with First-Year Experience and continues with four seminars, freshman to senior year, exploring prominent themes in the Dominican tradition.

When St. Joseph College opened its doors, Sister Francis Joseph Wright, OP, was a one-woman Humanities Department, handling all English, philosophy, and religion classes except for theology, taught exclusively by priests for some years. As Siena Heights evolved, so too did the humanities division, which in 2019 provides in-depth study for those students choosing humanities majors, and elective enrichment for all others.

Philosophy and Religious Studies: Although separate departments, philosophy and religion have always been closely aligned; and in the decades when all students studied theology and most attended daily Mass, these disciplines had a major influence on every student. Monumental faculty in the early years included Sister Benedicta Marie Ledwidge, OP '29, who taught religion for many years while serving as academic dean; Sister Mary (Patrick Jerome) Mullins, OP '33, a brilliant classical scholar who taught church history, Latin, Greek, and philosophy; and Sister Cyril Edwin Kinney, OP, who chaired the division of theology and philosophy into the 1960s.

- *Religious Studies:* Sister Carmelia "Carmie" O'Connor, OP joined the faculty in 1965 and led the department into the post-Vatican II era, engaging students in social service missions and nudging the faculty into new fields like liberation theology. Sister Donna Kustusch, OP '63, and Michael Donnellan helped rewrite the curriculum, introducing three "Values" courses and a Peacemaking and Spirituality Institute. In the 1980s, Susan Conley Weeks added "Values in Video," engaging hundreds of students in thoughtful evaluation of contemporary films, and reshaping Siena's general education requirements. Sister Pat Walter, OP, taught in the 1980s, and returned to the department twenty years later, joining colleagues Joseph Raab and Ian Bell, who helped craft the university's new liberal arts core courses.

Sister Carmie O'Connor, religious studies.

- *Philosophy:* Sister Pat (John Mary) Hogan, OP, began teaching philosophy at Siena Heights in 1966 and chaired the humanities division for much of the 1980s. As a scholar, mentor, and friend, she had an enduring impact on both students and colleagues. Mark Schersten joined the faculty in 1984, chairing the division from 1996 until becoming academic dean in 2011. He also coordinated the Chiodini-Fontana Ethics Lecture Series for its first ten years, bringing national speakers to campus such as Kerry Kennedy Cuomo and Morris Dees of the Southern Poverty Law Center. Kimberly Blessing brought national attention to SHU in 2002 with the class Animated Philosophy and Religion, co-taught with Anthony Sciglitano of religious studies, in which students culled timeless lessons on ethics, character, and other topics from episodes of "The Simpsons."

Sister Pat (John Mary) Hogan, OP, influenced students well beyond the Philosophy Department. In 2009, three Alumni Award winners—poet Tod Marshall '90, symphony conductor Jacob Chi '85, and lawyer Gabrielle Davis '85—all credited Pat Hogan as the professor and mentor who most influenced them, and best prepared them for their successful lives and diverse careers.

Off-Campus Theology

Since 1995, Siena Heights has collaborated with the Diocese of Lansing, preparing men and women for lay leadership in the church by providing a solid grounding in theology. Originally coordinated by Sister Jodie Screes, OP '53, with Susan Conley Weeks of the Religious Studies Department directing the academics, the theological studies program offers undergraduate credentials in theology through the College of Professional Studies. A majority of students complete the 36-credit certificate; but some go further, applying the certificate courses toward a major and completing a bachelor's degree at Siena Heights. Alumni include Mary Fairweather '01, who subsequently served on Siena's Alumni Board; Judy Drake '04, who received the Alumni Association's Recent Graduate Award in 2008; and Richard Haller '07, who became a member of the Board of Trustees. The theological studies program was offered briefly in the Saginaw Diocese, but in 2019 operates only in the Diocese of Lansing, which includes Adrian, Jackson, Ann Arbor, Flint, and other communities.

Known for her dramatic enthusiasm in class, English professor Sister Pat Schnapp, RSM told students that language was "the verbal expression of our unique selves. Befriend it and love it, and it will reward you all your life." Here, at one of the Shakespeare birthday parties she helped organize, she speaks with the Bard—aka, Patrick Wallace '17.

English: The department of Dominican Sisters Francis Joseph Wright, Mary Basil Sheridan, and Mary Jerome Kishpaugh remained largely stable through the first fifty years of the college; but social change and the arrival of Sister Mary Louise Hall, OP, in 1970 marked the start of a new era. "Mary Louise never backed down from any kind of confrontation, ever," recalled Father David Van Horn, who joined the art faculty at the same time. A "real scholar, very strong and pro-liberal arts," Mary Louise had an enormous influence on the English Department. As chair, she hired faculty like writer Simone Press Yehuda, who founded the literary magazine *Eclipse*; scholars Dan McVeigh and Nancy Schuman; and poet Sister Pat Schnapp, RSM, who taught African-American literature as well as Shakespeare and rhetoric. Course offerings expanded to include ethnic literature, film analysis, journalism, and creative writing. Poet Saleem Peeradina brought internationalism to the department. Brother Frank Rotsaert, CSC, produced a writing handbook for students in all departments in 2001, and added "Baseball in Literature" to the curriculum. *In 2019:* A new generation of scholars has ushered the English Department into its next phase, with courses such as contemporary adolescent fiction, postcolonial literature, and gender and sexuality in literature. English students focus on literary studies or secondary English education, or major in creative writing. Communications students can major in professional writing; or in enterprise, religious or digital communications. The College for Professional Studies offers a professional communications major.

Brother Frank Rotsaert, English.

Sister Mary Louise Hall, English.

History: Under Sister Ann Joachim's direction, history for many years was grouped with the social sciences but now falls within the humanities area. In the late 1960s and early 1970s, a new generation of historians arrived, including IHM Sister Jane Farrell, who noted that "Ann Joachim was, I think, a little nervous about us coming in." Teachers like Jane, Sister Theodora "Teddy" McKennan, OP, and Sister Jean Burbo, IHM, led the department through a tumultuous but exciting decade. Spencer Bennett, David Chelminski, and Sisters Peggy Burns, IHM, and Jeanne Lefebvre, OP '66, shepherded the program through the last decades of the twentieth century, adding Russian, Middle Eastern, U.S. intellectual, and U.S. ethnic history to the curriculum. *In 2019:* The History Department offers Native American, African American, Mexican American, and U.S. women's history, as well as traditional overviews and specialized courses on such topics as the American West and war in history. The program offers a major, a minor, and a museum studies certificate, as well as an interdisciplinary major in social studies which serves a number of teacher education students. Former program chair Julieanna Frost now chairs a new humanities program in global studies.

Sister Ann Joachim, history and political science.

Spanish: Languages, both classical and modern, were long a prominent part of the curriculum under the watchful eye of Sister Regina Marie Lalonde, OP, but declined in the 1970s, eventually leaving only the program in Spanish. Sister Evangeline Davis, OP, chaired the department in the 1980s. Professor Renato Gonzalez succeeded Sister Evangeline, directing the program for almost twenty years, and developing a semester program in Mexico. Renato was the face and force of Spanish at Siena Heights from 1989 to his death in 2007. Nicholas Kaplan '03 has directed the department since 2008, maintaining the passion of his predecessor and mentor. *In 2019:* Students may major or minor in Spanish, and/or prepare for teacher certification. An immersion program in Costa Rica has replaced the Mexico semester.

Right: Nick Kaplan '03, Spanish

Below: Renato Gonzalez, Spanish.

Engaging in a Widening World: The 1980s and 1990s

A Century of Study

1919–2019
SIENA HEIGHTS UNIVERSITY

THE PERFORMING ARTS

Music and theater have been part of Siena Heights from its founding. In the earliest years, student plays and concerts included St. Joseph Academy girls as well as college students. Before Walsh Hall (Sage Union) was completed, music lessons took place in Madden Hall; concerts and plays were staged in Madden's "Old Aud" (today's Adrian Room). With the opening of Walsh in 1924, music lessons moved into the teachers' spacious new offices, sized to accommodate concert pianos; students practiced in the small practice rooms lining the second floor balcony above the main stage. The theater program used the Walsh Hall stage as well as the "Little Theater" in the lower level of Sacred Heart Hall. When art vacated the fifth floor of Sacred Heart for the new Studio Angelico building, theater moved upstairs for two years. "What a wonderful place for theater!" Doug Miller '74 said of the fifth floor: "You would walk into an area where people would be rehearsing a scene. Then you'd slip through the darkness and there would be another scene rehearsing. It was magical!" The theater offices moved again in 1973–74, to the basement of Archangelus Hall, before both theater and music relocated into the new Verheyden Performing Arts Center. In 2018, the two departments dedicated their new campus home: the expanded and renovated Spencer Performing Arts Center.

MUSIC

Siena Heights has prepared many alumni for careers in music education, and provided others with a foundation for professional performance success.

St. Joseph College students studied piano with Sister Mary Louise Wald, OP, who began teaching in the 1920s. Sister Thomasine McDonnell, OP, directed the instrumental program into the 1940s, and was an "outstanding figure for those of us who were music majors," music education major Sister Leslie Hartway, OP '45, recalled. As head of the orchestra, Sister Thomasine insisted that "we had to all learn to at least play the scale on every instrument . . . (Her) ears must have been very much disturbed at us sometimes," Sister Leslie added. "(We) had practices down in the orchestra pit in Walsh Hall. The pit had a big brass rail around it, and poor Sister Thomasine . . . cracked many a baton over that brass rail."

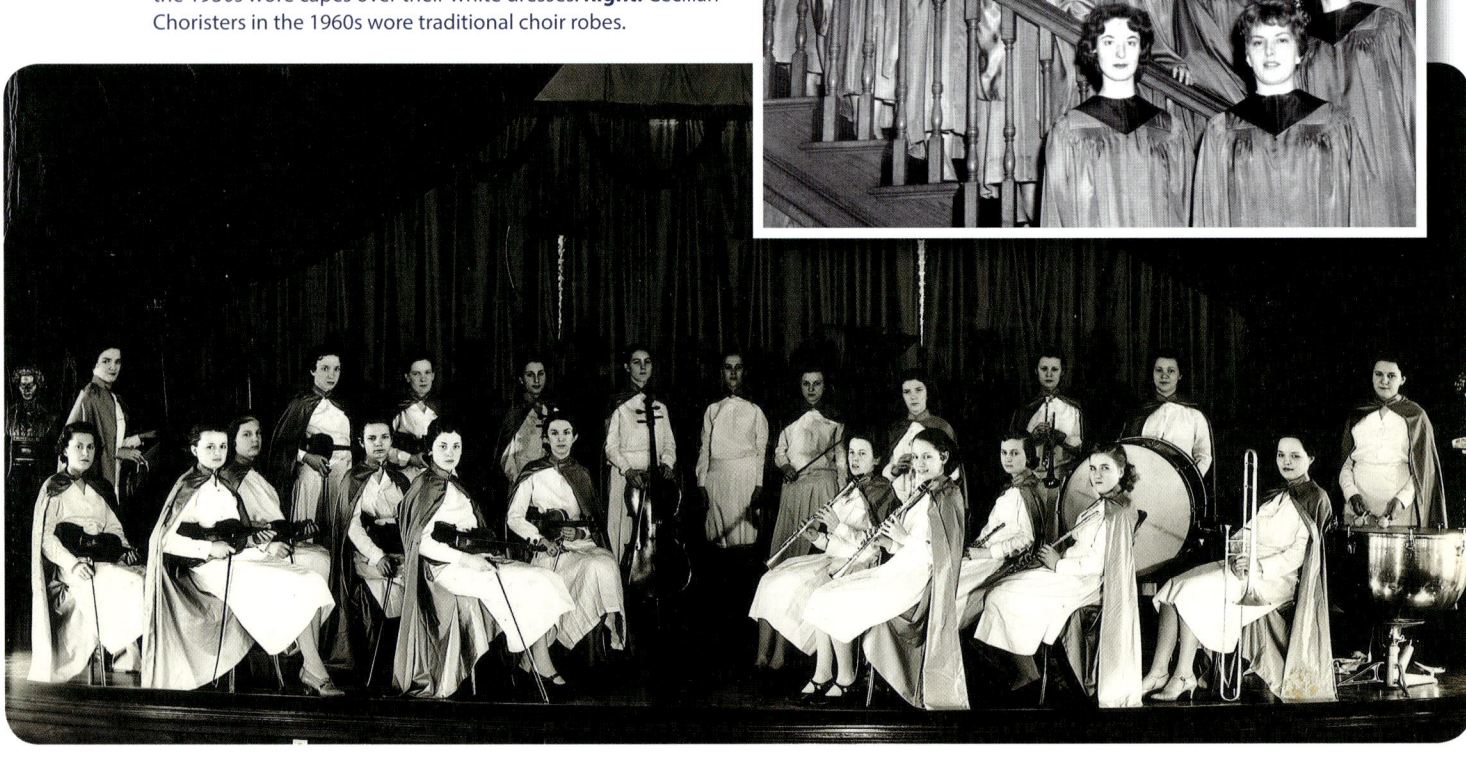

Dressed for performance success. **Below:** Instrumentalists in the 1930s wore capes over their white dresses. **Right:** Cecilian Choristers in the 1960s wore traditional choir robes.

HAIL, SIENA! Siena Heights University

The 1979–80 jazz band—the first jazz ensemble in college history—adopted a casual look: white shirts and dark pants.

Sister Philomena Murray, OP, taught music from 1939 to 1951, primarily directing the vocal program. She also established the Cecilian Choristers and briefly directed the orchestra.

In the 1950s and 1960s, Sisters Marie Madonna Oliver, OP (later Evelyn Evon), Denise Mainville, OP, Marie Paul Rist, OP, Mary Daniel Moran, OP, and Rose Therese Audretsch, OP led the music program. When Sister Maura Phillips, OP '39 began teaching, music at Siena Heights had become almost entirely vocal. Sister Maura was beloved as director of choral groups; and in the early 1970s, near retirement, she took Siena's Pops Ensemble to Disney World in Florida for a memorable week of magical performances.

Music from the 1980s to the twenty-first century was led by these three faculty: (above) Mike Lorenz, shown in the electronic and jazz recording studio, (above right) Sister Magdalena Ezoe, OP '55, with chamber musicians, and (below) Susan Matych-Hager '68, who directed all choral groups.

In 1968, pianist and composer Sister Magdalena Ezoe, OP '55, began her thirty-nine-year tenure on the music faculty, reviving the instrumental program. Magdalena established ties with Adrian's community symphony and soon was teaching chamber music. A few years later, Susan Matych-Hager '68 joined Magdalena and Sister Maura on the faculty—and music entered a new period of growth. Matych-Hager eventually took over the vocal program and built participation from about thirty to as many as two hundred students. She established a new group, the Madrigal Singers, and in 1979 initiated the Madrigal Dinner Concert, a rousing medieval Christmas celebration that was a campus tradition for twenty-five years. She also established the Siena Heights Youth Choir for local schoolchildren.

Jazz musician Mike Lorenz joined the department in 1980, founding the Freetime Jazz Ensemble. By 1990, the department had expanded to offer BA programs in music synthesis and music business. These three musicians—Matych-Hager, Ezoe, and Lorenz—largely defined the department up to the twenty-first century.

The Saints marching band and the university choir are two among many music groups at Siena Heights in 2019.

After a few transition years, a temporary dip in student interest, and a brief elimination of the music major, music has once more emerged as a vibrant part of the curriculum, and a prominent feature of university life. (Ironically, football, which prompted the start of a marching band, deserves some credit for jumpstarting the renaissance of music at Siena!)

. . . continued on page 142

In 2019: The university offers a BA in music with concentrations in voice, instrumental music, and music business; and a BA in music education, with concentrations in choral music and instrumental music education. The program also offers a professional teacher certification track. Choral ensembles include: University Chorale, Chamber Singers, SHU-Wops (men's barbershop), and Nothin' But Treble (women's barbershop). Instrumental groups include: Saints Marching Band, Concert Band, SHU Strings, Percussion Ensemble, and Jazz Band. A full schedule of concerts, recitals, and special event performances make music a regular part of university life. The music curriculum is available only on the main campus.

Engaging in a Widening World: The 1980s and 1990s

PERFORMING ARTS *continued from page 141...*

THEATER

Siena Heights has prepared graduates for success in a variety of theater careers, from theater education to set design, film technology, backstage management, front-of-house administration, and leading roles on Broadway as well as on regional and community stages.

Women played all the parts in early theater productions, from annual passion plays to this 1950s production of *Our Hearts Were Young and Gay* (right) starring Virginia Robertson Buckle '53, left, and Phyllis Coscarelly '53 in evening dress and quite a few women in tuxedos. (Below) Cross-dressing thespians in the 1940s, including Betty Theisen '44, far right, strike a jaunty pose as gentlemen in suits and fedoras.

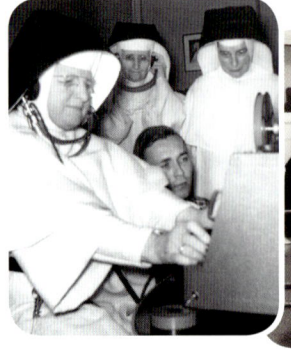

Sister Leonilla Barlage, OP taught speech as well as drama, and established a radio broadcasting studio in the 1940s in Sacred Heart Hall 112.

Sister Leonilla Barlage, OP, was the face of speech and drama through the early decades, teaching acting, puppetry, and radio broadcasting from 1934 to 1969. She directed legendary Passion Plays during Lent, as well as spring productions such as *Our Hearts Were Young and Gay*. (In the all-women years, tall students acted all the male roles.) Sister Leonilla also established the "Little Theater" in the northwest corner of Sacred Heart's lower level, where smaller performances and classes took place; across the hall (in the area occupied by university marketing in 2018), she established a radio studio where students produced live broadcasts for a local station. In the late 1960s, students had the opportunity to explore television broadcasting.

Sister Therese (Rose Terrence) Craig, OP '48, joined the theater faculty in 1965. Collaborating with Maura Phillips in music, she establishing a verse choir, in the tradition of ancient Greek drama; and directed *The Sound of Music*, the first modern musical produced on the Walsh stage. Therese Craig's biggest contribution to theater, however, was the introduction of child drama. With this innovative approach—engaging young children in learning and growth through creative dramatics—she created a dynamic program (initially called Studio 6–12, because it welcomed children aged 6 to 12) that has endured for five decades. Child drama has also built strong ties between Siena Heights and the community.

Sister Therese Craig started child drama in the 1970s. Now called Creative Stages, the program includes annual youth productions such as *Robin Hood* (2016) and *The Jungle Book* (2017).

HAIL, SIENA! Siena Heights University

In fall 1973, Trudy McSorley '70 joined Craig on the faculty, assisting with child drama and directing her first children's theater production (*Ice Wolf*) in April 1974. For thirty years, until she left teaching to become dean for students, Trudy McSorley was a pillar of Theater Siena, and director of child drama long after her mentor's retirement. (Professors Kerry Graves and Joni Warner '83, respectively, followed McSorley heading the program, now called Creative Stages.) Over the years, Siena students worked with hundreds of area children, in after-school programs and annual youth productions, and through "Troupe," which put theater students into elementary classrooms to explore contemporary issues through drama.

Siena Heights also developed a reputation for powerful adult theater. By the mid-1970s, the faculty included Bob Soller, Glenn Crane, and Sister Therese Tighe as well as Craig and McSorley. Later, Doug Miller '74 and Bob Hawley joined the department. The 1990s and 2000s brought Mark DiPietro '83, Graves, and Warner to the faculty. Dan Walker came to Siena as technical director in 2015. Through these years, the department has maintained a strong collaborative relationship with the Croswell Opera House in downtown Adrian.

Program alumni—including Trudy McSorley '70, Doug Miller '74, and Mark DiPietro '83, among others—have had a lasting impact as Theater Siena faculty.

In 2019: Theatre Siena students earn the BA in musical theater, theater and speech communication, or theatrical design and technology. The department presents four major stage productions a year, many student-directed one-act plays, senior performances, and youth theater productions, on the new Deborah Haller Stage and in the Stubnitz Lab Theater. Student performance groups include the Acapelicans, a theater improvisation group, and Troupe, a new version of the 1970s outreach program. Theater students assist with the Creative Stages and Youth Theater after-school programs and with a Creative Stages summer camp. Theater is offered only on the main campus.

On stage through the years: *The Lark* (1968); Glenn Crane directing a 1970s version of *Dracula* featuring Mary Fitzpatrick Thompson '76; *The Diviners* (2005); *Chicago* (2015).

Engaging in a Widening World: The 1980s and 1990s

PART 5

Technology and the Common Touch

The 2000s and 2010s

By the dawn of the twenty-first century, technology was embedded in every aspect of college life. The challenge of the new millennium would be to harness technology—as a way to improve teaching and learning—while balancing the budget, modernizing the campus, and keeping Dominican values at the heart of it all.

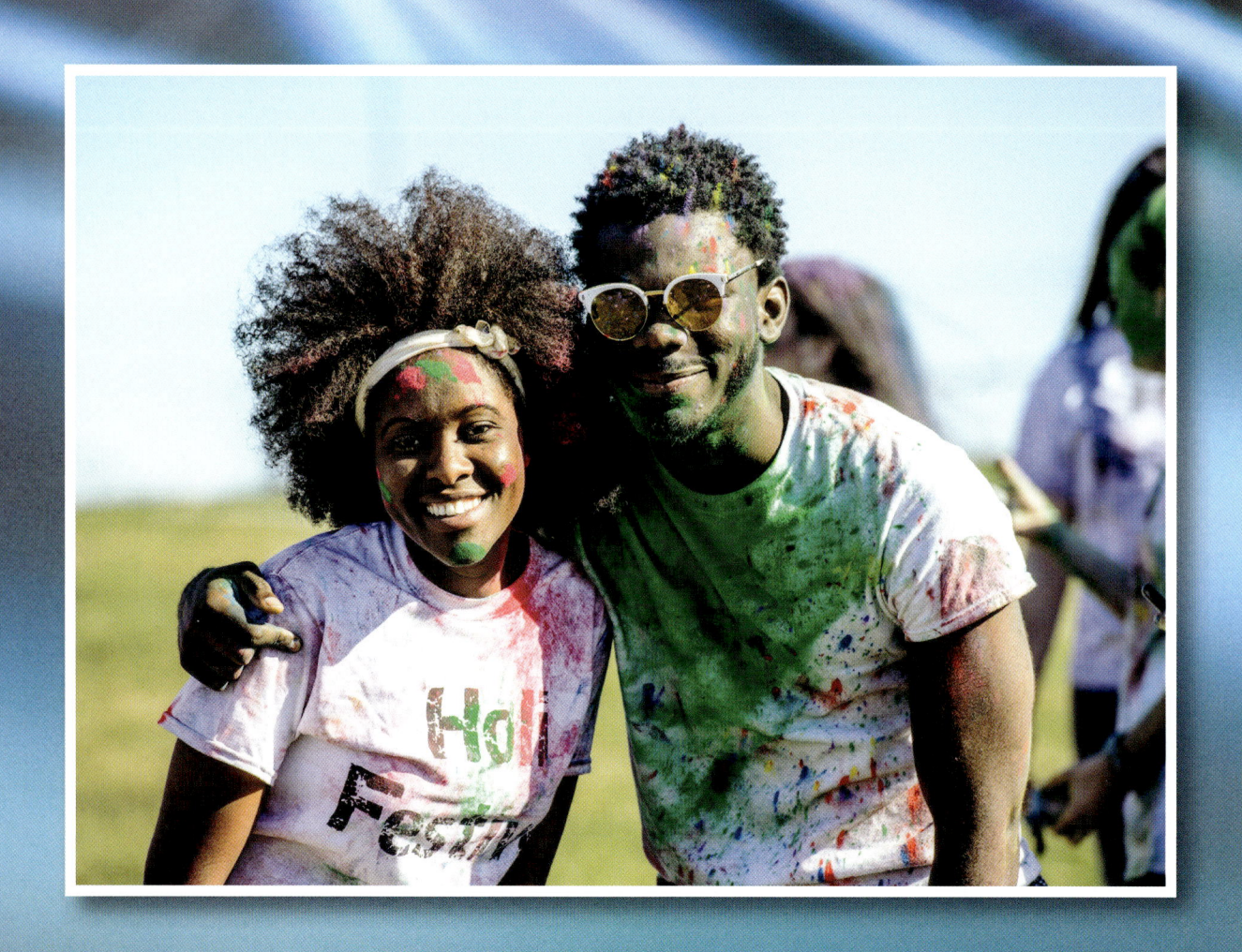

University life in the twenty-first century includes plenty of computer keyboards—but also the joy of faith (Father Tom Helfrich in St. Dominic Chapel in the early 2000s), the pride of academic achievement (Marcus Carter receiving his master's degree in 2016), and, on the Adrian campus, the lively energy of sports and student activities.

FROM CAMPOUTS TO COMPUTERS:
WORKING WIRELESS AND LEARNING ONLINE

In the fall of 1999, students camped out in Sacred Heart Hall for the last time. It was a semiannual tradition: The night before registration opened for the next semester, students with sleeping bags lined the hallway outside the registrar's office, in order to be first in line the next day, ensuring speedy registration and the best selection of classes. By spring, the world had survived "Y2K"—and students could register directly on the web. No more camping or waiting in long lines. Traditionalists worried about the loss of face-to-face interaction, but students welcomed the change. "It's nice to see Siena using the latest technology," one senior said.

About the same time, Sister Magdalena Ezoe, OP '55, a longtime member of the music faculty, released a compact disc of her "Non-Stop Piano Concert" honoring the 150th anniversary of composer Frederic Chopin's death. At Magdalena's request, sales of the CD would benefit a new electronic keyboard lab and recording studio for the department. Tradition and technology would make music side by side.

In 2000, Siena Heights offered its first five online courses through the Metropolitan Detroit Program in Southfield. Under the leadership of Norm Bukwaz, dean of off-campus programs, the university had been experimenting with limited amounts of online content, posting class schedules, assignments, and discussions on the World Wide Web. Now they would go further, introducing "blended online" courses that began and ended with in-person meetings, but relied on Web-based interaction in between. Some were skeptical; but the immediate success of those first classes led Siena to move confidently in the direction of online education.

When Deb Carter succeeded Bukwaz as dean, she pledged that off-campus programs—soon renamed the College for Professional Studies (CPS)—would "continually seek new and better ways to meet the needs of adult learners." Online education was just one of those "ways." No one yet knew how dramatically it would impact the university.

While CPS explored online learning off-campus, Siena Heights in Adrian became one of the first colleges in the nation to have a completely wireless campus. This meant that laptop computers could access the Internet and the SHU network anywhere on university grounds without "plugging in" to a telephone modem or a network outlet. Students could

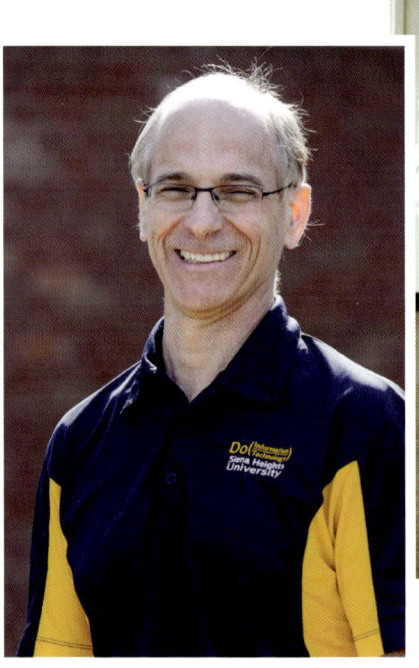

Computer guru Bob Metz led Siena Heights into the wireless age, giving twenty-first century students the flexibility to study with laptop computers anywhere on campus.

At the 2003 graduation reception in Southfield, *from left, standing,* then-Southfield director Carrie Jeffers, staffer Aimee Adamski, College for Professional Studies dean Deb Carter, President Artman, and, *seated,* staffers Cheri Betz '07, Khalilah Outlaw, and *far right* Angela Pinkett '07, '09 gather to congratulate 2003 master's degree graduate Lynn Kendrick, *front second from right*.

write and edit papers in Trinity Garden or Ledwidge lobby. Coaches could post up-to-the-minute scores from game sidelines. Teachers could check on research (or investigate suspected plagiarism) from the classroom, the library, the snack bar—anywhere on campus they carried a computer. "We looked at how computers would be used" in the future, Siena computer guru Bob Metz said, "and decided wireless would be the best way to go."

Across the curriculum, the classroom, the campus, and the state, technology was reshaping life at Siena Heights: how we worked, taught, studied, learned, and communicated.

THE RELENTLESS PACE OF TECHNOLOGY CHANGE: SHOESTRING BUDGETS AND CAPITAL CAMPAIGNS

Approaching the new century, the main campus mathematics faculty had begun a small-scale facilities upgrade, renovating the "math cave" in the lower level of the science building into a multipurpose student space. "People think all you need to teach math is chalk and a chalkboard, but that's not the way we do mathematics at Siena Heights," professor Tim Husband said in 2000, adding that Siena, then, was "one of the few liberal arts colleges that uses technology in every math class at every level." Resourcefulness, elbow grease, alumni support, and some well-placed dollars produced a model higher-tech study space for students.

The math cave was a small project, not a huge renovation—but it presaged improvements to come. Even when supported by large-scale fundraising, keeping up with the pace of technological change would require vision, a clear student focus, and the hard work of making limited funds go as far as possible.

When President Artman and the trustees kicked off the public phase of *The Campaign for Siena Heights University: Education with a Mission* in May 2001, the campaign's $12.5 million goal included almost $2 million for technology upgrades in computing, mathematics, and the sciences, and $1.25 million more for technology in the library, residence halls, and other areas. "Smart boards," interactive classrooms, computer banks, and high-tech instrumentation came out of that campaign. But newer and better technology would be needed before long.

Technology and the Common Touch: The 2000s and 2010s

PRESIDENTIAL PROFILE NO. 10

Sister Peg Albert, OP, PhD

President of Siena Heights University: 2006–present

Visionary Dominican.
Bold Risk-Taker.
Leader of Academic, Athletic, and Campus Expansion.

Raised in Florida, Sister Mary Margaret (Peg) Albert has left the sun country twice for Michigan: once to join the Adrian Dominicans, and again to join Siena Heights University.

The middle child of five siblings, Sister Peg grew up competitive and was voted "Most Athletic" in high school, where tennis was her sport of choice. Feeling called to religious life from a young age, she entered the Adrian Dominicans at age twenty. After graduating from Wayne State University with a degree in sociology, she spent a few years as a social worker in inner-city Detroit before returning to Florida to begin a career at Barry University that culminated in her serving as head of the Barry School of Law.

Since becoming tenth president of Siena Heights in 2006, Sister Peg has guided the university through a period of dynamic academic and athletic expansion and unprecedented campus growth. Challenging the community to "be bold" and "think higher," Sister Peg developed a three-question matrix by which, she said, every new proposal would be evaluated: Is it in sync with Siena's mission? Does it fill a need in the community? Is it financially sustainable? Using that analysis, she soon made two decisions that ignited optimism and energy on campus: to develop a nursing program, and to add football to SHU athletics. Other programs and sports followed.

While overseeing new academic offerings and an expanding athletic program, Sister Peg has been tireless as both friend-raiser and fundraiser. She has engaged many alumni and friends in significant support of university projects and scholarships—and has transformed the campus. The generosity of hundreds now lives and breathes in Siena's football stadium, athletic complex, university center, baseball stadium, St. Catherine residence hall, the "Chaos Getaria" sculpture, and the performing arts center and music hall. Thanks to the generosity of the Adrian Dominican Sisters, Sister Peg also has transformed the St. Joseph Academy building into a vibrant new part of SHU academic life.

During Homecoming weekend, which now attracts thousands of fans and former students, Sister Peg spends long hours hosting events, cheering Saints teams, and crisscrossing campus in the "Prezmobile," always looking for alumni to greet, supporters to thank, and friends to make.

Sister Peg's habit of hugging people has made Siena Heights a warm and welcoming place. Her social work background has shaped her response to students, from nurturing community spirit with a Siena Heights mascot to assisting homeless students on campus. Her deep faith has led her to promote awareness and appreciation of Siena's heritage and values.

During Sister Peg's presidency, Siena Heights has received numerous awards, including these:

- Recognition in *Money* magazine's 2018–19 list of "Best Colleges for Your Money."
- Repeated—2015–19—recognition in *U.S. News and World Report*'s annual rankings of the Best Online Learning Programs, with top state and national rankings and special recognition for retention and graduation rates.
- ATHENA Lenawee's 2010 Parthenon Award for Business Leadership in providing an institutional culture "that allows women to reach their full leadership potential."
- Repeated recognition as a "Military Friendly" university for veterans; and also as offering one of the "Best Online Programs for Veterans."

Sister Peg's friend and mentor Sister Jeanne O'Laughlin, OP '58, was a featured speaker at her inauguration.

The president has worked closely with Board of Trustees chair Margaret Scholz Noe '75, who joined her in welcoming Sister Peg's father, Ron Albert, to campus.

Sister Peg and, from left, benefactors Steve and Sally Hickman and Mary Spencer, cut the ribbon at the dedication of the University Center, named in memory of Mary Spencer's parents, Donna E. and Delbert J. McLaughlin.

SISTER PEG COMES TO MICHIGAN: DOMINICAN HEART, DOMINICAN DARING.

President Artman worked to revive the university's Catholic identity; but it was Sister Mary Margaret Albert, OP, PhD, the tenth president, who invigorated the Dominican spirit of Siena Heights. The first Dominican to hold the office in thirty-seven years, she was welcomed with enthusiasm—and she responded with hugs, establishing her trademark greeting almost immediately. Known to one and all as Sister Peg, she was quick to smile, quick to laugh, quick to become teary at the poignant stories of students or alumni. She was also ready to be a leader and a risk-taker. For her inauguration in November 2006, she adopted the theme "Be Bold. Think Higher." She would lead the way on both fronts.

Early on, Sister Peg developed three criteria by which she and the Siena community would evaluate any proposed new plan or program:

- Is it in tune with the mission of Siena Heights University?
- Is it needed in the community—locally, or societally, or globally?
- Is it financially sustainable?

Applying that matrix, she made a number of daring early decisions. Despite an economic downturn that prompted many colleges to cut back, Sister Peg chose to go forward:

- Yes, Siena Heights would start a nursing program.
- Yes, Siena Heights would bring football to campus.
- Yes, Siena Heights would support homeless students at the university.

Each of these initiatives could have been rejected as too expensive; instead, all had positive ripple effects at Siena Heights. Nursing prompted a significant boost in student interest in all of the sciences at Siena. Football led to a marching band, an expanded Music Department, varsity cheer and dance teams, and significant enrollment gains. Shedding light on the hidden problem of homelessness, even among Siena students, helped invigorate the spirit of service and faith on campus. Volunteerism and "giving back," always part of Siena, became even more lively and pervasive.

Other bold decisions included: bringing engineering to campus; establishing new majors in digital communications, global studies, and theatrical design and technology; initiating a gender and ethnic studies institute; further expanding the athletic program with men's volleyball, and men's and women's bowling and lacrosse, and eventually eSports; and reshaping the campus with new facilities supporting athletics, student life, and the arts.

HAIL, SIENA! Siena Heights University

ENSURING A STILL-DOMINICAN FUTURE

"Keep bright the fire, and high the flame!" Students, faculty, and staff sing those words from "Hail, Siena" at most official celebrations. The song continues, "Our patron is a holy name," referring to St. Catherine. The words echo Sister Peg's commitment to making sure the community knows the university's history and understands its core values. She has been keeping the fire bright and the flame high ever since her arrival; and as Siena's "encourager-in-chief," she is quick to echo Catherine's beliefs: *If you are who you were meant to be, you will set the world on fire.* Students in 2019 know those words almost as well as *competent, purposeful, and ethical.*

To heighten students' awareness of Siena's Dominican foundations, Sister Peg supported a revision of the university's general education requirements, linking liberal arts learning to Dominican values. Now, four required seminars (Diversity in Community, Inquiry and Truth, Contemplation and Action, Justice and Peace), taken freshman through senior year, provide a common interdisciplinary core built around prominent themes in the Dominican tradition.

To strengthen Siena's connection with its heritage, Sister Peg also established a new position—director of mission education—and hired Sister Mary Jones, OP, to develop a program to deepen the community's understanding of the Dominican charism. "Someday, hopefully not any time soon, the Adrian Dominican Sisters may not have a physical presence on the Siena Heights campus," Sister Peg said, explaining her intention, but "our Catholic identity and Dominican tradition must continue."

The Heritage Project, launched in 2015, touches everyone at Siena. Students explore Dominican themes through the liberal arts core. Employees participate in activities that highlight Dominican thought. And a few employees—faculty and staff volunteers—participate in the "Torchbearer" program, completing a three-year exploration of Dominican values and history, and working to inspire others with what they learn. *Contemplate, and share the fruits of contemplation.*

Since the late 1990s, Siena Heights also has offered scholarships each summer for two community members to participate in a two-week immersion into Dominican history called the Fanjeaux Seminar, for the location in France where St. Dominic established his ministry in the Middle Ages. Many students, faculty, and staff have traveled to Fanjeaux with participants from other Dominican colleges; upon returning, they have gladly shared what they learned about Siena's Dominican heritage.

...continued on page 152

The campus ministry team in 2005 included, *from left,* Father Tom Helfrich, April Gutierrez '02, and Tom Puszczewicz. Father Tom served Siena from 2005 to 2013. Tom "Push" Puszczewicz has been at the heart of campus ministry since 2000, continuing in 2019 to coordinate the "Siena Serves" community service program and to support the Champions of Character initiative in athletics.

Darius Price '18, *center*, helped organize Compel Ministry on campus, becoming as well known for his preaching and gospel singing as for his exploits on the football field.

Continued from page 151...

    Perhaps most importantly, Sister Peg has led the way in lifting up Siena's values by speaking directly to the community on matters of faith. On Catholic feast days or religious holidays (not just Christian but other faith traditions as well), or when current events seem to shake the foundations of everyday life, a "Message from the President" shows up, either in an email or in person in a ten-minute hallway prayer service. By sharing her own faith, and inviting others to reflect on their beliefs, Sister Peg models the importance of our Dominican roots.

Left: The words of Catherine of Siena, written almost seven hundred years ago, continue to inspire the Siena Heights community in its outreach and service.

Below: Father John Grace, campus chaplain 2013–18, engaged students in mission outreach, in locations near (including Flint, Michigan, during that city's water crisis) and far (including Home Boy Industries in Los Angeles).

STUDENTS FOR A WHILE. ALUMNI FOR LIFE!

Today—as in the earliest years of St. Joseph College—earning a degree is only the beginning of a lifetime connection between Siena Heights and its graduates. The 1928–29 catalogue stated that, "for the promotion of the interests of our Alma Mater and the continuation of friendships formed in school days," the National Alumnae of St. Joseph's Academy was organized June 22, 1904. After 1919, the association was renamed to include graduates of St. Joseph College, as well as the academy. Not until 1957 did college alumnae separate officially from the academy, establishing the Siena Heights College Alumnae Association. In the 1970s, after the college began graduating both men and women, the association dropped the all-female *alumnae*, adopting the Latin plural for a mixed group of males and females to become the *Alumni* Association.

Following the name change in 1998, the Siena Heights *University* Alumni Association came into being, claiming as its members all graduates of St. Joseph College, Siena Heights College, and Siena Heights University!

Catherine Clark '27, *right*, one of the first four-year lay graduates of the college, became one of its first alumnae leaders. Here, in 1932, she represents St. Joseph's College at a biennial meeting of National Catholic Alumnae hosted by Bishop Michael Gallagher.

During the October 19–20, 1957, alumnae meeting, members of the newly formed Siena Heights College Alumnae Association, elected and inducted their first officers: *from left: seated*, Dorothy Ward '45, president, and Agnes Binsfeld Crombe '45, first vice president; *standing*, Portia Beal Coury '50, second vice president, Agnes Finn Dombrowski '43, treasurer, and Doris Kish Heidenberger '50, corresponding secretary. Missing: Barbara Oess Dumouchelle '51, recording secretary.

Through the decades, volunteer service on the Board of Directors of the Siena Heights Alumni Association has been fun and rewarding for graduates of all ages, decades, and Siena Heights sites. Among many dedicated boards through the years have been, from the top, 1980, led by *standing, fifth from left* Jane Korte Waldo '53, president; 2006, led by *seated center in light blue shirt* Joe Balusik '90, president; 2014, led by *seated top row third from left* Mary Small Poore '76, president; and 2018, led by *front row right end* Dory Garcia Bryant '88, president.

Crowding into past Homecoming photo booths are past Alumni Association presidents Dennis Reeder '78, Keith Rusie '99, Mary Small Poore '76, Michael Lane '01, and Katie Hatch Massaro '07, plus then-alumni director Jennifer Hamlin Church, Honorary '13.

NEW ACADEMIC TRADITIONS:
EXPLORING IDEAS AND SHARING ACHIEVEMENTS

In the first two decades of the twenty-first century, Siena Heights added three significant traditions to academic life.

First, the university decided to take one day every year to engage the community in shared discussion of a significant topic. The first **Common Dialogue Day** took place March 21, 2001. Regular classes were replaced by a keynote address, a community lunch, dozens of breakout sessions, and a closing panel discussion—all on the theme of "Technology and the Human Spirit." It was "an opportunity for the whole community to come together to hear and think about the same idea," philosophy professor Mark Schersten said, and was successful enough to do again. The next year's topic was "Veritas," the search for truth that is a core Dominican value. "There is no single approach" to that search, keynote speaker Sister Jamie Phelps, OP '69, reminded everyone; break-out sessions explored truth in history, wartime, business, and the Bible—among many perspectives. Then-president Rick Artman called the day "a tribute to the intellectual curiosity" of the community. Eighteen years later, Common Dialogue Day is a cornerstone of the university calendar. Now held early in the fall, it introduces the theme for the academic year, and has grown to include live-streamed presentations from distance learning and the off-campus centers.

Second, in 2002, Siena Heights inaugurated the ***Chiodini-Fontana Endowed Lecture Series on Ethics*** with a presentation by human rights activist Kerry Kennedy Cuomo, who urged the community to fight injustice and "speak truth to power." Funded by philanthropist Catherine Reuther, the endowed lectureship brings acclaimed speakers annually to explore theoretical issues in ethics, current issues of moral importance, and the nature of Catholic identity.

Torch Night. The Torch Night ceremony, which dates at least from the 1940s, is one of the most cherished and enduring academic traditions at Siena Heights. Each senior passes the torch of learning and light of truth (a candle) to an undergraduate, who gives the senior a rose.

Halo Fest. A week of events marking the end of winter semester, Halo Fest is a new main campus tradition that concludes with a focus on unity and cultural diversity. The final event, *shown here 2018*, is a colorful celebration of spring based on India's Holi festival.

    Finally, in 2015, the **Scholarship Symposium**, scheduled in April a few weeks before graduation, provided another all-university academic event. The now-annual symposium highlights academic accomplishments of all kinds, in every part of the university, from senior projects to ambitious term papers to all kinds of research. The day features separate morning and afternoon poster presentations that fill Benincasa Hall, oral presentations in classrooms across the Adrian campus, arts exhibits and performances, and online discussions from the College for Professional Studies.

    Common Dialogue Day, the Ethics Lecture, and the Scholarship Symposium reflect Siena's continued commitment to Veritas, community, and the Dominican belief in contemplation and "sharing the fruits" of contemplation.

BUILDING BOOM:
PUTTING SHU "ON HIGHER GROUND"

President Artman focused primarily on upgrading existing facilities during his presidency: expanding the Fieldhouse; renovating the library, chapel, and residence halls; and upgrading technology in many buildings. One new facility, the Campus Village apartment complex, was nearing completion when Sister Peg arrived in 2006.

Five years later, Sister Peg launched *On Higher Ground*, a true "brick and mortar" capital campaign, and kicked off a period of remarkable campus growth. The twenty-first century building boom began with an outdoor performance stadium, providing an instant upgrade to the Saints' track-and-field, soccer, and lacrosse programs—and a home field for the brand-new football program.

Trustees, administrators, athletic leaders, and students joined Sister Peg in the former baseball field to break ground for O'Laughlin Stadium and the Dr. Mike and Lynne Dawson Field.

With the Spencer Athletic Building completed behind them, charter members of the football team model new uniforms by the stadium entrance.

The dedication of O'Laughlin Stadium and the Dr. Mike and Lynne Dawson Field during Homecoming 2011 was the first of many new-building celebrations:

- 2012: The Mary and Sash Spencer Athletic Complex (attached to O'Laughlin Stadium);
- 2012: The new Baseball Stadium next to the Fieldhouse (the old diamond was absorbed into Dawson Field);
- 2013: The Donna E. and Delbert J. McLaughlin University Center;
- 2015: The St. Catherine Residence Hall;
- 2018: The Mary and Sash Spencer Performing Arts Center, including the Deborah Haller Stage and the Sister Kevin McLaughlin Music Hall.

...continued on page 158

St. Catherine Hall, the newest residential option, offers small group living near the stadium and the Performing Arts Center.

Technology and the Common Touch: The 2000s and 2010s 157

Continued from page 157...

The campus has evolved in other ways, too:

- On the north side of Siena Heights, *a new entrance* from Oakwood Road leads into the university.
- In an area once paved for parking, *a spacious green quad* now invites walking and talking, meeting, reading, and studying. The quad is bordered by Archangelus, Ledwidge and Dominican halls on one side, with the Spencer Performing Arts Center and Studio Angelico on the other.
- *Chaos Getaria*, a monumental art piece by Jedd Novatt, anchors the west end of the quad. The eighteen-foot stainless steel sculpture was installed in April 2015.
- *Outdoor art on campus* also includes the meditative stone sculpture "Inverted Arch" by Ken Thompson '77 on the south side of the quad, and assorted pieces in the John Wittersheim Memorial Sculpture Park, which mounts a new outdoor exhibition each year at different locations around campus.

Below and right: A distinctive red sculpture by Rik Leichliter '73, part of the Wittersheim Sculpture Park, anchors the view of McLaughlin University Center in one direction and the Mary M. and Sash A. Spencer (inset photo) Performing Arts Center in the other.

Left: The University Center dining hall includes a variety of menu options; students including Najee Brazzle '15 appreciate the pizza oven!

Right: The monumental *Chaos Getaria* sculpture by Jedd Novatt stands in front of the Performing Arts Center, at one end of the new quad.

HAIL, SIENA! Siena Heights University

THE EXPLOSION OF ONLINE EDUCATION

Perhaps technology's most dramatic impact has been in the area of online education. Our Dominican founders could not have imagined today's online "classroom," but they would approve of the Dominican values that undergird this new kind of teaching and learning at Siena Heights. No doubt they would smile, too, to see the state and national honors SHU has won.

How it Happened:
Distance Learning, the Dominican Way.

Siena Heights was a pioneer with degree completion in the 1970s—the first (and for a while only) private liberal arts college in Michigan offering a degree path specifically designed for adult students. Like Dominic, who took the church to the people, Siena Heights met students where they were instead of insisting they come to campus, and worked around their needs rather than forcing them into a traditional mold. Today, degree completion is available from hundreds of providers in countless locations, but Siena Heights paved the way.

The story was different with online education—also called distance learning.

As technology made it possible to have classes without classrooms, and to teach students who never came face-to-face with each other or the professor, Siena Heights did not jump in immediately. Instead, Norm Bukwaz, Deb Carter, and the CPS faculty and staff reflected on the success of Siena's existing off-campus programs and partnerships. They asked what was distinctive about Siena's approach, what was Dominican about it, and what contributed to the success of those programs. Working with Siena's computer guru Bob Metz, they studied the new technology. Working with online teaching champion Jim O'Flynn, they studied which teaching methods would, or would not, be effective with technology. They studied anew the university mission (competent, purposeful, ethical, respect for all) and the Dominican pillars (study, prayer, community, preaching), which had always empowered teaching and learning at Siena Heights.

In short, they sought *Veritas* the Dominican way, through contemplation and sharing the fruits of that contemplation. At the end of the process, in spite of competition from other national providers, Siena Heights was ready to enter the online arena. In 2002, the university received approval from the North Central Association of Colleges and Schools to offer an entirely online degree completion program.

To ensure quality teaching, Siena Heights required every professor interested in online teaching to enroll in an online class—acquainting him or her with Siena's expectations of online education—before being approved to teach one. (Not all professors are comfortable with 24/7 involvement in "threaded" discussions, extensive personal feedback on written work, and rapid response to assignments and exams.)

...continued on page 160

NO.1 IN MICHIGAN
AMONG THE TOP IN THE NATION

In 2019, for the third year in a row, the Siena Heights undergraduate online learning program was ranked the best—No. 1—among all institutions in Michigan by *U.S. News & World Report* in its annual rankings of online bachelor's degree programs. For the sixth consecutive year, SHU was ranked nationally as well: No. 2 among all Catholic institutions in the country and No. 5 among all private colleges and universities—also earning top rankings for student engagement and faculty credentials and training. In 2019, Siena Heights tied for 29th among all institutions nationally, and has been ranked previously as high as 24th in the country.

Siena Heights pioneers in the development of online education include: *from left*: professors Tad Dunne, Jim Sam, and Jim O'Flynn; and *at right, from left:* Gail Ryder, Mike Winstrom, and Carol Himelhoch. Professor John Fick, *center*, is a core member of the Metropolitan Detroit Program faculty in Southfield.

Continued from page 159...

To ensure successful learning, the university required prospective online students to first complete an online orientation, confirming they had the computer skills to handle the work.

CPS began offering totally online degree completion in 2004. Two years later, Deb Carter observed that "our cautious, quality-focused approach to delivering distance education is beginning to bloom, as evidenced by record growth." *Indeed!*

- Siena Heights awarded its first degree to a totally online graduate in 2005. That year, there was one online graduate among approximately 570 new undergraduate alumni.
- Five years later, in 2010, the number of online graduates had increased to 125, more than 18 percent of that year's new bachelor's degree alumni.
- Five years after that, in 2015, 195 online graduates received diplomas, accounting for more than 22 percent of that year's undergraduate degrees. (The main campus accounted for another 28 percent of the graduates. The remaining 50 percent of that year's bachelor's degree graduates represented Siena's seven on-the-ground CPS sites.)

Distance learning was off and running. And earning rave reviews.

Redefining Time and Place:
Teaching and Learning Anytime, Anywhere.

At the College for Professional Studies commencement in 2015, members of the Alumni Board lined the walkway into the Fieldhouse, applauding CPS graduates as they processed past. Banners identified where each group had studied: Metropolitan Detroit, Monroe, Jackson, Lansing, Battle Creek, Benton Harbor. And then: Distance Learning. As that final group of graduates passed, Alumni Board members encouraged them to call out where they were from. Some lived not far: Blissfield and Tecumseh, Ohio and Indiana. Quite a few had come a long way: Texas, Washington (the state), West Virginia, Pennsylvania. And one came all the way from Saudi Arabia! Not all distance learning graduates participate in commencement (nor do all main campus graduates). But, remarkably, many who complete their degrees entirely online *do choose* to attend, often traveling long distances with family and friends, excited to see the university and claim it as "My Siena." Highlights of these first-time visits are many: not just graduation itself but meeting online classmates for the first time, shaking hands with faculty who have mentored them from afar, exploring a campus they now can call their own.

From the start of totally online degree completion in 2004 through fall 2018, Siena Heights enrolled online students from forty-six states and four countries outside the United States. (In fall 2018, online students represented thirty-seven states and one non-U.S. country.) In addition, some online graduates have worked on their degrees while serving overseas in the military:

Humanities professor Gail Ryder teaches her online classes anywhere she finds a computer connection, from her backyard to a hotel room in Italy!

- For Army Specialist William Good '09, the online program was "a Godsend" because he was able to complete his assignments "anywhere I can get an internet connection—whether I am in the DMZ [Demilitarized Zone] in Korea or the mountains of Bavaria."
- Completing his degree during a thirteen-month tour in Iraq, Michael Douglas '10 "learned a great deal" from classes that "taught me to think critically and look at all the issues." Like many online students, he appreciated that "everyone gets to have their say, as opposed to the traditional classroom, where sometimes it's dominated by one or two personalities. This way, you are able to hear everyone's opinion."

Online faculty enjoy the same geographic flexibility. Mary Brigham '97, the Outstanding Teacher for 2013 at Siena's Metropolitan Detroit Program in Southfield, taught some of her classes that year from an Internet café in Dubrovnik, Croatia. Online humanities professor Gail Ryder responds to emails and online discussions throughout the day, no matter where she is; she kept teaching all though a Siena Heights alumni trip to Italy in 2014.

Professors Gail Ryder, Jim O'Flynn and Jim Sam, congratulate online BAS graduate Helen "Cookie" Burkhalter '09 (second from left) at commencement. Cookie completed her degree at home, in Georgia; but—like many distance learning graduates—she came to Adrian to participate in graduation and receive her diploma in person.

Technology and the Common Touch: The 2000s and 2010s

Legends of the Faculty

The Architects of Off-Campus Education

NORMAN BUKWAZ

Hired to teach sociology in 1974, Norm Bukwaz has spent virtually all of his forty-four-plus years with the college, then the university, helping Siena Heights move boldly into off-campus education. After one year of full-time teaching, he moved into off-campus program development while chairing the general studies division. He pioneered the concept of degree-completion, administered the new bachelor of applied science (BAS) program, and played a key role in establishing the first two off-campus centers in Southfield, Michigan, and Sylvania, Ohio. In 1982, he was appointed dean of both admissions (replacing Sister Anne Marie Brown, OP) and off-campus programs (replacing John Hounker), responsible for recruiting students for all undergraduate programs. He led the modernization of Siena's admissions office for nearly a decade before turning his focus solely to off-campus programs in 1991. Having developed Siena's first community college partnership on the campus of Lake Michigan College in Benton Harbor in 1982, he went on to start four more degree-completion programs—at community colleges in Monroe (1990), Battle Creek (1992), Lansing (1996), and Jackson (1998)—recruiting and training staff for each site, and enrolling and advising each site's first generation of students. "Norm Bukwaz is one of the primary architects of the modern Siena Heights University," former provost Bob Gordon said in 2000, when Norm officially retired . . . sort of. In the nineteen years since his "retirement," he has worked nonstop as a consultant, assisting with research, analysis, and program development for what is now the College for Professional Studies. He continues to provide data-driven creativity and innovative thinking to Siena's degree completion programs. In Bob Gordon's words, Norm "has been the most important adult educator at the institution."

Norm Bukwaz has brought pioneering vision and energy to the university's adult learning programs since Siena Heights first ventured into nontraditional education.

DEBORAH CARTER

Educated as a teacher of hearing impaired children, Deb Carter was a young mother looking for part-time employment when she was hired by Norm Bukwaz in 1982 to help start a new Siena

As dean of the College for Professional Studies, Deb Carter, center front, focused on faculty development. She is shown here at graduation in May 2007 with, from left, full-time online and Southfield faculty Mary Raymond, Gail Ryder, Steve Ball, Jim Sam, Michael O'Connell, and Tad Dunne; and adjunct professor Peter Sagala from the Lake Michigan Center.

HAIL, SIENA! Siena Heights University

Heights program for adult students in Benton Harbor. "There was so much I didn't know" about higher education, she said later. "I was constantly calling" for advice and guidance from Norm, who helped her navigate the creation of Siena's first community college partnership, with Lake Michigan College. Under her guidance, the LMC program became a solid, successful model for future off-campus developments. Deb herself became a favorite of alumni of the LMC center, many of whom had her as a teacher in either the entry "Adult Learner" class or the final senior seminar, and still today refer to her as Mother Carter. In 2000, Deb succeeded her mentor, Norm Bukwaz, as dean of off-campus operations. Over the next fifteen years, she mentored off-campus faculty and staff across the state; developed a cohort degree-completion program for nuclear power workers in Southwest Michigan; established new programs in Port Huron (2001–2010), Ann Arbor (2004–2010), and Dearborn (2014–ongoing); laid the groundwork for a new center in Kalamazoo (opened after she retired); and guided the College for Professional Studies into the era of online education with the development of Siena's award-winning distance learning program. Her greatest accomplishment, however, may have been developing an outstanding, highly talented permanent faculty for CPS, which had previously relied entirely on dedicated part-time adjunct instructors. A tireless proponent of Dominican values and an energetic cheerleader for Siena Heights, Deb received the Michigan Academic Advising Association's 2015 Pacesetter Award. She retired later that year, shortly before receiving the Alumni Association's 2015 Honorary Alumni Award.

JAMES O'FLYNN

Jim O'Flynn was a recently retired IBM executive in 1998 when he joined the faculty at Siena's Metro Detroit center in Southfield, just as SHU began wrestling with the prospect of online education. In short order, he became "the architect" of Siena's distance learning programs, according to then-dean Deb Carter, immersing himself in the literature, creating course development and faculty standards, and establishing himself as "a standard-bearer for quality online education." In 2003, Jim became coordinator of distance learning, while also teaching five online courses and incorporating the kinds of innovations—streaming video, text animation, and audio-augmented presentations, among others—that characterize Siena's award-winning and nationally ranked online education program. Recipient of the first-ever Jack Bologna Award for Innovative Teaching in 2005, Jim was both a technical wizard (a self-described "propeller head") and a teacher of "infinite patience and deft human touch," according to faculty colleague Bill Blackerby. (Years earlier, Bill first glimpsed the possibilities of technology in the classroom when Jim, then an adult student in Bill's graduate business class, was called out of town unexpectedly but still presented his required project, speaking to the class via live online video.) In addition to his contributions in designing the distance learning program, "Jim was an outstanding teacher, both on the ground and online," recalled former student/now CPS dean Cheri Betz '07; he made "each student dig deeper in order to move each of us to a higher level." Deb Carter summed up his impact this way: "No one, since Norm Bukwaz, has had as much impact on adult degree completion at Siena" as Jim O'Flynn. Jim died in 2018.

Jim O'Flynn, lead architect of the online program, celebrates with the first cohort of totally online distance learning graduates in May 2006: from left, Jessica Brookshire '06, Anne O'Neill '06, Jim O'Flynn, Barb Kline '06, and John Anderson '06.

Athletics

A HALF CENTURY OF INTERCOLLEGIATE COMPETITION

From the beginning, Siena Heights embraced sports as an important part of a healthy life. The women and men who call themselves Saints in 2019 are the descendants of "Siena girls" like Beatrice Cunningham Meyer '32 and Michelena DeRose '45, whose half-court basketball skills were the stuff of legend among their classmates. The modern era of athletics began in the 1970s with the introduction of intercollegiate competition. The program grew slowly but steadily for three decades—then burst into the twenty-first century with a period of remarkable growth.

Who would have guessed, given our modest beginnings. . . .

"Tiny college starts sports."

That was the 1972 headline in the *Detroit News*, heralding the Siena Heights decision to offer intercollegiate athletics. Sports had always been part of campus life; there were academy-versus-college rivalries even in the 1920s. But "starting sports" was different.

When Hugh Thompson brought his coaching background to the presidency in 1971, he correctly guessed that varsity athletics would attract more male students to "tiny" and newly coeducational Siena Heights. He hired Sam Baughey '72, then working on a master's degree, to help him jump-start the program. Harvey Jackson signed on as the first athletic director in 1973. Jackson's first move was to enroll Siena Heights in the National Association of Intercollegiate Athletics (NAIA). Since the NAIA did not then sponsor women's sports, Siena's early women's teams played in the South West Athletic Conference, then in the Association of Intercollegiate Athletics for Women, until 1980 when the NAIA expanded to include women.

Once upon a time, "you were part of the team if you had a pair of black bermudas and a white t-shirt, and you showed up," recalled Anna Marie Moriarty '67 of the pre-modern era in athletics. "I was basically a benchwarmer; I tended to dribble on my foot. Those were the days of the old rules: six on a team but some players were never allowed to cross the center line." (Notice the half-court plan on the blackboard.)

Cheerleaders lead the 2018 Homecoming parade

164 HAIL, SIENA! Siena Heights University

Sister Mary Alice Murnen '54 joined the staff in 1974, becoming women's athletic director and coach of women's tennis and basketball. She began campaigning immediately to call female athletes women, not girls—since, as she said, male student athletes were always men, not boys. "It took time to educate people," she said. "We were always fighting that with the media. We had to educate the male coaches, too!"

The Siena program began with baseball and golf, "because, frankly, the investment would be very low," Baughey recalled. "We decided way back then that we couldn't do football; it was just way too expensive." But in short order, Siena had seven athletic teams, four for men (cross country and wrestling, plus baseball and golf) and three for women (tennis, basketball, and bowling). Women's volleyball came later, along with men's tennis, softball, women's cross country, and men's and women's track and field. Bowling disappeared early on (to reappear decades later). In the 1980s, Dean of Students Fred Dobens encouraged the start of men's soccer; soon after, students Jackie Battalora '88 and Sharon Barnes '88 successfully lobbied to add women's soccer.

"We started out as the Cannonballs, in honor of Sister Ann Joachim who at the time was fighting for the Wabash Cannonball," Sam Baughey said. "They eventually changed to the Saints." Team colors evolved, too, he said. The Dominican colors had always been black and white; Siena students through the 1960s claimed those as "their" colors, and the earliest intercollegiate teams did, too. But Harvey Jackson was a Michigan fan and he had other ideas. "I wasn't in on the decision," Baughey recalled, but "one day Harvey announced the colors were maize and blue." (Sister Peg Albert, not so much a U. of M. fan, corrected the record in 2018: "Yellow and blue," she said definitively!)

...continued on page 166

Harvey Jackson, the Saints' first athletic director, was also the first wrestling coach. Wrestling achieved success early, and in later years was coached by Gail Shinall and Pat Palmer.

In 1983, coach Doug Moss took men's soccer from "club" status to varsity level, beginning a strong and enduring soccer tradition at Siena Heights. In his third year, Moss, *at right in photo, with then-athletic director Pat Palmer and a soccer recruit,* led the 1985 team to a regular season record of 14-4-3; undefeated at home, the Saints went on to compete in the NAIA nationals—the first Siena Heights athletic team to make it that far—and finish the year 17-6-3. Mello soon began coaching varsity women's soccer, too, and in 1988 led the women's team to the NAIA national semifinals—and a 23-2-3 final record. Soccer was here to stay! One of Mello's (and Siena's) finest players, Andy Crawford '89, became head men's soccer coach in 2018, succeeding Aldo Zid. Since 2001, head women's coach Scott Oliver '97 has led his teams to numerous national tournaments.

Technology and the Common Touch: The 2000s and 2010s

Softball has been on the varsity schedule since the 1980s, before Siena had its own field; then-coach Al Sandifer can be seen at left rear. Since 2005, Laura Klutsaris has coached the program. **Above:** Hannah Bleikamp '17 goes for the catch in Christensen Softball Field.

Continued from page 165...

In 1971, the only athletic facilities on campus were the undersized gym in what was still called Walsh Hall and some decades-old tennis courts. Early basketball and volleyball contests took place at the Piotter Center (the former Adrian Catholic Central High School). Baseball played "at home" in Adrian's Riverside Park. Track teams ran down city streets and country roads, never hosting a meet. But President Thompson made athletics a priority. Zollar Field was dedicated in the fall of 1973 for soccer, followed by the new Thomas Emmett tennis courts in 1974. Thompson also began fundraising for an indoor facility for basketball, volleyball and indoor track, but it would be his successor, Louis Vaccaro, who oversaw construction of the Fieldhouse in 1978.

Early teams competed with few amenities. Basketball coaches hand-cranked the baskets into position, set up the Catholic Central gym, and sometimes cleaned it afterwards. Baseball players piled into the back of a panel truck to get to a game. Team meals for away games consisted of plain cheese sandwiches. "We didn't have a lot of anything," recalled longtime cross country coach Tim Bauer '82, who ran for the Saints as a student and began assistant-coaching in 1983.

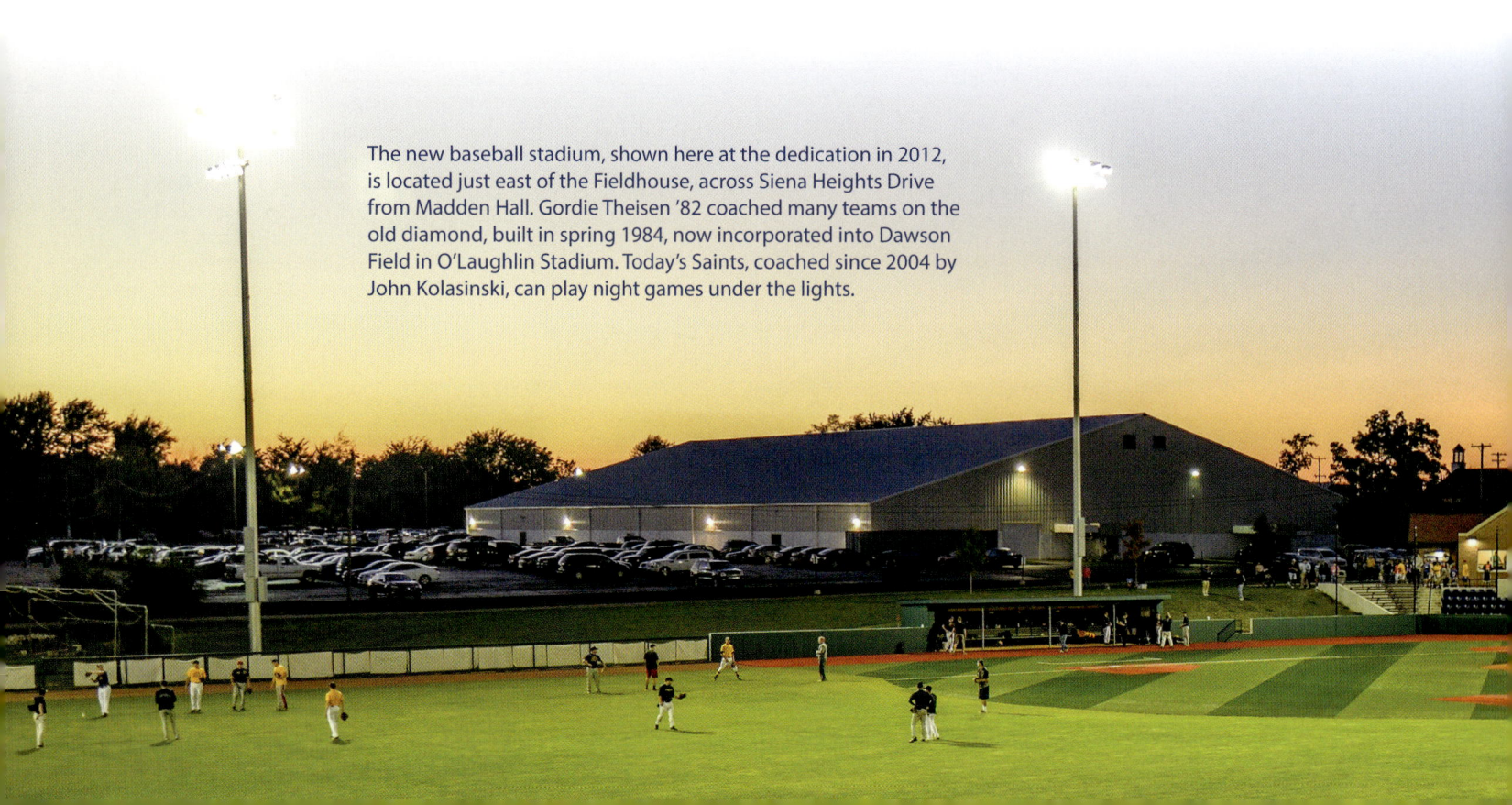

The new baseball stadium, shown here at the dedication in 2012, is located just east of the Fieldhouse, across Siena Heights Drive from Madden Hall. Gordie Theisen '82 coached many teams on the old diamond, built in spring 1984, now incorporated into Dawson Field in O'Laughlin Stadium. Today's Saints, coached since 2004 by John Kolasinski, can play night games under the lights.

Nonetheless, the Saints began to succeed. Cross country runner Jim Miller became Siena's first NAIA All-American in November 1978. Mary Alice Murnen led the 1978–79 women's basketball team to third place in the state tournament with a 27-2 final record. A young Ben Braun coached men's basketball into a force to be reckoned with, leading the Saints to seven consecutive winning seasons from 1979 to 1985. Soccer became the heart of Alumni Weekend festivities. Each year, a few more students came to play for the Saints.

After Twenty-Six Years, a Hall of Fame.

In October 1999, during what was still called Alumni Weekend, Siena Heights inducted the first honorees into its new Athletic Hall of Fame. Six alumni athletes (representing basketball, softball, soccer, and cross country/track & field), one former coach (Ben Braun), and one team (1988–89 men's basketball) made up the inaugural class. Over the next two decades, the Athletic Hall of Fame induction banquet and the Saints Golf Outing the next day would become perennial highlights of what was soon renamed Homecoming.

Night games—for soccer and football in the fall, and lacrosse in the spring—are common now under the lights in O'Laughlin Stadium.

Men's basketball maintains a lively cross-town rivalry with Adrian College, battling each year for the coveted Milk Jug Trophy. Tyrone Wilson and Al Sandifer, coached by Ben Braun, celebrate the Siena Heights win in 1980; while the whole Saints team, coached by Fred Smith, celebrates in 1996. Coach Joe Pechota succeeded Fred Smith in the head coaching spot in 2006.

When the Hall of Fame came into being, twenty-six years after the Cannonballs played their first baseball game, athletic director Fred Smith estimated that athletics enrolled about one hundred new student-athletes each year (roughly eighty-five freshmen and fifteen transfers). Siena Heights was fielding fourteen teams, seven each for men and women. And people knew about the Saints. Smith, who joined the coaching team in 1977 and became athletic director in 1983, recalled that "in the old days, we had to familiarize people at the high schools and community colleges with what Siena was about." No more! The growth of the program made him proud: "In the beginning, we were mainly trying to get on the field with eligible kids and just compete a little. . . . Now we have sports information, athletic directors and trainers, and a host of people doing things the right way," Smith said in 1999. "That is how far we have come."

Volleyball has been part of women's intercollegiate sports since the 1970s; *here,* the 2017 team strikes a pose for media day. Men's volleyball was added in 2010. Kim Berrington coaches both the men's and women's teams in 2019.

168 HAIL, SIENA! Siena Heights University

Business Professor Bill Blackerby has followed the Saints since he arrived on campus in 1979. Reflecting, in 2019, on "how far we have come," Bill observed that the creation of the Fieldhouse and Ben Braun's success with men's basketball were the major hallmarks of the "first era" of intercollegiate sports at Siena Heights. The second era, he said, was distinguished by the rise of "soccer as a premier sport on campus with a strong student fan base, soon followed by a dominating softball program." Along the way, Siena's track and cross country teams—though drawing fewer spectators—developed an award-winning tradition and national reputation.

The twenty-first century would mark the start of a third era in SHU sports history.

Dramatic Growth:
New Sports, New Facilities, New Halo!

The scope of present-day athletics at Siena Heights would astonish our first president, Mother Camilla, and also Sister Ann Joachim, our earliest proponent of organized sports. But if Camilla and "A.J." visited today, they would surely sidle up for a photo with Halo.

Halo, a husky dog chosen in a campus-wide contest, first appeared as the Saints' athletic mascot in December 2008. Choosing a dog made sense, because "the Dominicans were often called the 'Dogs of the Lord,'" Religious Studies professor Joseph Raab said. "They were known as the 'watchdogs' of truth." The name chosen for the dog reflected the new athletic logo adopted earlier in 2008: a halo, with a star for truth and light, hovering above the word SAINTS. Since his debut, Halo the husky has become a fan favorite, not only at games but at events of all sorts.

In 2006, Sister Peg Albert brought the enthusiasm of a former athlete to the presidency. It was she who proposed the search for a Saints mascot—and she who first posed for a picture with Halo. Since then, she has overseen dramatic growth in athletics. From 2008 to 2018, the university added nine new sports: men's volleyball, men's and women's lacrosse, men's and women's bowling (one of the original women's sports, but long gone until 2011), football, cheer, dance—and the latest addition: eSports. Siena Heights now sponsors twenty-two intercollegiate programs.

"This is a historic and significant day in the history of Siena Heights," Sister Peg Albert said May 3, 2010, introducing football to the athletic program and Jim Lyall as the Saints' first head football coach. SHU mascot Halo the Husky joined the celebration, which came after a comprehensive five-month analysis of the potential impact of football and its "fit" with the Siena mission. "Helping young men become competent; giving them purpose, meaning in their lives; and teaching and modeling ethical behavior—that has to be the foundation of the program," said Lyall. The Saints took to the field in 2011 and quickly began building a solid tradition. Lyall retired in 2016; Matt Kohn succeeded Lyall as head coach.

Cheer and dance were added to the coed varsity program in 2012. Madeline Soave '16, *shown,* was named an NAIA All-American in competitive dance 2014, 2015, and 2016. Founding coach Angie Heath directs both programs.

Under Sister Peg's leadership, athletic facilities also have expanded dramatically, starting with O'Laughlin Stadium (honoring Sister Jeanne O'Laughlin, OP '58) and the Dr. Mike and Lynne Dawson Field, both dedicated at Homecoming in 2011 as football kicked off on the Saints' home turf. Men's and women's soccer played night games under the stadium lights that same weekend. Lacrosse began practicing on the field immediately. The following spring, the stadium was the site of the inaugural Kleinow Invitational (named in memory of longtime coach Don Kleinow), the first-ever home meet for Siena's acclaimed track and field teams. Around the same time, the Saints played—and won—their first home game in the new baseball stadium next to the Fieldhouse. (Baseball's old diamond became part of Dawson Field.) At Homecoming 2012, Siena Heights dedicated the new Mary and Sash Spencer Athletic Complex (attached to O'Laughlin Stadium); now the athletic staff claimed offices on both sides of campus, some in the Fieldhouse, others in Spencer. A few sports still compete off-campus: Bowling adopted the Lenawee Recreation Center as their home lanes. Golf plays at the Lenawee Country Club. Cross-country competes at Heritage Park for home meets.

In 2018, Siena Heights welcomed its newest athletic team: eSports, or competitive gaming. Noting that "the definition of 'athletics' is constantly changing," athletic director Fred Smith reported that eSports had been embraced by a number of universities. "I am excited about the possibilities it presents for Siena Heights," he added. Sister Peg concurred. "We are at the beginning of a movement," she said. "Although this is certainly a nontraditional sport, it builds some of the same skills as our other athletic programs, such as teamwork, and the ability to think critically and solve problems." Sister Peg also noted that, in the spirit of the Siena Heights mission, Siena's eSports athletes play no first-person shooter games. The coeducational team has its own "arena" on the third floor of Dominican Hall, bringing the excitement of Rocket, League of Legends, and Overwatch into a venue steeped in Siena's Adrian Dominican roots.

A young Ben Braun began his storied national coaching career at Siena Heights in 1977. Upon hiring him, then-athletic director Orby Moss said, prophetically, "Braun is one of the young and promising coaches that will make his mark in athletics in the future." Braun laid the foundation of the Saints' men's basketball program with nonstop winning seasons, 1979–85.

HAIL, SIENA! Siena Heights University

A Legend of Athletics

1919–2019
100
SIENA HEIGHTS UNIVERSITY

Coach Fred Smith

Fred Smith '86/MA dates his time in intercollegiate athletics at Siena Heights from the start of the "modern" era in the mid-1970s, when he coached part-time while serving on the admissions staff. His early assignments included coaching golf and cross country, assisting head men's basketball coach Ben Braun, and serving as interim athletic director (AD). In 1983, he officially took on the job of AD and has guided the overall athletic program for thirty-five years.

Beginning in 1985, he was also head men's basketball coach for twenty-one years, becoming one of the winningest coaches in the country and leading the Saints to five 30-win seasons, one region four National Association of Intercollegiate Athletics title, two district championships, eight Wolverine-Hoosier Athletic Conference titles, and twelve NAIA tournament appearances. The 1996–97 Saints played for the national championship up to the final minute, emerging as runner-up only when the final shot circled the rim . . . but did not go in.

Since 2006, Fred has focused full-time on his job as AD, overseeing twelve years of remarkable growth in athletics. Over the years, he also has established Siena's Hall of Fame, annual golf tournament, and Saints booster club; served on the WHAC and NAIA executive committees; and received numerous coach-of-the-year honors (at the conference, district, and regional levels) and two-time recognition as district administrator of the year. In honor of Fred's four hundredth basketball victory and the sustained effort over many years that produced it, the university established the Fred Smith Champion Award in 2003; the award honors employees who demonstrate similarly devoted and sustained service, a caring attitude, and the ability to overcome adversity. Fred finished coaching with a 527-198 win-loss record, and in 2006 was inducted into the NAIA Hall of Fame. In 2011, Siena Heights named its new basketball court in Fred's honor. As Fred retires in 2019, he will be honored at Homecoming as the sole 2019 inductee into the Siena Heights Athletic Hall of Fame—literally and figuratively in a class by himself.

Fred Smith's 1996–97 team finished second only to one, with the outcome of the thrilling NAIA Division II national championship game up in the air to the last fraction of a second—when a Saints ball rolled off the rim, giving Bethel College the 95-94 win. Even so, the players returned to a champions' welcome, having gone further than any SHU basketball team before—or since.

Technology and the Common Touch: The 2000s and 2010s   171

Coach Tim Bauer has been a key figure in Saints athletics for 40 years. Since transferring in as a runner in 1979, he has built a powerhouse cross-country and track-and-field tradition at Siena Heights.

More Than Athletes:
Students and Champions of Character.

When the Hall of Fame came into being in 1999, Fred Smith noted that Siena's positive reputation was based in part on the fact that Saints athletics was about more than winning games; it was about helping students "to become more competent, purposeful, and ethical, to become educated, get jobs, and become pillars of our society." At Siena Heights, he said, athletes were not *only* athletes. "They're students who play. And that's the way we like it."

Two decades later, sports and academics remain closely linked. A member of the faculty serves as an official representative to athletics, overseeing player eligibility and consulting on academic issues. Coaches organize team study groups and consult with professors and advisors whenever a student-athlete struggles in the classroom. Both the National Association for Intercollegiate Athletics and the Wolverine-Hoosier Athletic Conference honor athletes for academic achievement as well as on-field performance. In 2014–15, eight Siena Heights teams were honored as NAIA Scholar Teams based on the combined grade point average of team members. In that year, Siena's women's golf team—with a combined GPA of 3.93—was the top team academically in women's golf, and No. 2 among all Scholar Teams in all sports.

Starting in 2001, the NAIA expanded and articulated its expectations of student-athletes by launching the "Champions of Character" initiative, still in place in 2019. Siena's campus ministry team partners with athletics to encourage student-athletes in embracing

SHU students—athletes and nonathletes—express gratitude to all the donors who helped build O'Laughlin Stadium, Dawson Field, and the Spencer Athletic Center.

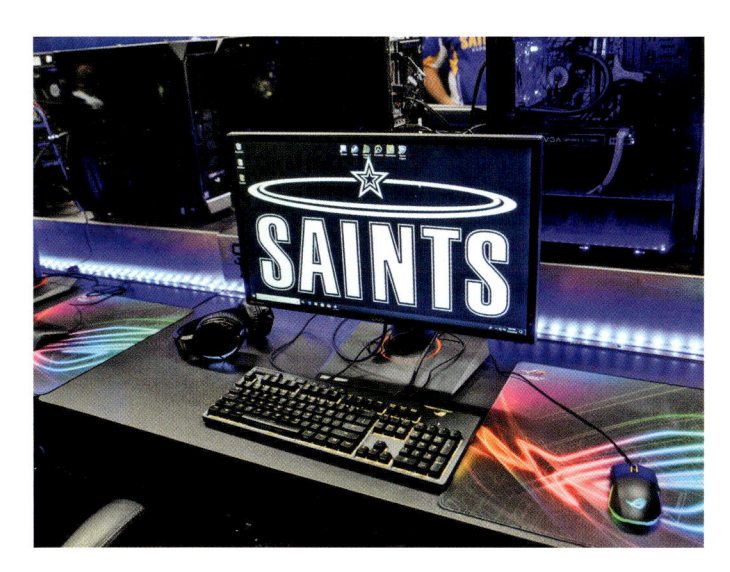

The newest addition to Saints athletics, eSports began in 2018–19. Team members practice and compete in their own "stadium" housed within the computer center on the third floor of Dominican Hall.

the five qualities that define true champions: integrity, respect, responsibility, sportsmanship, and servant leadership. Each year, in connection with fall convocation, Saints athletes pledge to live and play by these values. Siena Heights has been named a Champions of Character institution every year since the program began.

As the 2018–19 academic year began, 588 students on the main campus (including 229 new freshmen and transfer students) were listed on Siena's athletic rosters, intending to play sports. *And this was before recruiting began for e-Sports!* Siena's earlier alumni might be surprised that well over half of the 1,041 full-time undergraduates in Adrian planned to be athletes as well as scholars—but the prominence of athletics on campus in the twenty-first century merely reflects society's overall interest in sport and fitness.

As Siena Heights celebrates its centennial, one appropriate response might be: **Go, Saints!**

Siena's players have always been student-athletes: students first, and athletes in addition.

SPORTS DATA

Siena Heights Athletic Directors
Harvey Jackson	1973–75
Steve Balyo	1975–77
Orby Moss	1977–78
Fred Smith	*Interim, 1978–79*
C. Patrick Palmer	1979–83
Fred Smith	1983–2019

Saints Athletics at SHU's 100th
In 2019, Siena Heights fields twenty-two intercollegiate teams:
- **Men's:** baseball, basketball, cross country, football, golf, lacrosse, soccer, track & field indoor/outdoor, volleyball
- **Women's:** basketball, cross country, golf, lacrosse, soccer, softball, track & field indoor/outdoor, volleyball
- **Coed:** cheer, dance, eSports

Success by the Numbers
As of December 2018
63 total NAIA All-Americans
270 NAIA Scholar Athletes
12 CoSIDA Academic All-Americans
99 alumni athletes inducted into Siena Heights Hall of Fame
12 faculty/staff/coaches inducted into Siena Heights Hall of Fame for meritorious service

"Going to Nationals"
- Men's cross country was the first Siena Heights team to qualify for competition at the NAIA national tournament in 1983. Men's and women's cross country have qualified for nationals numerous times since then.
- Other Saints teams that have made it into the national tournament: men's soccer, women's soccer (eight appearances), men's basketball (twelve appearances), women's basketball (four appearances), men's baseball, women's softball, men's lacrosse (three appearances), women's lacrosse, dance (two appearances).

Leadership in the NAIA
Two SHU presidents have chaired the NAIA Council of Presidents**:**
  Cathleen Real
  Rick Artman
Six of SHU's 2019 coaches have served as president of NAIA coaching groups:
  Tim Bauer (track, cross country)
  Angie Heath (cheer and dance)
  Laura Klutsaris (softball)
  John Kolasinski (baseball)
  Scott Oliver (women's soccer)
  Sue Syljebeck (women's basketball)

AFTER A CENTURY OF SMOKING: WELCOME TO OUR SMOKE-FREE CAMPUS!

Smoking at Siena Heights has come full circle. It's a fascinating social history. Since 2011, Siena Heights has been a smoke-free university—no smoking anywhere, indoors or out, on the Adrian campus. Those who need a smoke break stroll the city sidewalk. This is not far from where we began, but we traveled a circuitous route to get here!

When St. Joseph's College began, girls were forbidden to smoke because it was considered vulgar and slightly immoral. But, even then, some students did smoke; and, years later, stories about where they went to "light up" became a staple of reunion conversations.

Mary Duker Barker '39 recalled late-night forays up a ladder to the attic above the fifth floor of Sacred Heart Hall. "We called it our 'ash tray,'" she laughed years later. "But, oh my, what a fire hazard. . . ." Alumnae of the 1930s and 1940s also spoke about an odd but pleasant outdoor smoking spot: "We went to the cemetery, and visited Jimmy Mahoney," who had a convenient bench at his grave, recalled Mary Pariseau Hintze '45. "We imagined he was always happy to see us!"

Girls who were brave sometimes sneaked onto the fire escape that zig-zagged down the west side of Sacred Heart Hall above Trinity Garden. Sister Julie "Pat" Sullivan, OP '47 wrote with regret to her class before their 50th reunion: "Fifty years ago I missed going to Innisfail with you all for our senior picnic, because Sister Miriam Michael caught me smoking on the fire escape. Now I will miss you all again." She was battling lung cancer.

For decades, the fire escape on the west end of Sacred Heart Hall—seen in this photo from a celebration in Trinity Garden, possibly the dedication of Benincasa and Archangelus Halls—was a not-so-secret smoking venue for students who felt the need to sneak out between classes. When, in the twenty-first century, the university built interior closed-door stairways, workmen removed the old steel fire escape.

"People who were at Siena in the 1940s or 1950s are certainly going to remember smoking at the big tree," Joan Robie '55 reported, describing a spot west of campus, just down the road. "It was this huge oak tree and there was no grass around it because, of course, no grass could grow with all those cigarette butts. Even if you didn't smoke, you went there because it was a sort of social club. I can remember standing there in the cold, stamping my feet and clapping my hands together in my gloves, trying to keep warm."

But those days were numbered, Joan said: "The student government was very much involved in the dissolution of smoking under the tree and the development of the smoker on campus. That was a really big step at Siena."

When Christa Marsik, OP '58, arrived as a freshman, the smoker was well-established in the basement of Archangelus Hall, but smoking was limited to designated evening hours, and upperclassmen still talked about going "down the street to the tree." A few years later, the rules loosened to allow smoking in the main floor parlors of Archangelus.

In 1964, the U.S. Surgeon General's Office reported that smoking was a definite cause of lung cancer in men, and a "probable cause" in women. In 1968, the Phillip Morris company introduced Virginia Slims, suggesting that women who smoked them were both liberated and sophisticated; glossy ads proclaimed, "You've come a long way, baby!" For a while, advertising was more persuasive than the surgeon general.

In the 1970s, most of the smoking rules at Siena Heights were tossed out along with dress codes and core requirements. Eventually, students, both male and female, could smoke whenever they wanted, everywhere *except* in elevators and stairwells.

A decade later at Siena Heights, the pendulum began, very slowly, to swing the other way. Step number one: No smoking in classrooms.

SMOKE SIGNALS! *REGULATIONS THROUGH THE YEARS*

1944: "Since smoking is not in keeping with the high standards of womanly dignity which it is the aim of Siena Heights to maintain in its students, they are expected to refrain from this vulgar and unhealthful habit, both on and off campus."

1960: "Smoking is forbidden except in the smoker located on the service floor of the dormitory (Archangelus Hall)."

1966: "Students may smoke in the large recreation room on the ground floor of Archangelus Hall and with their guests in the parlors on the main floor."

1970: "Because smoking may be a fire hazard and endanger the well-being of everyone in the residence halls it is forbidden in bedrooms and the second, third, and fourth floors of the residence halls."

1974: "Smoking is permitted in the following areas only: the Union, Library Lounge, designated areas of the Residence Halls, which include lounges, lobby and bedrooms, and main floor of Sacred Heart. Smoking in classrooms is left to the discretion of the instructor. Fire laws prohibit smoking in elevators and on stairways."

1983: "Smoking is not permitted in classrooms...."

1994: "As of July 1, 1994, all buildings will be smoke free. Those who live in the residence halls, however, are free to exercise a choice to smoke in their rooms."

2006: "All buildings on the main campus of Siena Heights University are smoke free."

2019: "The use of tobacco products and electronic cigarettes on Siena Heights University property is prohibited."

OUR STILL-CHANGING CAMPUS:
SAY FAREWELL. AND WELCOME BACK!

Along with all the additions of the 21st century campus building boom, there was one subtraction…and one return of an old friend.

In Memoriam: Walsh Hall/Sage Union.

Alumni and administrators alike mourned the loss in 2018 of Sage Union, previously Walsh Hall. The beautiful Tuscan Romanesque brick building, beloved of many generations, had become, at last, not only outdated but irredeemable. "We considered so many options," President Peg Albert, OP, said of the deliberations leading to demolition. "It pains me to take Sage down," she told the community, "but it is too costly not to do so. We also priced out saving the facades," but that, too, was prohibitive.

Many of the qualities that made the elegant edifice so popular and well used in past days—multiple interior levels, nooks and crannies of all sizes, stairwells leading up, down, and around the corner—also made it inaccessible. In earlier decades, only the able-bodied attended college; but in recent years, many in Siena's joyously diverse student and alumni populations were unable to use or even enter the Walsh/Sage building.

Historic Beginnings: Walsh Hall, a spacious facility for music and athletics, was the college's second building and part of Mother Camilla's founding vision. Opened in 1925, the building was named in Mother Augustine Walsh's honor, though for a time it was also called the conservatory of music. The main floor provided theater seating, slanted toward an orchestra pit and stage. A second-floor balcony connected with side aisles of practice rooms (each sized for an upright piano) overlooking the main auditorium. Larger studio rooms, above and behind the stage, housed concert pianos for the music faculty. Beneath the auditorium was a gymnasium with locker rooms and showers.

Adrian Dominicans, as well as students from both the college and the academy, made good use of the Walsh Hall stage and its excellent acoustics for concerts, recitals, and theater productions including the annual passion plays.

For forty-five years, Walsh was the site of noisy basketball contests downstairs; and concerts, movies, lectures, and performances on the main floor.

- Actress Helen Hayes is reputed to have performed on the Walsh stage. The Trapp Family Singers (of *Sound of Music* fame) appeared in 1947.
- Sister Leonilla's passion plays were staged there in the 1930s and 1940s, as were musicals like *The King and I* in the 1960s. Music and theater students presented senior shows and recitals there.
- Diplomat Clare Booth Luce, social worker Dorothy Day, and missionary doctor Tom Dooley inspired students in Walsh.

Generations of "valiant women" crossed the Walsh stage as freshmen to receive their caps and gowns at the fall "Investiture" ceremony; then crossed it again as graduating seniors to receive their diplomas. Dominican sisters gathered nervously in Walsh to receive their annual mission assignments, leaving the auditorium in joy or disappointment depending on where they were headed the next year.

New Life in the 1970s: When Francoeur Theater and Verheyden Performing Arts Center provided new space for music and theater, the college, now coeducational and expanding rapidly, opted to remake Walsh as a student center. With support from the Sage Foundation, Walsh Hall became Sage College Union.

...continued on page 178

After the Walsh-to-Sage renovation in the 1970s, the stage became a performance platform for rock bands—and later, a busy snack bar for students, faculty, and staff.

Continued from page 177...

Sage was the hub of campus life from the 1970s into the 1990s. Upstairs, practice rooms became student organization offices, and faculty offices housed Upward Bound. The main floor was perfect for dances, and the student mail room. The old stage became a snack bar, attracting students, faculty, and staff for lunch, or a bite to eat before an evening class. Downstairs, the observation room overlooking the gym became a locker room for commuter students. The gym eventually welcomed the bookstore over from Ledwidge Hall. Nontraditional student services occupied the large room beneath the stage but above the gym. Coffee houses, student activities, and Shakespeare birthday parties all used rooms on the winding lower corridors.

For ninety-four years, Walsh Hall defined the south edge of Trinity Garden, providing the backdrop to many activities and events—and a sound-track, as well. Music often wafted from Walsh into the garden, classical trills from the second story practice rooms, rock and pop rhythms from dances in the lounge, and finally, brass band favorites from the basement—where the 21st-century marching band practiced in recent years.

HAIL, SIENA! Siena Heights University

The Twenty-First Century: In recent years, Sage was considerably less lively, eventually becoming the fallback alternative for any operation that lacked space elsewhere. Prior to the expansion of the Fieldhouse, the old practice rooms served as overflow offices for coaches. When student mailboxes were moved to Ledwidge lobby, the former mailroom provided space for International Student Services—until they moved to Dominican Hall. When the bookstore moved into Archangelus Ballroom, the new football program moved into the gym/bookstore space; when football moved to the new Spencer Athletic Complex, the marching band used the old gym as a practice room, while waiting for new space in the Performing Arts Center. After campus ministry and Student Senate moved into McLaughlin University Center, the Graduate College operated out of Sage before relocating to a house down the street. Upward Bound was the last program to maintain operations in Sage before moving into Sacred Heart Hall.

When demolition began in June 2018, tears were shed. Many in the Siena community were bereft. But now, where Walsh/Sage once stood, Siena Heights enjoys an expansive new view of Archangelus and Benincasa Halls, bordering Trinity Garden at the foot of a graceful green hill. It is a lovely addition to the campus. *See the title page of this book for a picture.*

Reclaiming Past Ties: **St. Joseph Academy**

Siena Heights has strong historic ties to St. Joseph Academy. It was the success of the academy, founded in 1896, that enabled the Adrian Dominicans to charter the college in 1919; and the two schools were inextricably linked in the early years. Sacred Heart, Walsh, and Benincasa Halls, and Lumen Ecclesiae Chapel were all used by both the college and the academy for several decades.

The academy building was designed with a "front" door opening onto the lawn in front of Madden Hall; but in more recent years, when St. Joseph Academy was no longer a boarding school, this south end—facing Siena Heights Drive—became the primary entrance for students arriving by bus or automobile.

180 HAIL, SIENA! Siena Heights University

Both college and academy grew, however, and in 1948 Mother Gerald contracted with her nephew, architect Gerald Barry of Chicago, to design a new academy building. When it opened in 1950, the building was, for a while, called Dominicana Hall. Decades later, a second, much smaller, building was constructed across Siena Heights Drive for the academy middle school; elementary and Montessori programs remained in Dominicana, by then just called "the academy."

The academy's days were numbered, however. When the middle school closed, Siena Heights leased, then purchased, the smaller building as a home for the new SHU nursing school. The congregation closed the rest of St. Joseph Academy a few years later; and, in 2016, the sisters generously donated the Dominicana/St. Joseph Academy building to Siena Heights.

By 2017, the main floor of the academy building, newly outfitted with the latest technology, provided offices and classrooms for Siena's teacher education program. Students loved the wide hallways. Faculty remembered bringing their children, or grandchildren, to the spacious "St. Joe" classrooms. By 2018, Sister Peg had secured the funding to renovate the upper floors of the building. In 2019, as Siena Heights celebrates its centennial, the university will rededicate this historic building, so full of ties to our Dominican roots, as the Maureen M. McLaughlin, MSN, Center For Health Professions.

St. Joseph Academy—now the easternmost point of the Siena Heights campus—glows in the late afternoon sun of a cold winter day.

A Century of Serving Others

1919–2019 SIENA HEIGHTS UNIVERSITY

THE LEGACY OF CATHERINE OF SIENA

Responding to community needs has been a core value of Siena Heights ever since Mother Camilla saw that young girls in the wilds of Michigan needed opportunities to learn. Catherine Benincasa inspires today's faculty and students, as much as she did our Dominican founders. Through her devotion to the poor, the sick, and the hungry of *her* time in the fourteenth century, St. Catherine provides a model for trying to make *our* world a better place.

Sister Nancy Murray, OP has introduced many students and alumni to Catherine Benincasa through her live portrayals of the fourteenth-century saint.

THE GIRLS TRAINING SCHOOL

As early as the 1930s, faculty and students volunteered at the Girls Training School in Adrian. Education teacher Sister Ambrose Collins, OP "was involved with the 'wayward girls,' as they called them at that time" and often took college students with her, so the Training School girls would have "someone they could talk to," Lucille McCall Canzona '41 remembered. Sociology professor Sister Mary Therese Crimmins, OP '37, founder of Siena's social work program, continued that tradition in the 1940s and 1950s, providing counseling to the Training School teachers, and bringing Siena students to visit the girls. "I had never been in a place like that … I met a girl close to my own age from Kalamazoo who, I found out later from sister, was only there because she had no place else to go," recalled Diana Albera Luciani '58.

MIGRANT WORKERS AND THE HISPANIC COMMUNITY

Longtime language professor Sister Laurine Neville, OP, initiated Siena's ties with the Spanish-speaking community. By the early 1940s, she was taking upper-level Spanish students to the homes of Hispanic migrant families. Annita Galnares Cantu '77 remembers Sister Laurine often "at my grandparents' home, visiting." Thanks to Laurine's encouragement, Annita's aunt, Maria Guadalupe Galnares, graduated from Siena in 1961. Gloria Faz '91, the daughter of Mexican migrant workers, was a teenage bride and veteran field worker when she met Sister Laurine; before long, she joined the kitchen staff in Benincasa Dining Hall—where she became head of the food service, friend to students for decades, and a proud Siena alumna. When Patricia Siemen, OP '72 (now Adrian Dominican Prioress), began working with Adrian's Hispanic community, she found that Sister Laurine was still "very well known in the older Puerto Rican and Mexican-American families." When Siena Heights began its Upward Bound program in the 1970s, Karen Glaser and Annita Cantu continued Laurine's outreach, along with Dionardo Pizana in student development and Idali Feliciano in advising.

THE RURAL POOR IN APPALACHIA

Sister Carmelia O'Connor, OP, theology professor from the 1960s to the 1980s, was a favorite in the classroom, but may be remembered even more for the service trips she led to Appalachia. Inspired by Vatican II, Sister Carmie took Siena Heights students to economically and culturally depressed Appalachian communities, where they spent spring "vacation" living and serving with the poor. (Among the Dominican Sisters, it was said that anyone wanting adventure and surprise should travel with Carmie; perhaps that was one more reason why those service trips were so popular with Siena students.)

THEATER IN THE SCHOOLS

In the 1970s and 1980s, students in the "drama-in-education troupe" volunteered in Lenawee elementary schools. Directed by Sister Therese Craig, OP '48, and Trudy McSorley '70, troupe members engaged youngsters in creative improvisation, developing original stories related to their studies. Characters such as Adrian anti-slavery activist Laura Haviland sometimes figured into the stories. The children gained confidence and creativity while their teachers learned a new teaching tool; but troupe was equally meaningful to the Siena student participants.

A LOCAL NEED: HOSPICE

In the 1980s, Siena volunteers, including professors Kitty Madden and Barbara Wall, were leaders in community discussions of a new kind of service to the terminally ill. Though well accepted today, the concept of hospice care was revolutionary at the time and Siena Heights voices played a key role in winning acceptance for providing end-of-life comfort and dignity as an alternative to medically extending life at all costs. When a fledgling hospice program came into being, a recent non-traditional graduate of Siena Heights, Susan Jacobson '85, became its first director.

Service in the 21st Century:

SIENA SERVES

Incoming freshmen learn right away about the Dominican commitment to serving others. For two decades, main campus students have participated in a day of service as part of freshman orientation, working with groups and agencies throughout Adrian. Since 2010, service projects of all types, throughout the year, have been coordinated under the umbrella term, "Siena Serves."

SPRING SERVING. (NOT SUNBATHING.)

Campus ministry leaders such as Tom Puszczewicz, Sisters Barbara Blesse, OP, and Lorraine Reaume, OP, Father Tom Helfrich, Father John Grace, and Sister Mary Jones, OP, and staff such as Renee Bracy and Michael Orlando, have led hundreds of students on "alternative spring break" trips serving communities from Michigan to Florida, New Orleans to Los Angeles, El Paso, Texas, to Flint, Michigan. Siena volunteers have built houses with Habitat for Humanity since 2001 (thanks to Traci Stewart '02 who started SHU's Habitat chapter), provided post-Katrina support in Louisiana, shared faith with the women of Centro Santa Catalina, and met with former felons at Home Boy Industries. The common feeling is: "We receive more than we give."

SPREADING SUNSHINE

Siena Heights has built a strong relationship with Camp Sunshine in Casco, Maine, a retreat for children with terminal and life-threatening illnesses. Camp Sunshine declines many volunteer offers but welcomes Siena students, whom they have dubbed Sunshine Saints for their close connection in mission and quality service. The SHU delegation travels to Maine each spring after school ends. In 2019, the Sunshine Saints worked with children with limited (or no) eyesight due to retinoblastoma and other rare eye cancers.

SHELTERING THE HOMELESS

Share the Warmth, Adrian's shelter for the homeless, came into being in 2006, thanks largely to the passion and compassion of English professor Sister Pat Schnapp, RSM. Since then, Tom Puszczewicz in campus ministry has rallied one-hundred-fifty volunteers each year to provide meals and staffing for the overnight shelter, making Siena Heights one of the lead volunteer supporters of the program. Now an independent non-profit, the shelter continues to rely on the generosity of Siena Heights, the Adrian Dominican Sisters, and other community supporters.

FEEDING THE HUNGRY

Since 2004, Professor Jeff Lindstrom's social psychology class has sponsored a food drive every November supporting The Daily Bread, which provides free meals for the hungry in Adrian. Organized, promoted, and managed by Jeff's students, the food drive has been embraced by the entire campus, generating enough food and financial support to stock the food pantry for four to six months. The 2018 delivery from Siena Heights was the largest ever received by The Daily Bread. In another initiative, the dean for students office partnered with current undergraduates to respond to food insecurity on campus, establishing a SHU Pantry for student use in times of need.

LEARNING BY SERVING

For twenty years, community-based learning (CBL) has taken Siena classrooms into the community. CBL puts students into hands-on situations where they address real problems while applying academic skills. The students learn from, while serving with, people and organizations. Unlike an internship—which enhances one student's professional development—CBL is a group commitment, engaging with the community *for the good of the community*. CBL is embedded across the curriculum: Linda Easley's sociology and anthropology classes partner with the Boys and Girls Club. Sport management students also spend time at the Boys and Girls Club. Environmental science students work with the River Raisin Watershed Association.

LEARNING AND SHARING BEHIND BARS

Members of the Siena Heights community have served inmates at the Gus Harrison Correctional Facility since its opening in 1991. Sister Marcine Klemm, OP '55, helped begin the tradition of offering weekly Mass at the prison. Sister Pat Schnapp, RSM, has taught literature classes at Gus Harrison since its opening, often involving other Siena volunteers. Since 2008, SHU criminal justice program director Elly Teunion-Smith '89 has taught "Criminal Justice: Fact and Fiction" inside the prison for both "resident students" (inmates) and "commuters" (Siena undergraduates); the class routinely proves to be eye-opening for all: everyone teaches, everyone learns.

HERE, THERE, AND EVERYWHERE

In Adrian and at Siena's off-campus sites, students, faculty, and staff regularly "give back" with such initiatives as: TEACH's adopt-a-family program, Campus Ministry's Advent giving trees, annual blood drives for the Red Cross (a main campus tradition for decades), and the annual Gift of Life Challenge (signing up organ donors)—to name a few. Monroe Center students have gone bowling for scholarship dollars. Freshmen in a 2016 seminar taught by Joni Warner '83 raised $1,000 to support Lakota teens in South Dakota. And students have served impoverished communities as far away as Jamaica, the Dominican Republic, Mexico, and Nicaragua.

Right: Blood drives have a long history at Siena Heights. Here, Chris Pawson '83 rolls up his sleeve during the 1980 blood drive.

Below: Recent Habitat for Humanity volunteers help build a home.

Part 6
Hail, Siena!

Commencing into the Future

Commencement—graduation—is the biggest event of the year: the celebration of a job well done, a journey completed and destination achieved for every student who becomes, that day, an alumna or alumnus of Siena Heights University. Some graduates have spent four years, others decades, on the road to a degree; but all are proud to be alumni—and happy to be "done." But Commencement is also a beginning…

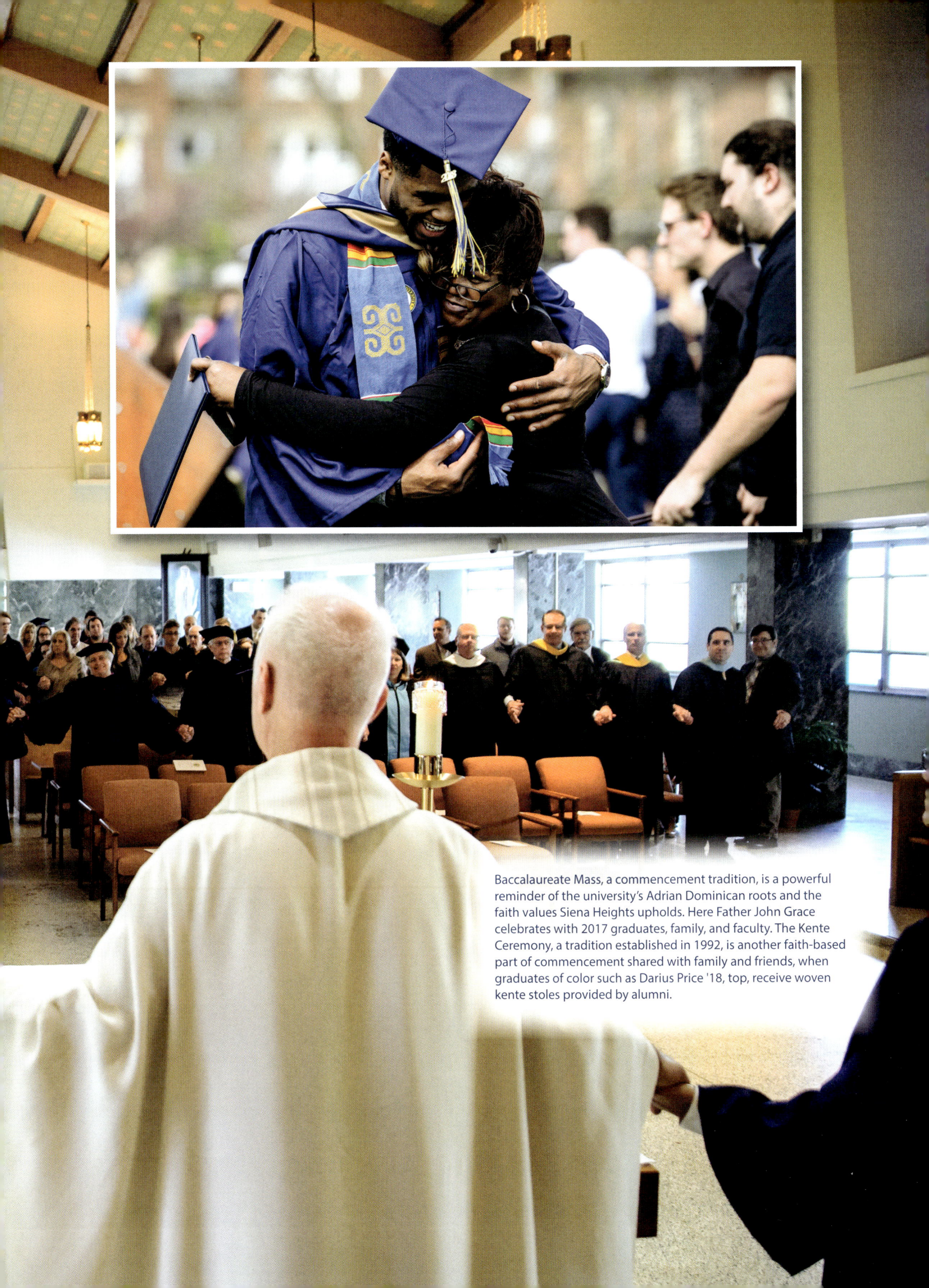

Baccalaureate Mass, a commencement tradition, is a powerful reminder of the university's Adrian Dominican roots and the faith values Siena Heights upholds. Here Father John Grace celebrates with 2017 graduates, family, and faculty. The Kente Ceremony, a tradition established in 1992, is another faith-based part of commencement shared with family and friends, when graduates of color such as Darius Price '18, top, receive woven kente stoles provided by alumni.

1930

1945

186 HAIL, SIENA! Siena Heights University

1950s

1964

1996

Graduation through the years! In 1930, white-robed graduates of St. Joseph College and St. Joseph Academy posed in front of the Grotto, that once stood near what is now the front entrance to St. Dominic Chapel; *college* graduates are distinguished by black ribbon ties. Graduation 1945 took place in Holy Rosary Chapel. In the 1950s, graduates, along with faculty (all sisters) and family, gathered in Walsh Hall for commencement. By 1964, graduation had moved into Lumen Ecclesiae Chapel. These 1996 graduates give a thumbs up to graduation in the Fieldhouse, where it continues to take place in 2019.

Hail Siena! Commencing into Future 187

"I hope the university will continue to be a home to many more students the way it was for me. Siena Heights changed me for good and made my wings bigger.

Arthur Gwoszdz '18

At graduations in the 21st century, colorful banners indicate all the sites where today's Siena Heights students find "a teaching and learning environment which respects the dignity of all."

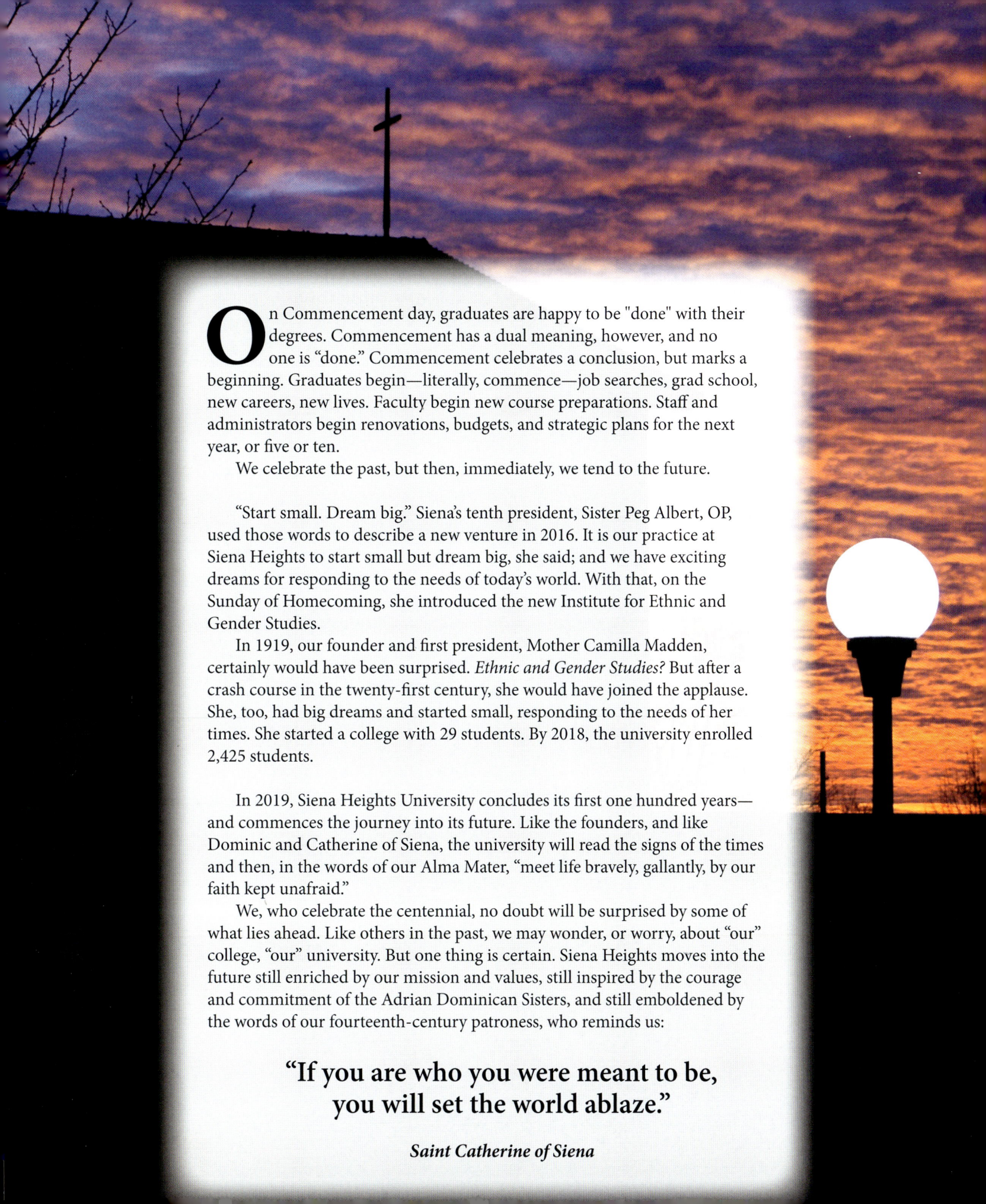

On Commencement day, graduates are happy to be "done" with their degrees. Commencement has a dual meaning, however, and no one is "done." Commencement celebrates a conclusion, but marks a beginning. Graduates begin—literally, commence—job searches, grad school, new careers, new lives. Faculty begin new course preparations. Staff and administrators begin renovations, budgets, and strategic plans for the next year, or five or ten.

We celebrate the past, but then, immediately, we tend to the future.

"Start small. Dream big." Siena's tenth president, Sister Peg Albert, OP, used those words to describe a new venture in 2016. It is our practice at Siena Heights to start small but dream big, she said; and we have exciting dreams for responding to the needs of today's world. With that, on the Sunday of Homecoming, she introduced the new Institute for Ethnic and Gender Studies.

In 1919, our founder and first president, Mother Camilla Madden, certainly would have been surprised. *Ethnic and Gender Studies?* But after a crash course in the twenty-first century, she would have joined the applause. She, too, had big dreams and started small, responding to the needs of her times. She started a college with 29 students. By 2018, the university enrolled 2,425 students.

In 2019, Siena Heights University concludes its first one hundred years—and commences the journey into its future. Like the founders, and like Dominic and Catherine of Siena, the university will read the signs of the times and then, in the words of our Alma Mater, "meet life bravely, gallantly, by our faith kept unafraid."

We, who celebrate the centennial, no doubt will be surprised by some of what lies ahead. Like others in the past, we may wonder, or worry, about "our" college, "our" university. But one thing is certain. Siena Heights moves into the future still enriched by our mission and values, still inspired by the courage and commitment of the Adrian Dominican Sisters, and still emboldened by the words of our fourteenth-century patroness, who reminds us:

"If you are who you were meant to be, you will set the world ablaze."

Saint Catherine of Siena

Sources

Books

Foley, Nadine, OP, *Mother Mary Gerald Barry, OP, Ecclesial Woman of Vision and Daring* (Adrian, MI: Adrian Dominican Sisters, 2000).

Foley, Nadine, OP, *Seeds Scattered and Grown, A History of the Adrian Dominican Sisters, 1924–1933* (Adrian, MI: Adrian Dominican Sisters, 2006).

Foley, Nadine, OP, *To Fields Near and Far, Adrian Dominican Sisters History 1933–1961* (Adrian, MI: Adrian Dominican Sisters, 2015).

Ryan, Sister Mary Philip, OP, *Amid the Alien Corn* (St. Charles, IL: Jones Wood Press, 1967).

Tsuji, Jun, *The Soul of DNA, The True Story of a Catholic Sister and Her Role in the Greatest Scientific Discovery of the Twentieth Century* (Coral Springs, FL: Llumina Press, 2004).

Unpublished Histories

- Beaubien, Mary, OP, Collected Historical Contributions to the Daily Announcements at Siena Heights University (Siena Heights Marketing Office, Online Archives)

- Lefebvre, Jeanne, OP, "Celebrating Siena's 70th Year, 1919–1989" (Siena Heights Archives, "History—Box No. 1")

- McKeough, Noreen, OP, with research assistance from Helen Duggan, OP, "Ascent to the Heights: An Informal Account of the Beginnings and Growth of Siena Heights College, 1919–1969" (Siena Heights Archives, "History—Box No. 1")

- Ryan, Mary Philip, OP, "Brief History of Siena Heights College" (Siena Heights Archives, "History—Box No. 1")

- Ryan, Mary Philip, OP, "Early History of Siena Heights College," Speech given for the President's Cabinet Dinner, June 13, 1987, at the Pontchartrain Hotel in Detroit (Siena Heights Archives, "History—Box No. 1")

- Stimson, Miriam Michael, OP, Speech given to Phi Sigma Sigma, October 30, 1985 (Siena Heights Archives, "History—Box No. 1")

Oral Interviews

- Transcriptions of 150 Interviews, conducted primarily by Helen Duggan, OP, with occasional interviews by Marie Irene Miller, OP, and Jeanne Lefebvre, OP, 1989–1993 (Siena Heights University Archives)

- Transcriptions of several dozen interviews conducted by Amy Garno Anderson as part of a senior project and a graduate assistantship. (Siena Heights University Archives)

- Fact-checking in-person, telephone, and email interviews by Jennifer Hamlin Church with many Siena Heights faculty, administrators, and alumni, especially including: William Blackerby, Norman Bukwaz, Deborah Carter, Doug Goodnough, Robert Gordon, Trudy McSorley '70, Carrie Mitchell, Mary Small Poore '76, Mark Schersten, Fred Smith, Jun Tsuji, and Sister Sharon Weber, OP '69. Brief fact-checking conversations with many others, especially including Katie Hamilton. (Author's records)

Publications and Periodicals

All in the Siena Heights University Archives.

- *Eversharp*, student newsletter of St. Joseph's College.

- *Sienae*, alumni association newsletter of Siena Heights College.

- *Reflection*, official newsletter of Siena Heights College, 1972–1977.

- *Reflections*, official newsletter/magazine of Siena Heights College/University, 1978–2019.

- *Academic Catalogues*, St. Joseph's College and Academy, Siena Heights College, Siena Heights University, assorted from 1923–24 to 2018–19.

- *The Valiant Woman*, yearbooks of the classes of 1945, 1946, 1947, 1948, 1949

- Other yearbooks, classes of 1979 and 1980.

- *Student Handbooks*, assorted from 1920s to 2018–19.

Letters, Documents, Minutes, Reports, and Miscellaneous

Individual files, departmental files, divisional files, history files. *(Siena Heights Archives)*

Congregational Biographies of Deceased Adrian Dominican Sisters

(Archives of the Adrian Dominican Sisters)

About the Author

Jennifer Hamlin Church worked at Siena Heights for twenty years in communications and alumni relations. During that time, she edited *Reflections* for eight years, coordinated communications for the change from Siena Heights College to Siena Heights University, organized annual class and special interest reunions, welcomed 50th anniversary classes from 1945 through 1965, coordinated alumni events on campus and across the country, and reached out in friendship to countless graduates and former students, engaging them in the life of Siena Heights. In 2005, she received the Distinguished Service Award from the Great Lakes District of the Council for Advancement and Support of Education. At Homecoming in 2013, she received the Honorary Alumni Award from the Siena Heights University Alumni Association. Upon retiring in 2015, she was granted *Emerita* status by Siena Heights University.

A graduate of Middlebury College (Vermont) and the University of Minnesota, she previously worked in public relations at Ohio Wesleyan University, Adrian College (Michigan), and Greenwich House Settlement (New York), and as a free-lance journalist. *Hail, Siena!* is her second book.

VERITAS
LAUDARE
PRAEDICARE
BENEDICERE